POISED FOR GROWTH

POISED FOR GROWTH

TAKING YOUR BUSINESS TO THE NEXT LEVEL

GABOR BAUMANN

AND JACOB WEINSTEIN

McGraw-Hill
New York San Francisco Washington, D.C. Auckland Bogotá
Caracas Lisbon London Madrid Mexico City Milan
Montreal New Delhi San Juan Singapore
Sydney Tokyo Toronto

Library of Congress Cataloging-in-Publication Data

Baumann, Gabor.
   Poised for growth : taking your business to the next level / Gabor
Baumann, Jacob Weinstein.
      p.   cm.
   Includes index.
   ISBN 0-07-006016-9 (hardcover)
   1. Industrial management. 2. Strategic planning. 3. Success in
business. I. Weinstein, Jacob. II. Title.
HD31.B369932   1997
658.4—dc21   96-36830
                                             CIP

McGraw-Hill

A Division of The McGraw-Hill Companies

1 2 3 4 5 6 7 8 9 0 DOC/DOC 9 0 1 0 9 8 7 6

ISBN 0-07-006016-9

*The sponsoring editor for this book was Susan Barry, the editing
supervisor was Jane Palmieri, and the production supervisor was
Pamela Pelton. It was set in Fairfield by Renee Lipton of
McGraw-Hill's Professional Book Group composition unit.*

Printed and bound by R. R. Donnelley & Sons Company.

McGraw-Hill books are available at special quantity discounts to use as
premiums and sales promotions, or for use in corporate training programs. For more information, please write to the Director of Special
Sales, McGraw-Hill, 11 West 19th Street, New York, NY 10011. Or
contact your local bookstore.

To the memory of my parents
G.B.

CONTENTS

ACKNOWLEDGMENTS

The authors would like to thank the following prominent people in the industry, with many years of experience in the business, who contributed their time and insights in personal interviews exclusively for this book. Henry Taub—cofounder of one of the best companies in the world, the $3 billion ADP, and currently a director, honorary chairman, and chairman of the executive committee—shared with us in an extensive interview some of his experiences during the emerging growth years of ADP. Bill Green—former Grand Union board member, Wall Street lawyer, and 14-year U.S. congressman representing Manhattan's East Side who now runs the family's Green Fund, actively invests in emerging growth companies and is on the board of ClientSoft, Inc., Energy Answers Corporation, General American Investors, New York City Campaign Finance Board, New York City Housing Development Corporation, and the Space Studies Board of the National Research Council—gave us his time in an extensive interview. Victoria Hamilton—executive vice president and chief operating officer of General American Investors Co., a closed-end investment company, and previously with SRK Management Co., a New York-based venture capital fund—gave us ample time and insights. John C. Baker—president of Baker Capital, and formerly senior partner at Patricof & Co. Ventures, the huge international venture and investment company—shared with us generous time and his extensive experience. Michael T. Moe—principal and emerging company analyst at Montgomery Securities in San Francisco, and formerly senior emerging company analyst with Lehman Brothers in New York—shared with us his vast experience in an extensive interview. Chip Ottness—a billion-dollar small-cap fund manager at J. P. Morgan—gave us his experience from putting his money where his mouth is. Michael M. Connors—senior vice president and divisional president at America Online—shared with us a few of his observations. Brenda Manning—manager of licensing and acquisitions at Ciba-Corning, now part of Novartis—shared her views on corporate partnering. Thomas W. Itin—CEO extraordinaire of the $70 million Williams Controls, and formerly cofounder of the now $900 million Roadmaster, known throughout the industry as one of the most astute managers—shared with us his experience and philosophy in an extensive interview. Stanley Trilling—senior vice president investments, and *Money* magazine's top broker for consecutive years—provided concise yet to-the-point input. Richard Frank—director of the University of Maryland TAP incubator—helped us identify a company we feature in the incubator chapter, and over the years has been very helpful in conveying the incubator concept. Terje Skotheim—founder and president of Moltech—agreed to share detailed information in spite of the fact that Moltech is a private company. The people at the National Business Incubation Association also furnished us with very helpful information.

We would like to thank our agent Ruth Wreschner, our McGraw-Hill editor Susan Barry, senior editing supervisor Jane Palmieri, and publisher Philip Ruppel as well as the creative, production, and marketing staffs of the McGraw-Hill Professional Publishing Group. Gabor Baumann would also like to thank Tina Baumann and Rae Hoffman for their encouragement and support.

POISED FOR GROWTH

DEFINITIONS, PURPOSE, AND FOCUS

In many ways, this book is a combination of *In Search of Excellence* and *The Only Definitive Guide You'll Need*—for emerging growth businesses. We accomplish this by what we call the EAIR method—examples, analysis, insight, and rules. You might even be tempted to play with the words, and say that in searching for business excellence and guidelines for company success, you must tune your EAR to what's in the AIR—hence, EAIR.

We opened with the words "In many ways" because much has changed in the 15 years since the publication of the megahit bearing the title *In Search of Excellence*. In fact, in light of major problems encountered by some of the large corporations which were used as models in that book, many of the hypotheses were revised a few years later by one of the book's authors, Tom Peters, in *Thriving on Chaos*. And if the chaotic hurricane winds of uncertainty and fast change that Peters talks about play a crucial role in the lives of well-rooted huge trees—the large corporations—you can imagine how they affect the survival and growth prospects of the weaker trunk and branches of emerging growth businesses.

There are a number of Growth Factors which facilitate excellence and success in the emerging growth company. The three most critical ones are good people, quality capital, and the right corporate partners. These three Growth Factors—people, capital, and corporate partners (PCCP)—in their proper formats, are so vital to the growth of an emerging business that the ability of an emerging company to attract PCCP determines whether it will be given the chance to grow or whether it will be doomed to shrivel or find its place among the "walking dead."

For the public company, or the would-be public company, there is a fourth Growth Factor: appealing to Wall Street. As we refer to it in this book, Wall Street is not a place, but rather a concept: the vast network of worldwide public capital. Although we shall discuss the magic of appealing to Wall Street quite frequently in the book, we chose not to count it as a completely separate Growth Factor, mainly because Wall Street represents capital. Furthermore, a company with high appeal on Wall Street will usually attract PCCP—because everyone makes money. Key people receive stock options; investors will be lured by the famous ROI (return on investment); and corporate partners will be more attracted to the company for one of two reasons: either because equity can appreciate—if they buy a stake in the company—or because money raised through public offerings or private placements pays for much of the costs, from which these strategic investors also benefit.

Frankly, we consider the terms *excellence* and *success* to be superlative clichés that are used too loosely. We shall, therefore, refer to them only implicitly. Excellence and success are obviously the "end" goals, but it is much more practical to focus on the "means to the end," because of the chaotic nature of the process, and hence the "end." America Online (AOL) is one of the most important growth and success stories of the first half of this decade—a company whose revenues grew from $30 million in 1991 to $1 billion just 5 years later. A senior vice president and division president of AOL relayed to us in an interview that one of the company's founders "crashed" a few businesses before he hit the "jackpot" with AOL. You see, chaos, uncertainty, and change always compete with order, logic, and predictability.

Attractiveness is, on the other hand, a very practical term to refer to when discussing the emerging growth business. Yet it's not in the mainstream vocabulary of business "how-to"; we usually use more objective, pragmatic terms to describe a company's appeal: annual rate of growth, sales volume, profit margins, reinvestment in infrastructure, and other such "measurable" benchmarks. Attractiveness in business is an analyzable and qualifiable factor that determines an emerging growth company's ability to attract good people and quality capital, as well as important corporate clients and strategic partners—all of which *empower* the business. These are again the three Growth Factors—PCCP in acronym.

There is an important blessing or malaise—it depends on which side of the trend you are on—that strongly affects the emerging growth sector. We call it the *chain reaction of attractiveness*, or what Microsoft's Bill Gates calls positive and negative spirals. A company with a product that starts winning markets gets positive public relations (PR), and soon good people flock over, private investors and venture funds offer their money, large strategic partners commit their resources, and Wall Street starts luring the company to the pot of gold of the public markets. The company is rich in PCCP—the positive Growth Factors. The major boost in talent, capital, and marketing or other resources of corporate partners propels the business ahead, and the company becomes even more attractive and starts growing even faster. When, conversely, a negative trend gets triggered by a bad product, by grossly underestimated trends and competition, or by financial improprieties, the company gets bad PR and good people start leaving, capital becomes scarce, and the chain reaction of unattractiveness pulls the company down the helix of a negative spiral.

Is there a connection between the chain reaction of attractiveness and the chaotic patterns of uncertainty and change? Absolutely. Are these phenomena random, or completely beyond your control? Absolutely not.

Peter Lynch, manager of Fidelity's highly visible Magellan Fund until 1990, makes a point in his book *Beating the Street* that, often, there is no correlation between the success of a company's operations and the success of its stock over a few months or even a few years (that points to an element of randomness). In the long term, however, there is a 100 percent correlation between the performance of the company and the success of its stock (which demonstrates that events are not really random). Since Wall Street is a measure of attracting attention and with it public capital, it seems that some experts do not believe in complete randomness when it comes to predicting the long-term success of businesses.

Another important characteristic of business uncertainty is that within chaos there is a degree of randomness—not total randomness. It is somewhere between total predictability and total unpredictability. And that's what we mean by chaotic markets—they are *somewhat,* but not fully predictable. In fact, some situations are more chaotic than others. All can't be just "noise," it's a "signal" *with* "noise." And it's your job to develop your own noise reduction Dolby system. As the cliché goes, the *optimist* sees the cheese, the *pessimist* sees only the holes in it—and the *realist* sees cheese with holes. The optimist sees a glass half full, the pessimist sees it half empty, and the realist says: "Hey, one half of this glass is full, and the other half is empty."

The same applies to *analyzing* the Growth Factors of the emerging growth company. These factors do not constitute a prescription for *success,* but they put you on the road to it. Still, final results depend on *other* factors which are out of your control—those associated with uncertainty.

In identifying and analyzing the ways in which emerging growth businesses can boost their Growth Factors, we have interviewed successful company founders and managers, as well as private investors and experts from the venture capital and securities industries. We combed through a large number of company reports—the business literature, magazines, and newspapers—to try to be as current and up to date as possible. Finally, we blended all the above with our own experience and insights and devised rules.

In presenting concrete examples and case studies throughout the book, we needed to make trade-offs—sometimes tough ones. On the one hand, we wanted to present companies which are going through various emerging growth stages *currently*—sort of a contemporary snapshot. On the other hand, we felt that a more reliable lesson may be learned from companies that already "made it through the rain." Backtracking a successful large company to the emerging growth years—in 20-20 hindsight—is actually a very effective proposition for getting a reliable measure of what it takes to grow a business successfully. In this book you'll learn lessons from America's most successful and not-so-successful companies.

Backtracking can be divided into far hindsight, near hindsight, and nowsight. We look back at the emerging growth years of companies like ADP, Wal-Mart, Microsoft, and Apple, which made their transition to fully grown large corporations in the 1970s and 1980s. Then we look, for example, at the emerging growth years of Starbucks and America Online—companies that made their transition in the first half of the 1990s. We also analyze in hindsight some of the Growth Factors of companies that have just recently made the transition—such as Boston Market and Fore Systems. We look at quite a number of companies that are midway in their emerging growth stages, like Williams Controls and Nobel Education Dynamics, and at some which are at earlier stages. And then we sprinkle here and there some negative examples—to contrast what works with what is proven not to work. For obvious reasons, all negative examples in which companies' names are provided are based on facts from publicly available media. We believe that a good balance has been achieved in presenting things from all angles—in foresight, nowsight, and hindsight.

When we discussed the concept and premise of this book with Victoria Hamilton, executive vice president and chief operating officer of General American Investors (GAI)—a closed-end investment company with more than half a billion dollars in assets—she made a very important comment. Hamilton, who was with the private New York venture capital firm of SRK Management Co. until joining GAI in 1992, pointed out that she doesn't believe one can "quantify" the ingredients for a company's success. The decision, for example, of whether a company gets funded or not involves a large element of luck—according to her venture capital experience. Call it luck or call it uncertainty—both allude to a degree of randomness.

We do agree that for startups or very early-stage emerging growth companies, luck, or being in the right place at the right time, plays a crucial role. But we believe that for most of the emerging growth contingent, we are in a position to analyze to a great extent the Growth Factors that will put a company on the right track to success. In fact, we agreed to Victoria Hamilton's suggestion to adopt the term *analyzable* or *qualifiable factors*, instead of using the term *quantifiable factors*. These are the kinds of factors that put you on the correct road, and help you make the right turns.

Some of these observations are in line with the opinions of one of the most successful investors of our time—George Soros. In his books *Soros on Soros* and *The Alchemy of Finance*, he stresses the fallibility and unpredictability of financial markets, because of the reflexive nature of the processes that determine their outcome. Simply stated, reflexivity refers to the fact that investors' actions will affect the market—which in turn will affect investors' actions. Unpredictability, of course, usually implies uncertainty—maybe that's what gave Soros the idea to call his fund the Quantum Fund. Sounds disappointing; not only are we fallible but the financial markets are too! Well, there is an optimistic way to look at all this: Hey, we still manage to create complex mechanisms that don't go haywire that often.

In fact, even George Soros—whose meteoric success was associated more with currencies and international markets than with emerging companies—couldn't have performed under totally random conditions. Many of the very profitable steps he took, including his home run with the pound sterling in 1992, were based on careful analysis and probabilistic predictions. No guarantees—just well-calculated risks.

As you might surmise, a great divide separates the emerging growth stage from the fully grown company stage. Searching for *excellence* in a company's critical, fast-growth stages resembles searching for the perfect, smooth trail when the horses must pull a wagon up the hill. It's true that the smoother the trail, the better the trip—and there's less chance that the horse will break a leg, that the wagon will lose a wheel, or that the whole kit and caboodle will tumble, roll back down, and disintegrate. But if this were a wagon of pioneer settlers in the Old West—being chased by bandits, with dwindling supplies of food and ammunition and an approaching storm, to boot—the wagon would have to cut across in a direction that would get it up there fast. Once it arrived at the plateau on the top, it could design its route under more favorable conditions.

While excellence is always something any company must strive for, it is generally easier to prescribe it for the large corporate entity than for the emerging growth constituency. But as we mentioned earlier, in the new chaotic age of business, even the large companies that were selected as role models in *In Search of Excellence,* such as IBM and DEC, couldn't thrive on excellence alone, and had to adapt to a scenario of change and uncertainty.

In fact, some large companies have started imitating internally the emerging growth business models. They are becoming more lean and entrepreneurial, they structure themselves around smaller teams and product-based units, and they transfer the decision-making process to lower levels of management. But there is no paradox here. The restructuring we just mentioned is intended, in most cases, to provide a more independent, creative environment that would also enable the large corporation to respond faster to change. And a large corporation has some advantages, emanating from its massive internal and external networks. It has less of a problem maintaining a pool of good people, it is usually well capitalized or is able to pull together capital when it wants to develop a product or conquer a market, and of course it has less need for the resources of other large strategic partners.

Finally, the prescription for *success* has to be questioned too. For if, in the age of chaos, there's no one-to-one correlation between the rules you follow and the outcome, then there's no prescription for success either. Under such circumstances, we can discuss the means but we can't discuss the end. Being an attractive company, in the context of this book, means doing your best to create a framework for excellence and success— and putting your best foot forward within this framework. "Dress up," "create a positive aura"—produce the framework— then use your brain and savvy. This still might not be *guaranteed* success—because there are so many other factors that do not depend on you—but you have created the environment for achieving your company's goal.

Just what range of companies are we talking about in this book? *Business Week* publishes annually, in the month of May, its list of 100 Hot Growth Companies. To qualify for this list, a company, among other things, has to be publicly traded and its annual sales have to be between $10 million and $150 million.

Although we find this definition very useful, we want to adopt a more flexible definition for our emerging growth companies. We will include *privately* held companies. Also, in order to allow the inclusion of companies with especially long development cycles which might have no revenues yet, but whose valuation (or market capitalization in the case of public companies) can reach tens of millions or even exceed $100 million, we replaced the requirement for a minimum of $10 million of revenues by a minimum "objective" valuation of $10 million. By "objective" valuation we mean (1) for the private company, a valuation by private investors or large corporations that made investments in the company; or (2) for the public company, market capitalization—the number of outstanding shares multiplied by the stock price. We also decided to be more flexible with the upper limit, simply because we are not restricted to a finite list of 100 companies. We'll, however, stay in the same ballpark as *Business Week*—an upper range of $150 million to $200 million in sales.

Let's compare these definitions with some other criteria used to define the statistical range of companies. A study conducted by Merrill Lynch divides the U.S. equity market by market capitalization. Companies with $5 million to $50 million market capitalization belong to the microcap category. Those with $50 million to $500 million market capitalization belong to the small-cap category. If a company's market capitalization ranges between $500 million and $2.3 billion, it is a midcap company. And a capitalization over $2.3 billion earns the company a place in the large-cap sector.

How does our emerging growth company categorization compare with the Merrill Lynch formula? It is quite simple: 93 percent of the companies on *Business Week*'s 1995 Hot Growth

Companies list and 83 percent of those on *Business Week*'s 1996 list belong to the microcap or small-cap sector. Only 7 percent of the companies in the 1995 list and 17 percent in the 1996 list belong to the midcap sector. If we extend the range to around $200 million in sales, we increase the companies that belong to the midcap range by a few percentage points in each year. The higher percentage in the larger market capitalization categories is attributable to the much higher valuations in the 1996 equity markets.

Since the general populace of companies is underperforming the *Business Week* list, we can safely conclude that the vast majority (over 90 percent) of the companies that fit the definition of emerging growth businesses in this book are microcap or small-cap companies, and a small minority (10 percent or less) are midcap companies. Are there any emerging growth large-cap companies? As always, there are exceptions, but one can count them on one hand (or perhaps one finger). In December 1995, the emerging growth Internet "play" Netscape Communications, with $42 million in sales for the four previous quarters, had a market capitalization of over $5 billion— definitely a large-cap. When an emerging growth company is at the same time a large-cap company, we call it *Netscapism*.

How do our definitions of the emerging growth sector compare with the government's terms for small business? Is there a correlation? According to the U.S. Small Business Administration (SBA), a small business is any business with up to 500 employees. This definition evidently covers a wide range of small to midsize companies—close to 99.7 percent of all the businesses in the United States. One might even argue that when a business has 499 employees—which often can put its revenues close to or above $50 million—it's not such a "small" business any more. And, indeed, that's just exactly the range we want to cover in this book.

How many small businesses are there? The Internal Revenue Service reported that over 20 million small businesses filed tax returns. American Business Disc (ABD), an information service which classifies businesses on the basis of revenues and number of employees, has a record of only half that amount, approximately 10 million. Perhaps the difference lies in the many small-scale individual home businesses which are below the radar of an information-collecting service, such as ABD. In fact, from the perspective of this book, we feel more comfortable with the conservative figures of ABD, because it includes only the more substantive companylike entities. In actual number there are 9,845,033 businesses with fewer than 500 employees, out of a total of 9,866,327 businesses in the United States.

How do you correlate the small business sector with the emerging growth sector. Well, the correlation is not direct, but again, if we follow the ABD data, we will find that there are approximately 8,785,000 businesses in the United States with revenues under $200 million. The total number of businesses studied in this "revenue cross section" is only 8,796,266. If we subtract the approximately 6,000,000 businesses with less than $500,000 in revenues or fewer than 5 employees, we are left with 2,785,000 businesses which have the potential to fit into the emerging growth category.

The small business sector is an important national economic factor. In a position paper for the task forces preparing the 1995 White House Conference on Small Business, the SBA reported that close to half the employment opportunities in the United States are provided by small firms. Furthermore, close to half the new jobs are created by small businesses. In certain states the percentage is even higher. Case in point: In the mid- to late 1980s, more than 85 percent of the new jobs created in the state of Washington were by small businesses. Small businesses originate more than half of the nation's technical and industrial innovations, close to half the gross domestic product (GDP) of the United States, and more than half of all domestic sales. Not only are these firms creative, but they grow rapidly and boost the nation's economy. Average assets of these firms increase typically at a compounded annual rate of 23 percent, export sales at 136 percent, and tax payments at 233 percent.

Another reason this range of businesses is important is that large corporations looking to expand into new markets, to add new product lines, or simply to inject "new blood"—without the need to develop those assets internally—routinely joint-venture with and buy out successful and promising emerging companies. Finally, you can't underestimate the importance of the hopes and expectations of the entrepreneurs that founded these companies.

But the small, emerging business reality is not simple at all. Only a fraction of the millions of companies become successful and contribute to real personal and economic growth—not to mention climb to the heights of companies like Starbucks, Boston Market, Amgen, and America Online. Others either disappear or survive in the form of "walking dead."

There has been some debate in the world of journalism (*The New York Times, Success Magazine*) whether the myth that small businesses are the job engine of the United States is indeed true. In a *New York Times* article (March 25, 1994) titled "Myth: Small Business as Job Engine," Sylvia Nasar claims that large companies are the real source of new jobs, quoting numerous economists and professors. In *Success Magazine* (July–August 1994), Wilson L. Harrell challenges Nasar's claims and proves that big business is definitely not the job engine—we've lost millions of jobs in that sector since the 1980s. So, if neither big business nor small business is the job engine of America, what is? Who created, for example, the 3 million new jobs between 1987 and 1991? The answer is: It's the entrepreneurial, fast-growing emerging growth companies that create the jobs during their initial growth cycles.

But in order to make it to the "next step," emerging growth companies today must find a hedge against the small business manifestations of chaos and change. These universal problems are compounded with issues that are unique to emerging companies, such as the shortage of capital, labor, experience, and credibility.

This book explains how to replace the parallax view of the typical entrepreneur with a view that's more consistent with that of experienced professionals and managers (or potential critics), especially the type whom you'll need to help you financially and otherwise, and whom you must convince of the value and profitability of your business. It will give you a "behind the scenes," *third-party* view of correct strategic and business planning, the hazards of business valuation, the options of financing, the new revolution in pooling resources, the importance and pitfalls of management, the power of strategic alliances, access to megainformation, and much more. Since the focus of this book is on *attracting third parties*, it is unique in its point of view.

Many books are written for the entrepreneur-with-an-idea—this is not one of those. It's for the entrepreneurs and business managers who already have something going, and for the dreamers who look ahead into the future. In a seed or start-up business, the founders have a lot to gain and little to lose; an investor, key employee, or corporate partner in a startup, in turn, takes a very high risk. For an emerging growth company, the risk-reward distribution between founders and owners, on the one hand, and third parties such as investors, key people, and corporate partners, on the other, is much more balanced. It's a more analyzable business sector, one in which careers and fortunes are made—the cradle for the future Intels, Microsofts, or Staples.

This book is also recommended for managers in many large corporations who are constantly scouting for strategic partners and acquisition candidates. You'll get an interesting frame of reference on candidate companies, the price they are worth, and the probabilities that they will be able to fit into your strategic goals.

SEVEN THINGS YOU MUST KNOW TO BE TAKEN MORE SERIOUSLY

How to Get Important Third Parties to Accept You for Real

"Netscape" they all cried; that is, they all cried for more stock. Priced at $28 for the initial public offering (IPO), the stock "net escaped" the gravitational pull of conventional equity valuation and entered into the realm of cyberspace (i.e., hypercyberspace) by increasing severalfold in price before it closed that hot day in August of 1995. An interview with the jaded Wall Street investment bankers who priced the IPO would have revealed that the offering went just as planned. "Nope, the issuer didn't leave anything on the table."

Let's not conjecture whether the investment bankers had it right or not. Instead, let's take a look at the Netscape levitation through the eyes of a leading emerging growth company analyst, Michael Moe, principal at Montgomery Securities. "It's a castle in the sky," Moe commented to us when we interviewed him about emerging growth companies. The company presents an "open-ended growth opportunity led by people who have made Wall Street a fortune before." The people or person to whom Moe was referring is Jim Clark, one of the founders of Netscape, who previously was with Silicon Graphics.

But let's look at it this way. The company was formed in April 1994. In the third quarter ending September 30, 1994, Netscape was a private company with no revenues to speak of (less than $200,000). One year later it was a public *large-cap* company with annual revenues of approximately $40 million and with a market capitalization over 100 times those annual revenues. Since the company had no earnings when it went public, its levitation was due to a "feel" of the analysts and investment bankers. These guys must have taken Netscape very seriously.

But Netscape's aura reached beyond the so-called fickle Wall Street. The multibillion-dollar Microsoft—one of the most prestigious corporations in the world—had to compete with this "fragile" emerging growth company in trying to win clients and strategic partners such as the two major on-line service companies: America Online and CompuServe. And the result: a tie. Each, Netscape and Microsoft—David and Goliath—got a piece of the pie of these services' lucrative Internet browser business. It seems that some established corporations must be taking Netscape quite seriously.

And talk about market share. Netscape had, in early 1996, 85 percent of the Internet browser market. The Internet user community must be taking Netscape quite seriously, because there are quite a number of alternatives out there. So whether because of its management, the quality of its product, its understanding of the market, or people's affinity to the smart and agile underdog "Davids"—or most probably because of a combination of all the above and more—Netscape has been taken very seriously right from the start.

Even a cursory review of books on the market tells you that "seven" is the most important number when creating an attractive book for best-sellerdom. Adding to his credentials as a master of longevity, Deepak Chopra has become a prophet of profit by proclaiming *The Seven Spiritual Laws of Success*. In an offering the size of a small prayerbook, Dr. Chopra has already rivaled the previous new-age consultant Stephen Covey, who wrote *Seven Habits of Highly Effective People*. While Dr. Chopra was turning his attention from health to wealth, the Book-of-the-Month Club tapped Henry Dreher's *The Immune Power Personality: Seven Traits You Can Develop to Stay Healthy* to tell executives how to have their success and eat it too.

Far be it from your authors to undermine a trend. We too have chosen *seven knowledge points* that will enable an emerging growth company to be taken seriously by investors (public and private), corporate strategic partners, and the all-important human capital needed to drive the emerging organization. Indeed, there are more than seven attributes, but after culling through case studies and our own personal experiences, we believe that the seven points listed in this chapter are the more compelling attributes.

PREVIEW: THE CASE STUDY APPROACH

Before we roll up our sleeves to convince you of the relevance and importance of our Magnificent Seven, let's review several additional fascinating examples that will drive home the concept behind "Seven Things You Must Know to Be Taken More Seriously." Later in this chapter, as the seven knowledge points unfold, these and other case studies will aid you in understanding the specific importance of each individual knowledge point.

ALDUS CORPORATION

Aldus Corporation, a high-flying, trailblazing innovator of desktop publishing software, was featured on *Business Week*'s Hot Growth Company list for 4 years straight; that was in 1991. Yet by 1993 it was billed a "laggard" by the same prestigious publication. After profits tumbled 70 percent in 1992—because Aldus spent heavily on new-product and market development to fend off the encroachment of fierce competitors—the company's stock dived to 25 percent of its 1991 value, a fourfold drop. The explanation given, at that time, by Aldus CEO Paul Brainerd—"The market is totally unforgiving....There's no in-between"—doesn't seem good enough. After all, many companies spend heavily on product and market development—and very often Wall Street views those expenses as positive. (Some emerging public companies, in fact, become darlings of the market before earning a penny.) Logic says, therefore, that a company like Aldus, whose stock was at a low and whose extensive resources were being plowed into developing new products and markets, should be a *buy*, because of the large *potential* growth it was facing. Evidently, there must be another explanation to the market being "unforgiving"—somehow investors stopped taking Aldus *seriously.*

NOBEL EDUCATION

There are few things more noble or serious than education. Nobel Education Dynamics has made a noble business of education. In 1982, the company was in its infancy as the Rocking Horse Child Care Centers of America. It sounds like child's play, but in 1992 the company graduated from the child-care business, or at least the company underwent—as the accountants put it in the footnotes to the financial statements—a "change of control." With a change in control, also, came a change in focus and a change in name. Not quite overnight, the Rocking Horse was transformed into Nobel Education, which proclaims itself as one of the leading companies in the "rapidly emerging private education market."

In 1995, Nobel began to make the grade with its newly focused strategy. Revenues in 1995 increased 28 percent to $44.5 million from $34.4 million. More impressively, net earnings for the year ended December 31, 1995, rose 64 percent over 1994 net earnings. Nobel is still moving to the head of the class. In the first quarter of 1996, its revenues increased 50 percent—from almost $10 million in the first quarter of 1995 to close to $15 million in 1996, or $60 million in annualized revenues. Net income for the 1996 quarter increased a healthy double digit—15 percent. The company is being touted by many securities analysts as one of the leaders in the future delivery of education in America.

Merryhill Country Schools is the company's Nobel prize. Small classes (maximum of 22 students) afford an individualized "nurturing" environment. After that statement alone, we want to go to school again. The company also offers an education that uses advanced technologies such as interactive learning via CD-ROMs. Early development is encouraged by the introduction of a second language to 2- and 3-year-olds, with total immersion into a second language by first grade. If nothing else, these students will be well prepared for the global marketplace.

Forbes took the Merryhill schools seriously when, in a line-by-line comparison, the program was favorably compared with the prestigious Sacramento Country Day School. There was one difference: The tuition at Merryhill is $4750, which includes day care before and after school, whereas at Sacramento Country Day the tuition is $7750, with an additional $2300 for day care.

Nobel, in a sense, has graduated into the Ivy League. In 1996, Nobel established a cooperative working relationship with the University of Pennsylvania and its Wharton School. Graduate students of the university's education/child-care/business programs will be provided internships at Nobel. In addition, the university is cooperating with Nobel in creating a program for the continuing development of Nobel's lower and middle management in disciplines required to properly provide an education/business combination.

As Bill Gates commented in his book *The Road Ahead,* a lot of credit goes to people who turn around companies. Once a company is caught in a negative spiral, it is hard to reverse the trend. Nonetheless, Nobel Education did take charge of its future and successfully changed its focus, and it must be taken very seriously. Securities experts, such as Stanley Trilling, a leading stockbroker with the Los Angeles office of PaineWebber, recommends Nobel as the best education "play" on Wall Street. *Money* magazine takes Trilling seriously, since he has been ranked more than once as a top stockbroker.

TRANSMEDIA NETWORK

Transmedia Network, Inc., an emerging growth company with revenues of more than $65 million, has nothing to do with media or the omnipresent information superhighway. The company has addressed the needs of restaurants and consumers in this era of cautious spending. Transmedia's core business is based on financing restaurants and is, thereby, able to offer Transmedia members a discount on their restaurant bills through its Executive Savings card. The service is offered in most major cities in the United States, through company-owned or franchised operations. The equation is simple: A restaurant bill is split 50 percent for the restaurant, 25 percent for the customer, and 25 percent for Transmedia (or the operating franchisee). The restaurant also receives free listings in a booklet that is distributed monthly to the cardholders. What's more important, the restaurant receives the money in advance, which it can use for its own corporate purposes. When customers eat up the money, a new check arrives.

To draw an analogy, some have characterized Transmedia as in the "yield management" business. Just as the airlines have brought down the price of visiting grandma to keep those empty seats full, almost 6000 restaurants have decided to sell their empty seats to the clients of Transmedia. A restaurant is saddled with high fixed costs along with its variable cost, primarily food, constituting 30 percent of the total cost of doing business. The logic from the restaurant's point of view is that it gets $50 on a $100 check. Of that $100 check, the variable cost is $30 and thus, the restaurant pockets the difference between $50 (which it receives from Transmedia) and $30 (which constitutes its variable costs). The restaurant is pricing its services at its marginal cost. If it works in one industry, why shouldn't it work in another? We suggest that Transmedia use this approach to blow some life into the retail apparel industry. Maybe the Chapter 11-in-bankruptcy-reorganization Barney's can give 25 percent discounts to Transmedia customers. Better yet, give the customers a choice: They could get a 25 percent discount or an extra pair of pants or a bottle of their favorite perfume. And Transmedia pays in advance—which is not bad for cashflow either and would make even Barney's creditors happy.

Getting little restaurants to sign up for a program that puts advance cash in their pockets and sends customers over would not qualify Transmedia, in our view, as a company that has been taken seriously. But look what else is happening—this time in the strategic partnering arena. *The* (mighty) *New York Times* became one of Transmedia's strategic partners in late 1993 by offering the Transmedia/TimesCard. The joint card is easier for *Times* home delivery subscribers, offers access to more cultural and entertainment events than ever before, and brings in the 75,000 or more TimesCard cardholders.

In mid-1994, Transmedia also signed deals with Prodigy Services Co., Amtrak, and credit card issuer MBNA America Bank NA to distribute its card as value-added premium to customers. More recently, in 1995 and 1996, Transmedia entered into an agreement with GE Capital, one of the largest purchasers of telephone long-distance time, that brings the cost of long-distance calling to Transmedia cardholders below the cost of calling through AT&T, Sprint, and MCI. Just to make the airline analogy complete, Transmedia cardholders can get "frequent flyer miles" from United Airlines and Continental Airlines as an alternative to cash savings on restaurant purchases made with the Transmedia card.

What is, however, even more interesting is that Transmedia is going global. A British merchant bank obtained the rights to market the service in Australia, New Zealand, and certain other parts of Asia. Next, we may be reading about people in Tokyo dining on discount sushi. Transmedia Network—a good idea that has no borders— is being taken very seriously.

WILLIAMS CONTROLS

Not every emerging growth company is an overnight success and not every emerging growth company is created in the imagination of an entrepreneur. But a leading CEO can transform an emerging company to his or her imagination. Williams Controls, a company that is broadly classified as a manufacturer of heavy vehicle and automotive parts, dates its origins to 1938. The company was acquired in 1988 from Dana Corporation, the global automotive parts manufacturer, by Thomas Itin, a financier and cofounder of several other businesses, including Roadmaster, a bicycle manufacturer. It might appear that Itin went from "footpower" to "horsepower"; others say he went from one success to another.

For the fiscal year ended September 30, 1995, revenues of Williams increased to over $60 million, compared with 1994 revenues of slightly over $40 million, or an increase of 45 percent. For the first 6 months of FY1996, *annualized* revenues increased again to $70 million. As we said, Thomas Itin is a financier—that is, a financier who feels comfortable with the art of the deal and believes that a company should grow through a combination of internal growth and acquisitions. As such, acquisitions accounted for 16 percent or almost one-third of the company's growth for the 1995 fiscal year.

Itin's clearly articulated goal is that the sales of Williams will grow at a 15 to 20 percent compounded rate until the year 2000. He projects that half of that growth will be internal and the remainder will be through acquisitions. Itin's efforts have been acknowledged by many analysts and stock pickers that follow small-cap, lower-priced companies. Once again, Stanley Trilling, PaineWebber senior vice president of investments in Los Angeles, who has been voted *Money* magazine's top-rated broker more than once, told us in an interview that Williams is one of the best emerging growth companies. And certainly, Trilling puts his money where his mouth is. His company and his clients hold 20 percent of the public shares of Williams. And in spite of temporary setbacks in the growth of Williams' earnings per share, Trilling predicts a bright future. He is looking for a quadrupling of the stock price in the next 4 years.

Just as important, when we spoke to Itin about the most recent results, he was already "turning around" the problems. New management was installed in one of the lagging divisions, and Itin continues to diversify. Quoting one of his favorite management gurus, Peter Drucker, Itin said that he plans "to stabilize Williams' existing businesses, extend but not overextend, and build a better platform for Williams." As he summed it up, "innovate, innovate, innovate."

AURA SYSTEMS

Aura Systems, Inc., a public company with fiscal year 1996 revenues of $82 million that employs around 250 employees, is an ideal case study for this book. We've known about the company for a couple of years, especially from stockholder friends and associates who have been riding the rollercoaster movements of its stock that would put Coney Island's best-known amusement ride to shame. Someone told us jokingly that he hardly knows anyone who doesn't own Aura stock.

Even though the company's fundamentals have been improving over the past few years, from $11 million revenues in 1993 to $16 million in 1994, $44 million in 1995, and $82 million in 1996 with earnings (loss) per share (EPS) of −$.36, −$.35, −$.07, and −$.48, respectively, the stock has been falling each year to a low that equals approximately one-third of its previous year's high. In the most recent quarterly result released by the company, Aura is at the breakeven point—for the 3 months ended May 1996 revenues have increased again and a net gain of 1 cent was reported—but its stock is still being left behind in the market rally; on October 16, 1996, it was $2.34 a share. And in the past three years, Aura's stock has been unable to break the $10 barrier. Specifically, in the years 1991, 1992, 1993, 1994, and 1995, the lows were $1.31, $2.50, $2.93, $3.75, and $3.06, respectively, and the highs were $9.25, $12.25, $9.56, $9.43, and $7.75, respectively, and the latest 52-week high and low were $6.75 and $2.25, respectively—a true rollercoaster that seems to go in circles. Dan Dorfman, the man who moves markets by touting stocks on CNBC, named Aura as one of his favorite *short sells* for 1995.

What's going on with Aura that its stock doesn't react to fundamentals? We think that perhaps investors are no longer taking Aura seriously. We got our first glimpse at the reasons from an investment banking colleague. He said to us: "The company is all over the board. Aura is in too many products and markets." We wanted to verify those statements and we didn't have to dig deep. Before even accessing detailed financial information, we looked at Aura's company snapshot in the basic CompuServe service. Here, Aura is presented as a company that develops, commercializes, and sells systems which use proprietary *magnetic technology* developed for electromagnetic high-force actuators and *magnetic bearings*; researches and develops advanced electro-optical *projection systems*; designs, develops, and markets *computer*-aided design and manufacturing *software*; and designs, manufactures, and sells *microwave components* for *commercial communications* and *military defense* systems.

To top it all, *The Economist* of August 27, 1994, reports on page 55 (ProQuest ABI/INFORM Abstract) that *youngsters and parents* who have tried the *Interactor*—a trim electromagnetic *backpack* that pummels the wearer in response to the *video-game* bangs and crashes on screen—swear they love it. Aura Systems of El Segundo, California has been looking for a block-buster product since it started to apply its aerospace know-how to the commercial world. Amazing!

Now, back to you—the emerging growth company. In order to attract people, capital, and corporate partners you must be taken *very seriously*. What can you learn from Aldus, Nobel, Transmedia, Williams Controls, Aura, and others? Dictionaries are a good starting point for people to make sure they are speaking the same language. The old *Webster's Collegiate* says: "Serious implies a concern for what really matters." This chapter will tell you how the "antennas" of third parties—investors, key people, and the corporate world—pick up that *you and your company really understand what matters*.

Let's start with an interesting observation from the culinary realm. The Italians have hundreds of types of pasta, the French produce as many types of wine, and the Japanese enjoy a large variety of sake. Often outsiders wonder what the minuscule differences are between, say, spaghetti and linguini, or two very similar-tasting Bordeaux wines, not to mention some nearly indistinguishable varieties of sake.

Does a minor difference in content, texture, or taste justify defining a new entity? The simple answer is: Yes, because it works. The profound answer, however, takes into consideration the "whole picture"—that a small difference in the source can end in major differences as it develops. Case in point: Different types of pasta are used to create different dishes; a different wine or sake goes with different types of food. To put it in another context, two human beings may look very similar at inception, but they sure are different at the age of 20. Or, in geometrical terms, two slightly divergent lines look parallel on an 8.5″ × 11″ sheet of paper, but will show a major divergence and change in spacing when drawn on a football field.

If the "devil is in the detail," so is success. The fact that small, apparent differences in the basic ingredients can make a major difference in the outcome is well known to people involved with evaluating emerging growth businesses. And this is a major dissimilarity between startup companies and emerging growth businesses. In startups, it is much easier for the keen eye of the expert to see who has got it and who hasn't—you can clearly discern the good from the bad. However, to evaluate and predict which emerging growth business will become a fully grown star, you need to differentiate among good, better, and best. Just as the approximate 1 percent difference in the content of the nuclei of different uranium isotopes causes major distinctions in their energy-releasing fission characteristics, so apparently similar, yet slightly different business teams come up with very different business performance.

When you deal with differentials, you have to know the laws of calculus—regular math won't do. And that is how we came to the concept of being taken more seriously. ("More," because the fact that you are where you are shows that you have already been taken seriously to a certain extent.) Being taken seriously is not the opposite of being laughed at. What it is, is the subtle association of what you say and represent with a high probability of practical potential. It is the yes answer to the question "Are these guys *really* for real?" Achieving this status as an emerging growth company requires that you know seven things that we believe are the underlying differentials in getting important third parties to take you for real. For the sake of being taken seriously, let's get started finally with our Magnificent Seven.

KNOWLEDGE POINT 1: ONLY PRIORITIZED KNOWLEDGE IS POWER— KNOW THY MARKET NICHE EVEN BETTER THAN THY PRODUCT

In the overused world of advice we always hear: "Do you want to be a big fish in a small pond or a small fish in a big pond?" We believe, however, it's less a question of what size fish you are and more a question of whether you understand the pond.

The pond is the market and, like any ecosystem, it's constantly changing. In order to be attractive to investors or others, an emerging company must know the market better than any outsider (and probably better than any insider): You are the expert of your domain; just knowing your product is not enough.

Being an expert in your world entails being able to address many issues, but first and foremost you have to determine where to point your arrowhead—what market niche you should focus on to penetrate the market "shields." Figuratively speaking, the market has an immune system of its own—its tendency is to reject foreign, unfamiliar objects. The roadblocks that this "immune system" puts in the way of new companies or products are in the form of competition, credibility, fear of the unknown, unproved cost-effectiveness, and many more such factors. Proving to the "immune system" of the market that you are a "positive" entity requires that you focus on what you do best and try to establish roots in your niche.

Spreading your efforts in many areas, unless you are Procter & Gamble or Philip-Morris, raises doubts in the minds of many third parties as to whether you can focus and achieve well-targeted goals—and they might not take you seriously.

Then you must show that you understand whether the market is presently big enough for you and the other competitors to operate profitability. Will the market grow enough in the future (say, over the next 3 to 5 years) for you and your prospective competitors to operate profitably? What's the life cycle of your product? Is your product a fad or will it have a long enough life cycle to penetrate both national and global markets? My pet rock is around here someplace, but the company ain't. Finally, is your product proprietary? Can it be patented? How can you protect your know-how? Starbucks doesn't have a patent on its roasting process, but its coffee flavors are unique and the double-back-flip latte keeps flowing.

Now for a concrete example. In 1993, the year *Business Week* designated Aldus as "laggard" of the class of 1991's Hot Growth Companies, American Power Conversion (APC) was designated as valedictorian of the class. APC describes itself in typically modest New England terms: a company which designs, develops, manufactures, and markets a line of uninterruptible power supply (UPS) products, electrical surge protection devices, and power-conditioning products (mainly for use with computers). Although that may sound *mundane,* somehow the meteoric success of the company tells you that there must be something behind those technical terms.

And, indeed, there is. What APC is selling is "insurance." The company has an awareness of the unparalleled importance of the computer in the work environment and the mindset of "technology officers" in corporate America. The United States has the best power grid in the world; yet the fear of a PC, or worse yet LAN, "crash" turns otherwise pallid computer junkies greener than their monitors. The title of its 1994 annual report captures the true product that APC is selling: *Pervasive Power Protection.*

We all buy insurance because of the fear of the unknown. We can hardly avoid hearing the elegant FDR saying at the abyss of the Depression: "We have nothing to fear but fear itself." Some companies, such as APC, understand that basic human concern so well that they become successful emerging companies.

You have to know what you have to know in a prioritized manner. It is apparent that APC produces a superior product, since the brochure accompanying the annual report lists APC as the recipient of virtually every award that a producer of UPS products could receive: *PC* magazine's "Editor's Choice" for UPS, *LAN Times'* "Best of Times" for UPS, and on and on. Just to make sure that you know APC is more than just a superior product manufacturer, the brochure also advises you that APC was selected as "Entrepreneur of the Year" by Ernst & Young and Merrill Lynch. From what we have seen, APC understands its products well and understands the market in which it operates even better.

As you can glean from its huge success, its position on *Business Week*'s list, and the accolades it received, APC was definitely taken seriously in its emerging growth years. So much so that larger competitors imitated APC's success, and the company, now over the $.5 billion revenue mark, is experiencing some pressure on its profit margins. Sometimes being a celebrity can lead to being stalked.

Nobel Education reinforces the premise that knowing your business and prioritizing your goals are the keys to success. Although the company began by catering to the two-parent working family and operated day-care centers, that business did not enable the company to sustain its growth and profitability. If nothing else, the children graduated from day care. Even children can't spend their entire childhood in a sandbox. With a new management team and an enhanced concern over the quality of America's public educational system, Nobel changed its focus to offering reasonably priced, quality elementary and middle-level education. Perhaps education could be viewed as a natural evolution, but it is an evolution that required an outside catalyst—understanding your market even better than your product—and it's an evolution that not all companies achieve.

By contrast, Aldus Corporation, the maker of desktop publishing software, failed to keep a prioritized focus on the market. Aldus knew its product well, and many users worshipped it as a desktop publishing savior. Enter Microsoft with its Windows on the World, and Aldus went from deity almost to dodo. Its customers claimed they had difficulty working with its software on Windows. An awareness by Aldus of a fundamental shift in the business market (IBM was "in") would have saved the company agony, and its shareholders would have had a less bumpy ride. Instead, it was eventually merged into Adobe. When Aldus lost a proper focus on priorities, its excellent technology and know-how didn't help. Even though the company started investing heavily in developing new products and markets, its customers and its investors lost interest. Aldus wasn't taken seriously any more.

Aura is another poignant example of Knowledge Point 1. In spite of its revenue growth and reduced losses, the company's stock, which fluctuates vehemently under the $10 resistance level, reflects clearly that the company is not being taken seriously by analysts and investors. Aura is even one step ahead of Aldus. While Aldus might be forgiven for missing the Apple-to-IBM shift, Aura doesn't seem to decide what market it is in. Aura's strategy could be perceived as random: the "Russian roulette" approach. For Aura's sake, let's hope it'll change. At least, it looks like things might be improving somewhat.

KNOWLEDGE POINT 2: YOUR PERCEIVED VALUE *IS* YOUR VALUE—"SOMEONE ELSE WILL TELL YOU WHAT YOU'RE WORTH"

We start with the basic premise that your company is "invaluable." After the time and effort you've put into your company— or the amount of stock you were given when you joined it—this dream is part of who you are as a human being. As is the case with all "relationships" (your marriage or the pet turtle you had in your childhood), you can't put a value on your company. To be taken seriously, you must realize that your company has a perceived value.

In other words, to be taken seriously you will have to distance yourself from your feelings about your company and project that you can objectively think about your company's value. How did you price your product or service when you first brought it to market? No doubt a combination of factors was involved, but certainly you looked at directly competitive or comparable products and placed a price on your product. That same analytical process that you went through in pricing the product is the process through which the financial community goes when it values your business (i.e., when it puts a "price" on your company). To be taken seriously, you have to realize that in the eyes of others, your company is a product.

Yes, you are a product. This is the good news, since you can prepare for an objective discussion about the merits of your company. The better prepared you are for the objective discussion about value, the more seriously you will be taken.

Indeed, we would like to think that value is a science or at least that the market is an objective arbiter of value. As we were writing this book, we became aware of several situations in the efficient market that gave us some pause to reconsider just how to explain value to the uninitiated. It was a week when a stock, Comparator, a manufacturer of fingerprint identification equipment or some such thing, traded more shares on the NASDAQ than any company in that market's history. The only problem was that the company had never sold its product to any reputable end user, and the company's balance sheet was qualified in its accountants' opinion; that is to say, the company's accountants believed that Comparator was overstating the value of its assets. Whoever was hyping the stock left no fingerprints, not even fingerprints that Comparator's prime product could detect, but the newly armed NASD regulatory agency decided to suspend trading in the stock.

You might say that Comparator's flight from reality is a "one off" situation where things got a little out of hand. Yet, in the same week, Alan Abelson, the stock market pundit at *Barron's*, passed up taking a swipe at Comparator and instead picked apart another company, Zoltek. "Zoltek" sounds like the name of the lead act and star magician at the circus that children usually attend in the summer months. It is also the name of a carbon fiber manufacturer that comes from the "show me" state of Truman's birthplace: Missouri. The buck definitely stopped at Zoltek; in fact, a lot of bucks stopped at Zoltek. In May 1996, the market valued Zoltek at $600 million. The magical part of the story is that Zoltek barely has $13 million in revenues, although it is profitable with earnings of $2 million. You might be saying that we either have too many or too few zeros attached to these numbers, but the proofreaders have checked the text.

According to Zoltek, the company will be, maybe in 7 years at most, the leading producer of carbon fibers. Carbon fibers are like Superman. They are stronger than steel and lighter than aluminum and faster than a speeding stock. You know, the fibers are used for space travel and things like that, sometimes golf clubs.

Zoltek is not your average $13 million manufacturer of carbon fibers; it thinks global. So in December 1995, Zoltek goes Hungarian and buys a company that produces acrylic fibers whose facilities will be expanded to produce low-cost feedstock for the Superman fiber.

That's as far as the good news goes. First of all, Zoltek doesn't really make the Superman-type carbon fiber. Instead, the company makes a not so "Wonder Boy" low-end carbon fiber. The only thing tougher than carbon fiber is the competition that Zoltek faces. The Dutch chemical conglomerate Akzo Nobel, operating out of the Volunteer State of Tennessee, upped its carbon fiber manufacturing capacity in its spare time. At the same time the Japanese, who may have been wounded in "Follywood," still have plenty of industrial strength when it comes to chemicals and fibers, including manufacturers with exotic-sounding names like Toray and Toho Rayon. Yes, Zoltek, it is a global marketplace, especially when you don't want it to be.

As for its foreign foray into the eastern European orbit, for which Zoltek spent close to $17 million, the Hungarian company has revenues, but its profits are closer to a dark red shade of one of Hungary's most appreciated spices, paprika. Still, people believe in the magic of Zoltek. Although the company earned 42 cents in its fiscal 1995, the consensus says despite all the red paprika from its foreign venture, it will earn 75 cents in the next fiscal year. That would value the company at over 100 times earnings, a multiple that many thought should be reserved for the most optimistic of Internet stellar performers. So put your mental armor on when you begin to discuss value, because it has its irrational components as well. And don't expect that just because one company obtains a hypervaluation for whatever reason, your company will be similarly endowed. Yet, if you see a crack in the clouds, grab the sunshine. Chapter 7, which covers valuation, will tell you how to make the most of that sunshine.

Meanwhile, how do you prepare to discuss the value of your "invaluable" company? First, when you deal with the big guys, don't try to show that you are on equal footing—'cause it won't work. Rather, arm yourself with the information about the market, especially its growth prospects in the United States and elsewhere in the world. Remember you are the expert of your domain. Even if you go to an investment firm that specializes in your industry, you should still know more than anyone at that firm about your market.

Demonstrate why your product is better than competitive products; in fact, show how it's unique. Just as important, highlight how your company's human resources put you above not only competitors within your industry, but competitors from other emerging companies. You're the best among the best.

You may have to accept that a value will be placed on your company, but you'll have significant influence over the valuation by preparing yourself. Not only will you be taken seriously if you project the "correct" objectivity, but you will be able to walk out the door with a check from the financial types that really will make you feel "invaluable."

When talking about value, we think it's valuable to close on a philosophical note. We heard Dan Lufkin, one of the founders of the highly successful investment banking firm DLJ— Donaldson, Lufkin & Jenrette—expound on his life experience as an investor. He spoke, among others, about looking for growth values in small-cap stocks. The title of his talk sums up the message: "Opportunity Is Where You Find It—Watson, You See But You Do Not Observe." You don't have to be Sherlock Holmes to find the right value for your business, but try to find those financial partners who will see and observe your business for the opportunity it is.

KNOWLEDGE POINT 3: *BUSINESS* IS THE GAME

Psychology is not the game—business is the game. Form will open the door, but substance is needed to consummate the deal.

The Spectrum Technology/Sculley episode highlights how a company can "bootstrap" itself into being taken seriously by attracting a high-profile CEO. Unless the company is really for real, it just can't succeed.

The Spectrum Technology/Sculley affair began in July 1992 when mastermind Peter Caserta became CEO of Spectrum, a somewhat well-known "wireless data transmission" company. In his first year, sales declined only 8 percent, but expenses rose 53 percent—aided by the addition of over a dozen of Caserta's family members and friends to the management and board. Losses increased more than fivefold, from $1.6 million to $10 million. The stock languished in 1992 and most of 1993.

Then Caserta levitated the stock by announcing in May 1993 that a new agreement with AT&T would produce "hundreds of millions of dollars in royalties." That announcement caused the stock to triple, even though AT&T called the claim a "gross exaggeration." Building on the strength of the new license and not wanting to let a good opportunity slip away from him, Caserta began to look for a new CEO who had some cachet.

In October 1993 John Sculley, former chairman of the Apple of Almost Everyone's Eye, joined Spectrum. On the basis of that news, the market took Spectrum seriously by running its stock up 46 percent. Many people speculated about what Sculley knew that no one else knew about Spectrum. The cynics said he did it for the money. Whatever his motives, by February of the following year Sculley resigned.

Issues surrounding Spectrum's accounting practices arose, and many called into question the uniqueness of its patents. Also, a few federal and state agencies have been investigating Spectrum. Spectrum was being taken seriously, but not by the people you want to take you seriously. Psychology without solid substance backfired.

You don't have to be rich and famous to be taken seriously or just to be taken in. Sometimes an enterprising company such as Spectrum Technology can attract a high-profile executive and the company ends up being taken seriously for the wrong reasons. Then again, sometimes a supposedly successful executive can attract a company to him and, like the innocent fly to the web of the spider, the company gets tangled up in the web woven by the clever executive.

Some say that Paul G. Kahn was a Mr. Fix-It. In the case of Ideon, the former Safeguard Services, the company should have first asked what he was going to fix. Kahn had all the right credentials to attract any company. As the credit card honcho for AT&T, Kahn grew the Universal card business to become just that: "universal." The company started with 40 employees and by the time he left, the company had 2000 hired hands and was able to walk away with the Malcolm Baldrige National Quality Award in 1992 from President George Bush.

Kahn was not only responsible for the universality of AT&T's card operations; he also turned Mellon Bank's credit card business into a juicy proposition. As head of its credit card operation, he developed "lifestyle" cards aimed at golfers, sailors, and skiers and increased the division's profitability 10 times over. The word was out: Kahn was the man to hire if you wanted to make your credit card business happen.

So, enter Safeguard Services into the arms of Paul Kahn. Safeguard is not quite a credit card company, but it is close enough; it is a credit card registration company. Kahn had great plans for Safeguard. Not only was he a big spender; he persuaded the company to enter into "related" businesses, such as tracking down missing children. And before you know it, the company was tracking down its missing profits and Kahn left in a puff of smoke.

We will talk throughout this book about the importance of an emerging growth company attracting the right people, and we will even point out to you that some investors will invest only in companies with experienced management in place; in fact, some investors will place their bets only with management that has had experience within the same industry. Nonetheless, the business of every company is to attract the right management, whether experienced in that industry or otherwise, and it may be self-evident, but you do really have to do your homework, even when it comes to people who look as qualified as Kahn. Hoping that psychology—dropping big names or, more accurately, picking up big names—will do all the work not only is naive, but can be detrimental to your wealth.

KNOWLEDGE POINT 4: WHAT'S YOUR SOURCE OF CREDIBILITY?

You need serious third-party credibility. That means publications, advisory boards, boards of directors, references, and the people who financed you (banks or venture capitalists versus friends and family). As we have said before, being taken seriously means *demonstrating* a concern for *what matters*. But that's still only your word—and that's not enough. You must have someone ascertained with your company who already has credibility in the industry.

The Wall Street Journal wrote a story about one of the affiliations of Mr. LA Olympics (Peter Ueberroth) with Doubletree, a hotel management company. When you've been *Time* magazine's "Man of the Year," you don't need a business card, and the company you decide to associate with generally does well—some time, at least.

Despite Ueberroth's many successes, his critics are quick to point out his failed investment in Hawaiian Airlines (HAL). You may recall that Ueberroth became a millionaire when he sold his LA-based travel agency business Ask Mr. Foster, a close fit with the hospitality industry. Also, Ueberroth admits that HAL was a mistake, and we suspect he's learned from it. Nonetheless, Doubletree has performed well and it's more in line with the bedrock of his original success.

The point of the Ueberroth story is that a *prestigious* outsider—a person or other entity—can help an emerging company be taken seriously. This outside entity should preferably have experience in the industry you are in, and should be there permanently rather than scarcely. One of the criticisms of Ueberroth's involvement with Doubletree is that he may have too many commitments to contribute value to the company. Analysts may be split on the outlook for Doubletree, but the market is taking it seriously, since it was trading at 30 times P/E.

Clustering in incubators can definitely add to your credibility. ThermoElectron, Safeguard Scientifics (no relationship to Safeguard Services), and Teknekron present examples of how companies can short-circuit the startup phase and be taken seriously at an earlier stage in their development than might otherwise be so. ThermoElectron, praised for its innovative practices in Tom Peters' megabook *Liberation Management,* is an eclectic "technoglomerate."

At the "egg stage," an employee-innovator within the ThermoElectron group is given an "incubator" environment: availability of capital, technical and administrative support, and so on. After sufficient incubation, the company is "spun off" and left to fly on its own. ThermoElectron has spun off close to a dozen companies. It also helps to be taken seriously when the chairman of ThermoElectron declares: "We won't let them fail."

Teknekron, and interestingly the recently deceased venture capitalist Wallace Steinberg of Healthcare Investment Group, pursues a different approach to enable a company to be taken seriously. Teknekron searches out entrepreneurs in university research departments. (Steinberg went to the ultimate research department for one of his ideas—the National Institutes of Health.) In addition to providing capital, the business incubator provides a "knowledge network," according to Teknekron's CEO. Teknekron, however does not make declarations like ThermoElectron—some of its companies have failed.

Safeguard Scientifics is more akin to ThermoElectron, but it is far more focused. Whereas ThermoElectron is a nonsynergistic business incubator, Safeguard Scientifics bills itself as an incubator concentrating on information technology. Rather than spinning companies off to its shareholders, Safeguard Scientifics offers its shareholder "rights" to buy shares in some of its best "partners." In 1995, Safeguard Scientifics gave its shareholders the right to subscribe to USDATA. USDATA provides software, hardware, consulting, and support services that enable its customers to greatly improve productivity, monitor automated processes, and optimize inventory management and distribution systems. USDATA was the most successful rights offering to Safeguard's shareholders. In June 1995, a share of USDATA could have been bought from Safeguard for $5; by late 1995, it was trading hands at five times that amount—over $25. USDATA has been taken very seriously, but not the least because of its association with Safeguard. (Due to fluctuations in company revenues and earnings, in February 1996 the stock slipped to $14.5, then it ascended to $25, and in early October 1996 it is nearing the $10 mark.)

Finally, the Spectrum/Sculley episode shows that for the 4 months that John Sculley was associated with Spectrum, it was taken quite seriously—more than ever before, because of Sculley's past accomplishments at Apple and PepsiCo.

KNOWLEDGE POINT 5: DON'T THINK *BIG*, THINK *GLOBAL*

Thinking global has, at least, three dimensions to it. First, as we all have read time and time again, the world is becoming an integrated marketplace (NAFTA, the EU, and other common markets). Just as important, thinking global means an awareness of "megatrends" as discussed by futurologist John Naisbitt or the "third wave" of the Tofflers. For example, how is the fundamental nature of business being changed by technologies (e.g., cyberspace) or by social trends (e.g., baby boomers are aging and Generation X is beginning to put its hands on the reins of power)? Finally, thinking global means a realization of all the potential dimensions of your niche.

You're never too small to think *global*—even when you are too small to think *big*.

So what's all the hype about Hyperion? Hyperion embodies a company that captures the aspects of thinking globally as discussed above. As Corporate America's business became diffused over more and more departments and as financial managers became increasingly cost-conscious, the CFO needed more timely consolidated information than was previously provided by either monthly or quarterly reports. In addition, the need that Hyperion sought to address was even more crucial at companies that not only operated over many departments, but also operated over many time zones around the world.

Hyperion, a company with $173 million in revenue for FY 1996, began its life under the name IMRS and the backing of major venture capitalists, such as Greylock. Hyperion is an excellent example of a "small company" that thinks globally. Almost singlehandedly, Hyperion has created the world of "enterprise software." As Hyperion states, its software meets the diverse accounting, financial consolidation, management reporting, budgeting, planning, and information access needs of the major international corporations in the world. Hyperion's mission statement puts it more concisely: "A strong product line; technology vision; commitment to service; and comprehensive global capabilities allow us to deliver the world's best software solutions to our customers." While many companies claim to be global, Hyperion backs up its claim by including a *10-page* brochure that lists its *worldwide clients*. This list not only reads like the "who's who" of corporate America, but also includes major corporations from around the world.

As is demonstrated by Hyperion's early stage of success, size is not important to be taken seriously. You can be taken seriously if you provide a solution to a global need. In 1994, *Forbes* magazine recognized Hyperion as one of the World's Best Small Companies.

As we engaged in research for this book, we were able to interview several successful and well-known executives on Wall Street and in corporate America. One such individual is John C. Baker, formerly senior vice president of Patricof & Co. Ventures, Inc. (PCV), one of the leading venture capital firms in the world. Baker now operates Baker Capital, his own firm. Among other companies, he spoke to us about Fore Systems, Inc. Fore quite simply calls itself the worldwide leader in the design, development, manufacture, and sale of high-performance local area networking (LAN) products based on asynchronous transfer mode (ATM) technology. Just to put things in perspective, Fore's revenues grew from less than $1 million in FY1992 to $235 million in FY1996.

Before finalizing PCV's investment, Baker told us, he put three explicit requirements to the founders. One of those requirements was that Fore must sell globally—and that was at a time when the company's sales were very modest. The other two requirements are discussed later in this book where they are relevant. Today, Fore has offices located in Europe (UK, Netherlands, France, Germany) and the Pacific Rim (Japan, Hong Kong, Singapore). Fore also covers Latin America from a base in Coral Springs, Florida.

Transmedia and APC are other poignant examples of companies that thought global. Transmedia's management has realized that its basic formula is applicable across many industries, countries, and business models (such as company-owned versus franchised territories). APC knows that concern over power outages or surges certainly is not limited to the United States. Already APC has a significant presence in Europe, and it is considering a manufacturing site in Florida to better service Latin America. APC also realizes the wide implications of the computer power "insurance" niche.

KNOWLEDGE POINT 6: DESIGN TO FIT STRATEGIC AND CAPITAL SOULMATES

Design to fit is not the sequel to Robert Altman's less than successful movie *Ready to Wear*. As an emerging growth company, you can begin the move from "emerging" to "fully grown" by "designing" or focusing your company in such a way that its business will fit or meet the strategic and financial interests of prospective corporate or financial partners.

Although in this book we will generally talk about name-brand companies, about which it is likely you have heard, we will also expose you to stories encountered from our experience that demonstrate the point we are making. QLT PhotoTherapeutics (QLT) proclaims itself as "a leading light in health care"; that is a literal description. QLT is a world leader in the development of light-activated drugs in the treatment of cancer and other diseases and is a leader in attracting corporate strategic partners. As stated in its annual report, QLT has a well-articulated strategy for strategic alliances: QLT will endeavor to strike a reasonable balance among upfront cash infusions, by way of licensing fees or equity purchases, milestone fees, and development cost sharing and retention of downstream profit sharing.

In 1987, QLT acquired from Johnson & Johnson the bedrock technology on which QLT's cancer therapy rests—Photofrin. However, since QLT was but a struggling company in the northern reaches of Canada (to be precise, Vancouver, British Columbia), the acquisition of Photofrin was made possible by a strategic alliance with and cash infusion from American Cyanamid. In a sense, QLT had designed itself to fit the corporate needs of two major pharmaceuticals companies. On the one hand, J&J no longer wanted to invest in the light-activated cancer therapy; on the other hand, American Cyanamid wanted to fund the development of a promising treatment, but did not want to take the research in-house.

American Cyanamid has gone through some changes of its own: The pharmaceuticals group was acquired by American Home Products. Nonetheless, the relationship between QLT and American Cyanamid continues to exist, albeit in an altered form. In 1994, QLT reacquired certain rights to Photofrin from American Cyanamid, since QLT believed that the product was not receiving the attention and focus that it warranted. That reacquisition was made possible because QLT saw great benefit in a new alliance it had formed with CIBA Vision. QLT is dancing with a strategic partner in virtually every continent in the world.

QLT is also dancing with investors in every market. Besides an infusion of over $15 million over a period of a few years by American Cyanamid, the company raised a total of $39 million in two secondary offerings, in 1992 and 1993. Then, in April 1996, this yet-to-turn-a-profit biotechnology firm sold over 3 million shares in a Canadian and American underwriting. With the likes of the powerful Canadian underwriter Nesbitt Burns and the prestigious Dillon Read and UBS Securities, QLT pocketed over $73 million; that's a lot of money for R&D and marketing.

You might ask: Why does everybody take QLT so seriously? Yes, its products are very promising, but how did it get to where it is today? The answer is: by a focused design-to-fit strategy. And the proof is conclusive.

If you look in the company's 1986–1988 annual reports, which cover QLT's activities primarily prior to the strategic partnering with American Cyanamid, you will find that QLT has been involved in the development of a large array of products. In its recent report, however, you'll notice that the company is practically *focused* on one area: photodynamic therapy. This is of course the area that was launched in a big way by the J&J/Photomedica acquisition, and the Cyanamid alliance. In fact, to reflect this focus, the company changed its name to QLT PhotoTherapeutic, Inc.

Can you imagine a more design-to-fit strategy than to completely reorganize and refocus a company around a strategic alliance? We couldn't. Does it work to enhance the degree to which the company is taken seriously? Well, if we look at QLT's recent huge cash infusion, and the quality of its corporate partners, *yes, it does.*

Where do you fit into the investment capital pool? Who's your strategic soulmate? Banging on the wrong doors and tooting your horn all over, can be not only frustrating but potentially damaging.

KNOWLEDGE POINT 7: NO SOLO FLIGHTS ALLOWED, EVEN FOR ACROBATIC PILOTS

What can be said about management that hasn't been said yet? Probably nothing. So we thought about skipping this topic. But you would have accused us of producing the less than definitive book that we hope this will become. Beside, any list of attributes that will make your company be taken seriously will be significantly deficient unless it includes the human element that runs the company.

If it's your money, you can do whatever you want. But with OPM (other people's money), that's different. Third parties want to see, not trickle-down management, but across-the-board management. They want to see you as a conductor of an orchestra, rather than a soloist with background music.

You have to know that you can't fly solo even if you feel that you can—you must be the roots of an organization. You will be taken more seriously when you project yourself as a person who wants to have the company last beyond your tenure there. Even people who like to do everything themselves don't trust "one-man shows" when they're on the giving rather than the receiving side. You can show up with an entourage of five people, but if you don't train to be a team player, your chances of being taken seriously diminish in an exponential manner. There are very few lone-star managers who are given the chance to find out whether they can take their companies from emerging growth to star-grown businesses. The rule in emerging growth businesses is: Dictatorship *out*—leadership *in*.

The word *company* should tell you something: You are creating a business that is not a one-person operation. Indeed, it's important that you project to people that the business will last beyond the years of your leadership.

The authors of *Built to Last,* who studied corporations which they believed could evolve and last "forever," very appropriately chose the charismatic Sam Walton as a man who knew how to build a company to last. Stories about Sam Walton abound, and he became a modern-day myth by constantly topping the *Forbes* billionaire list. Still, he was a man who knew he had to sublimate his own personality if his company Wal-Mart, was to succeed after he left. From his autobiography, it is clear that Walton wanted his company to be taken *seriously* during his lifetime and beyond: "What nobody realized, including a few of my own managers, was that we were really trying from the beginning to become the very best operators—the most professional managers that we could," he said. Every employee, especially at the stores, is encouraged to make suggestions to improve the operations. Wal-Mart sounds like a company that could be based in Osaka rather than Arkansas.

We turn from the Smokies of the southeast to the Green Mountains of Vermont, where a different group of people was building a company, now with approximately $140 million in annual sales and 500 employees, that made premium ice cream—Ben & Jerry's. Two idealistic individuals bred in the ethos of the 1960s seemed more interested in putting catchy names on their ice cream (Cherry Garcia became a member of the Grapeful Dead), and operating their company with a social conscience, rather than making profits. In fact, in 1994, the company posted a loss; people were scooping up Ben & Jerry's ice cream, but its stock was in the freezer. That year, the stock hit a low of $9.25, a level not seen since 1991.

Recognizing that they owed a duty to their public share-holders, the founders agreed to step down from the management of the company when they realized that the company needed the talents of an outside manager. In typical Ben & Jerry style, they announced that people should send in their résumés for the job with a poem on why they should be president of the company. Nonetheless, the founders hired a prestigious executive recruitment firm to find an appropriate individual to fill the top slot. In fact, it was the recruiter rather than the poetry contest that brought a new chief executive to the job of top scooper at Ben & Jerry's. Even idealists can learn to let go of their dreams, when those dreams no longer serve the interest of their public shareholders.

Letting go of your idealism is one thing; it's even better, if your lifestyle change works. For 1995, Ben & Jerry's net sales increased 4.4 percent to over $155 million, but the profits finally began to look a lot more cheery—net income was almost $6 million compared with a 1994 loss of almost $2 million. And, the results for the first 6 months of 1996 are even better—$86 million in revenues and $3.3 million in net income. The new president and chief executive officer, Robert Holland, proclaims that Ben & Jerry's still faces a relatively mature domestic market in the superpremium category, so he doesn't want to minimize the challenges the company must meet. Well, onward to new markets: Ben & Jerry's has set up a "scoop shop" in Karelia, Russia.

We can't predict whether all the companies mentioned favorably in this chapter will be successful into the next millennium and the one after that. It's difficult enough for most of us to predict what we will be having for breakfast tomorrow. We do, however, believe that emerging growth companies that grasp some or all of the seven knowledge points expressed in this chapter will significantly improve their chances of attracting the three crucial Growth Factors for their success: good people, quality capital, and the right corporate partners.

TWO

SEVEN RULES FOR ATTRACTING KEY PEOPLE

How to Get Top-Notch People into Key Positions in an Emerging Growth Company

"Good people" are the number-one Growth Factor for the emerging growth business—no debate about that. But the debate still rages on: Who are these "good people," especially at the upper levels of management? Is the emerging company better off with "repeater" *professional management,* whose previous experience in building companies (preferably in the same sector) is a central quality, as in the case of the veteran executive who has been three times around the (same or similar) block? Or can the highly motivated, open-minded, visionary, and inventive hungry entrepreneur—who is relatively new to business—do as good a job or better at the upper levels of management?

Mulling through many case studies, and seeking other expert opinions—all of which will be presented throughout this chapter—we realized that the answer to this question is much more complex than the reader might initially surmise. Still, we don't have the luxury to leave this apparent dilemma unresolved. The identities and qualities of upper-level management will always drastically affect an emerging growth company's ability to attract quality capital, the attention of Wall Street (when applicable), large corporate partners, and *other top talent*—the PCCP Growth Factors.

We also find it critically important to identify the factors that determine an emerging company's "people magnetism"—that essential ability to attract top talent to the various key positions in the first, second, or even third layers of responsibility. The emerging growth company manager will find in this chapter a range of diversified yet converging expert guidelines which will assist in increasing the company's people-related "magnetic field."

MANAGEMENT BY INEXPERIENCE

There is almost no book about growing a business in which Microsoft is not mentioned as an example—of course, in 20-20 hindsight. As they say, all's well that ends well. But the fact is that from the perspective taken by this chapter, there are many other companies with similar characteristics; only the Microsoft story is better documented and attracts more attention. So we'll open with Microsoft, followed by Apple, and move from there to deal with a variety of other poignant examples.

TWO LEGENDS

Microsoft, which was started by Bill Gates and Paul Allen in 1975, was run for the first few years by these two young entrepreneurs who had absolutely no previous business or management experience. We emphasize both business and management separately, because the head of department in a university and the manager of personnel in a midsize company might not have what we call business-building experience per se, but still they have experience in managing people. The founders of Microsoft had neither business nor management experience. In 1979, when Microsoft, with its 12 employees, moved from Albuquerque to a suburb of Seattle, Washington, it was entering its emerging growth phase. Bill Gates was still running the business, but he felt that he needed help in doing so.

The common practice in such a case would be to look for an experienced veteran executive, or at least someone with a few "notches" on the résumé. But that's not how Bill Gates handled the situation. He brought in Steve Ballmer, his old economics course pal from Harvard. Ballmer dropped out of the Stanford Business School—after finishing only 1 year—to join Microsoft. When Ballmer joined the company, it already had 30 employees. He, however, wanted to hire 50 more immediately. And, indeed, these three inexperienced-in-business people—Gates, Allen, and Ballmer—kept growing the company's head count as fast as they could find good people, and with it Microsoft's revenues. The rest, as they say, is history.

The Microsoft story is not the only one with the same motif, whereby a company experiences significant growth and is taken way beyond startup by top managers who have no extensive prior business experience. You might even say that they grow into the role. Usually as the company gets halfway through, or graduates the emerging growth stage, the picture changes to a certain extent because marketing and financial management become too complex, and the company tends to hire professionals in these areas.

In the case of Apple Computer, Steven Jobs and Steven Wozniak started the company as inexperienced in business as Bill Gates was. Jobs took Apple through its emerging growth stage, but with the company already generating revenues of over $500 million, he was forced to relinquish the top management spot to John Sculley, PepsiCo's former president and marketing whiz kid.

Some people, however, say that it was not Steve Jobs but Mike Markulla, a director, one-time CEO, and vice chairman, who actually took care of the critical business issues right from the beginning until Sculley's arrival. Sculley describes Markulla in his book *Odyssey: Pepsi to Apple* as someone whose breadth of business knowledge was expansive—a multifaceted talent who could speak authoritatively on technical, sales, marketing, and financial issues.

Yet, from the perspective of what we consider today a "previous track record in growing emerging businesses," even Mike Markulla was inexperienced. Before joining Apple, he was an engineer and product manager at Fairchild and Intel. Markulla doubled as a technologist. He designed a predecessor to the computer—an electronic slide rule, and he wrote one of the first software programs for the Apple II Computer. When Markulla started "growing Apples," he was not what they call today a "repeater" in terms of professional management with a track record in building emerging growth companies.

Three Rising Stars

The phenomenon of managers running their first entrepreneurial businesses way beyond startup into the emerging growth stage is not limited to those legendary big-name success stories such as Apple and Microsoft. The new stars, in fact, are slowly becoming legendary on their own merit.

Take, for example, Howard Schultz, chairman and CEO of Starbucks Corporation—the coffee bar conglomerate—now a household name. With 700 stores and $465 million in revenues in 1995, and with a projected 950 stores and $700 million in revenues in 1996, Starbucks actually reached the upper limit of what we define as the emerging growth sector not too long ago, in 1993, with sales of $177 million. But its phenomenal growth between 1987 and 1993, from 17 stores at the end of FY1987 to over 270 stores at the end of FY1993 (and to 676 at the end of FY1995), can be closely associated with Howard Schultz's management. (This is not to diminish from the role of the current president and COO—Orin Smith, who became president in 1994 and from 1990 to 1994 was first VP & CFO and later EVP & CFO—and from the roles of what some call an all-star management team.)

But who was Howard Schultz before? "He didn't have tangible experience [in building a company] and he hadn't shown a track record before," Michael Moe, a principal and emerging growth company analyst at Montgomery Securities in San Francisco, told us in an interview. "He was a sharp, disciplined, fanatical [in a positive sense], on-the-ball guy, with a vision and a plan."

It should, however, be noted that from 1982 to 1985, Schultz was the director of retail operations and marketing for Starbucks Coffee Company, which some refer to as the predecessor of the current Starbucks. This reference needs clarification, because the original Starbucks Coffee Company, which was founded in 1971, focused primarily on whole-bean sales—a business that's different from and smaller in magnitude than the now-ubiquitous coffee bar system of the current Starbucks Corporation and other coffee bar chain operators.

In fact, today's Starbucks is the derivative of a company Schultz founded in 1985—Il Giornale Coffee Company, which modeled the popular espresso bar concept Schultz saw in Milan, Italy, and which consequently offered brewed coffee and espresso beverages made from Starbucks coffee beans. In 1987, Il Giornale acquired the old Starbucks and renamed itself Starbucks Corporation—the company we acknowledge today as the unquestioned leader in the coffee bar industry.

Of course, the point we are trying to make is that Schultz's experience at the old Starbucks Coffee Company cannot be considered as a track record in building and navigating an emerging growth company. This brings us back to our previous contention that Howard Schultz, the founder and builder of a company with sales exceeding $0.5 billion, didn't have tangible prior experience in the sense of a "repeater."

From Starbucks Corporation we move to Fore Systems, Inc.—another company featured in this book. Whereas in Starbucks case you could argue that Howard Schultz had *some* related business experience, in the context of being in charge of retail operations and marketing for the predecessor company, the four researchers from Carnegie Mellon University who started Fore Systems had no previous business experience per se to speak about.

In December 1992, as a senior vice president and partner in Patricof & Co. Ventures (PCV)—the large and world-renowned venture capital firm—John C. Baker made an early (but not startup) investment in Fore. He told us in an interview that the only management-related requirement he presented to the company before investing was that the group choose a CEO. "Apparently the four partners were running the company as a partnership without hierarchy," Baker explained in that interview. "I told them to go away somewhere for a weekend, discuss the issues, consider the personalities, and come back to me on Monday morning with a name they picked as the CEO. The person they chose was Eric Cooper, who still heads Fore's management team." Note that Baker didn't try to land on Fore an outside executive who possessed the so-called previous experience in growing companies.

The seeming original naiveté of the Fore team in managing a growing company by committee without a designated CEO—which might make some veteran executives giggle—should be viewed in light of the meteoric growth of Fore. The company has increased its sales from $1 million in FY1992, to $5.5 million in FY1993, to $23.5 million in FY1994, and $76 million in FY1995. Sales for FY1996 amounted to a whopping $235 million, which includes the sales of the recently acquired ALANTEC. Fore also increased its valuation from $12 million after PCV's investment in December 1992 to nearly $3.5 billion in October 1996. And, guess what? The company still has the same CEO and the same top management. As the company grew, however, it did add professional managers such as a CFO, marketing director, manufacturing director, and director for European and Asian operations.

From Fore to another shining star: America Online (AOL). AOL, with revenues of $38 million, $50 million, and $115 million in fiscal years 1992, 1993, and 1994, respectively, was within the range of what we define in this book as emerging growth companies. In FY1995 revenues grew to $394 million, and FY1996 revenues exceeded $1 billion—which, of course, puts today's AOL outside the range.

Of course, the much publicized service blackout of August 1996 didn't go unnoticed—especially on Wall Street, where AOL's stock plummeted to half of its May 1996 value. In fact, AOL's stock, which on August 29, 1996, closed at around $30, had a previous 52-week high of $71. But, let's face it: there is no fail-safe system—the laws of entropy practically guarantee that. Therefore, as much as we sympathize with the likes of Andrew Plesser, who runs a New York PR firm and who, according to *The Wall Street Journal* of August 8, 1996 (a day after the blackout), couldn't use his AOL "essential link" to zap documents to his customers for approval, things shouldn't be blown out of proportion. We had electrical blackouts and cable TV blackouts, we lost time from plane malfunctions, traffic jams, subway accidents, and we often lose a day or two just because of a simple illness.

Therefore, we believe that the blackout issue was only a trigger to start dealing with the more underlying problems—that of subscriber churn rate (percentage of subscribers who quit each year), which some estimate at 50 percent, and future sources of revenue, which today relies mainly on subscriber fees, but which AOL's CEO Steve Case projects to gravitate toward advertising fees and royalties from retailers—all of which are catalysts for an industrywide uncertainty, which particularly affects a super-fast growing entity such as AOL. Having said all that, we wish to remind the reader that AOL is currently way beyond the emerging growth stage (as defined in this book), therefore its *current* state of affairs is not a relevant topic for this book.

But who was the CEO responsible for AOL's meteoric growth throughout the emerging growth years—specifically, FY1992, FY1993, and FY1994, and beyond? It was Steve Case. Can anyone claim that Steve Case's stints at Procter & Gamble, Pizza-Hut (tasting new toppings across the country), and even the more related Control Video were the "track record" and "previous experience" that would make him one of the most successful CEOs of the decade in building America Online into a name brand, and a company whose revenues increased tenfold between 1993 and 1995? Even his "incubation" at Quantum Computer Services can't be considered the classic "previous track record in growing a business"—a term many textbook investors like to use.

So here are three recent huge success stories—Starbucks, Fore Systems, and America Online—all taken through and beyond the so-called emerging growth years, by founders and top managers with no significant previous track record in company building. Is this the norm or the exception? Later in this chapter we will provide you with a satisfactory answer to this question.

"REPEATER" MANAGEMENT

Before we drift too far into the euphoria of a world in which every entrepreneur can become a successful business leader, and attract quality capital, the right corporate partners, and other good people, there are other examples that remind us of a more realistic view of the emerging growth business world.

Executives at the Sprout Group, one of the largest and most successful venture capital funds (an affiliate of the Wall Street securities firm Donaldson Lufkin & Jenrette, now owned by the Equitable), will make it clear to you, over and over again, that Sprout will consider investments only in companies whose CEO is a "repeater"—that is, he or she has previously grown a successful business in a field that is directly related to the one in which the company is seeking an investment from Sprout.

Now, you might think that the above guideline is more like a "target goal" than a make-or-break requirement, and you might speculate that if Sprout likes a business it becomes more flexible about its management's backgrounds. But think again, because you are wrong. The requirement for a "repeater" top management is actually in the charter of Sprout's mission. Therefore, if a company's business plan doesn't demonstrate this point clearly, the company will not pass even the preliminary screening, no matter what other great things it has going for it.

(Evidently Patricof & Co. Ventures, another major fund, doesn't have such strict guidelines. As we know, it invested in Apple, Fore, America Online, and other companies that were run in their emerging growth years by fresh company builders.)

But strangely enough, the investment banking division of Donaldson, Lufkin & Jenrette (DLJ)—a sister company of the Sprout Group—apparently does not share the same views about management. Why is that strange? After all, DLJ and Sprout are independent entities in terms of decision making. Well, the problem is that things seem upside down. Most experts will tell you that as companies grow larger—say, beyond $100 million—the entrepreneurs-founders should relinquish the reins to professional management. As an investment banking firm, DLJ usually gets involved with fairly large companies, whereas Sprout, as a venture capital firm, is naturally more involved with earlier emerging growth situations. As such, you would expect a more stringent requirement for professional, "repeater" management from DLJ than from Sprout. But that's not the direction in which the facts point.

Case in point: While the Sprout Group has been sowing seeds in the world of adventure capital, the investment banking division of DLJ has been sowing its seeds elsewhere in search of excellence or in search of Excel.

Excel Communications, a company which DLJ took public, is one of the fastest-growing providers of long-distance telecommunications services. With revenues of little more than $20 million in 1991, for the fiscal year ending December 1995 it had revenues of over $0.5 billion, and for the first 6 months of 1996 its revenues grew to $477 million. How did Excel excel to such heights? It is using a tried-and-tested technique of marketing: "network" (not phone network) or what many refer to as multi-level marketing. Instead of Avon calling, Excel has hundreds of thousands of independent representatives calling to bring in the business.

The management must be old hands from competitors AT&T, MCI, and Sprint, you say. Would you believe that the IPO prospectus for Excel lists as the first risk factor that the company's officers have had limited experience in managing companies as large and as rapidly growing as Excel?

We certainly agree with the prospectus. But, furthermore, we are also missing from the "repeater" management equation that part which relates to company building experience in a *similar industry*—which Sprout, for example, puts a high value on. Specifically, the founder, chief executive officer, and chairman of the board, who received $3.4 million in compensation in 1995—more compensation than his counterparts at MCI or Sprint—has no previous experience in the telecommunications field. He began his business career in 1970 when he founded Kenny Troutt Construction in Omaha, Nebraska. In 1982 the call of the oil patch brought him to Dallas, where he founded and operated SunTex Resources, an oil and gas exploration firm. Maybe he had experience in pipelines, but before he founded Excel in 1988 he had no experience in telephone lines.

So, you say, he must have brought in some seasoned heavy-hitter company builders from the phone industry for the *top layer* of management. Well, not really. The EVP/CFO had no previous experience in the industry. The marketing VP's previous telecommunications experience involved 4 years as an independent representative and consultant for various network marketing organizations. And the prospectus tells us that the brother of the CEO—the vice president and treasurer of Excel, who received an almost-seven-figure compensation package in 1995—served, prior to joining Excel in January 1996, as accounting systems coordinator at Lincoln Telephone and Telegraph Company, a local telephone company in Lincoln, Nebraska. Prior to that he held various accounting positions with the same company. From an accounting systems coordinator in a local telephone company in Lincoln, Nebraska, to the world of international telecommunications is an impressive leap for this 43-year-old executive.

Then again, there are other issues related to the company, as an article in *The New York Times* of April 28, 1996, points out. Many people are skeptical about the ability of the company to keep growing in view of prior experience with multilevel marketing schemes. At a certain point, multilevel marketing schemes begin to level out. Since sales representatives are busy recruiting other sales reps instead of focusing on getting phone customers, the pyramid grows. Some states like Texas and Arkansas are still investigating the marketing practices of Excel. Furthermore, a whopping 86 percent of the half million sales reps from last year chose not to renew their representative status. At the same time, however, the prospectus tells us that there were 461,158 new applications from independent representatives. What a turnover!

Another issue with the company is it ability to retain its customers. The multilevel marketing has enabled the company to attract customers, but Excel has experienced an attrition rate in its customer base of 48 percent a year. Then, there is a question of how it accounts for certain of its expenses. Unlike more conservative companies, Excel has capitalized the commissions it pays to acquire customers, who as we mentioned don't stay very long with the company. This capitalization increased the bottom-line earnings as the company was entering its IPO.

Still, Wall Street is a wondrous place. Excel's IPO in May 1996 was priced at $15, and its stock nearly doubled in one day. The case clearly demonstrates that timing is critically important in tapping the IPO market. It is quite possible that in a less buoyant and less cash-flush IPO market, a company like Excel would have a difficult time "going public," especially "going public" with a highly reputable underwriter like Donaldson, Lufkin & Jenrette.

A TRACK RECORD OF BUILDING COMPANIES

Now back to our discussions about management. Even though Sprout may apparently differ from its sister company, DLJ, it is not alone in its opinion that a "repeater" top management is more attractive to investors and corporate partners than the "new kids on the block," even if those "new kids" possess a fanatical determination, discipline, freshness, and vision, and a great plan.

Thomas Itin, the charismatic veteran executive—an acclaimed business personality, and president of the approximately $70 million Williams Controls—clearly believes in what he himself represents: a well-proven professional manager. His previous experience as cofounder of Roadmaster, now an $800 million company, his achievement at a number of other companies that grew under his leadership, and the rave reviews of his peers leave no doubt that Itin has a powerful experience and track record in growing companies. In fact, Stanley Trilling, senior vice president of investments at PaineWebber's Los Angeles office—and *Money* magazine's repeating top-ranked stockbroker—not only praised Itin to us as an excellent company builder, but named Williams Controls as one of his favorite emerging growth stocks.

Itin told us in an interview that he doesn't believe in giving people a second chance (in the context of business performance), because "you can predict with accuracy the future based on the past." Therefore, he argues, if you look at what someone has done in the past, you'll know what to expect in the future. And what about those who built their first company—the Gateses, the Schultzes, the Coopers—or those we mention later, like Taub from ADP and Zandman from Vishay—people who proved themselves beyond our wildest imagination? Itin responds with an apropos story from his days at Mobil Oil.

He was instructed to hire only high school graduates for certain types of jobs—even if those positions didn't require a specific education. He asked the makers of this policy why he couldn't decide case by case, and make the decision after interviewing the candidate. Perhaps, this way, he could find people who didn't have a high school degree but would do a great job. Management told him that it had been demonstrated statistically that high school graduates were better in certain positions. Therefore even if a few nongraduates could do a great job, it was just not worth it for the company to spend the extra effort in interviewing a much larger constituency of candidates, and perhaps take a chance with some who didn't fit into the statistics. They felt that with this policy they could save a lot of time and lose very little in the tradeoff.

We are sure that for many large corporations, establishing strict guidelines—for who fits a position and who doesn't—probably pays off overall in reducing the time spent on paperwork and interviews. Again, they may lose some talented people who don't fit into the "box," but statistically speaking that doesn't mean much. In fact, we are hearing lately that software programs which were created to analyze and store résumés may replace a significant portion of the "legwork" in recruiting. Personnel will be able to narrow down the range of potential candidates by plugging in a few search criteria.

Opponents of these methods will argue that with such a selection system, résumé reengineering will become more important than substantive qualities. The proponents of this policy might, on the other hand, tell you that first they check for the rigid criteria, for which the computer can be very helpful, and once they narrow down the search, they select the finalists on the basis of a multitude of objective and subjective criteria. So, the personal touch is still there.

This reminds us of an old caricature that demonstrates the true meaning of the "personal touch." It depicts two peasants who are hanging on to a camshaft-type bar which is supported on two poles. The camshaft is driven by a belt that's attached to a motor. Much like a car camshaft, which moves the pistons back and forth as it rotates, the camshaft in the caricature moves these two guys vertically, up and down. On the floor there is a large tub filled with grapes. You can imagine that as the motor turns, the shaft moves the guys up and down—to the effect that they are actually crushing the grapes.

Now, you may say: What a complicated way this is to prepare our favorite French wine! Realizing that an outside visitor might think just that, the president of the company, who is standing next to the contraption with a VIP visitor, explains in the caption: "In order to keep up with the times and stay competitive, we had to automate. But we still manage to keep the 'personal touch' in our products."

So, on the one hand, we have a mountain of evidence that people with the proper qualities—such as fanatical determination, great discipline, freshness, a powerful vision, and a good plan—can found, build, and manage major successful companies *without* having to have tangible previous experience and a track record in building enterprises. On the other hand, the policies of the Sprout Group and the arguments of Itin—which point in the opposite direction—make a lot of sense and are very easy to understand.

And, just to complicate matters further, the lead story of the Money and Business section of the March 26, 1996, *New York Times* has the headline: "How a Would-Be Mr. Fix-It Left a Company in Ruins." It tells the amazing story of Paul G. Kahn, who in 1992 received a Malcolm Baldrige National Quality Award from President George Bush after his phenomenal success with the AT&T Universal card. Kahn was hired in 1990 by AT&T to grow this new division, which offered a combined calling and credit card.

As president and CEO of AT&T Universal Card Services Corporation, Kahn started small with approximately 40 employees, and built the company into almost 2000 people—a major organization. You might justifiably argue that this is the same as growing an independent emerging company. The Universal card was not Kahn's only big accomplishment. As head of Mellon Bank's credit card operation, he developed "lifestyle" cards aimed at golfers, sailors, and skiers, and increased the division's profitability tenfold. Actually, throughout the industry he was getting to be known as the man with the golden touch.

So what happened at Safeguard Services, the credit card registration company, which Kahn renamed the Ideon Group? Safeguard Services had revenues around the upper limit of the range for the emerging growth sector. In less than a year and a half after Kahn joined as chairman, the company stunned everyone with the announcement that the new businesses it was entering had failed. Following the announcement, Ideon's stock collapsed, and within a couple of months hundreds of employees who had just moved to Jacksonville, Florida, to take their jobs were laid off. Losses actually reached $50 million in a quarter.

Some attribute the reasons for the problems to a clear pattern of gross overspending on behalf of Kahn. So the simple explanation might be that while a division of AT&T or Mellon Bank could carry his expenses, an independent emerging growth company couldn't. But that doesn't cut it, since AT&T Universal Card Services Corporation was a separate entity, an emerging growth company with its own P&L balance sheet.

It is now obvious that there is no singular simple explanation. We know that Kahn failed in a previous attempt to run *his own company.* Some interpret the Ideon saga as resulting from "the reckless action of a single *poorly supervised executive,*" trying to contrast it with the fact that Kahn's previous positions supposedly involved some kind of supervision from the parent company. But are those speculations or explanations?! Your guess is as good as ours.

So we see "new kids on the block" who successfully make the grade through the emerging growth stage. We see very successful "professional managers" who also take companies through the emerging growth stage. Then we have failures on both fronts.

MATCHING GUIDELINES

The question that evidently follows from the above analysis is: Does a state of randomness prevail when it comes to qualifying emerging growth company management which will attract people, capital, and corporate partners—or is it rather a matter of a certain elasticity within the framework of well-defined rules? The examples presented here might point toward a certain set of guidelines—which are not ultimate paradigms but definitely have a significant degree of validity.

For example, professional managers might have more aptitude to grow an emerging company by synergistic acquisitions—what Bill Sahlman of Harvard Business School calls small-company consolidation. Thomas Itin is using such strategies to grow Williams Controls. You might also argue in favor of professional managers in growing a retail, distribution, or franchising operation in which the products or services and/or markets may be innovative but not new. George Naddaff was perfect for Boston Chicken (now Boston Market)—he had 20 years of franchising experience before he first set foot, in 1987, in a Boston Chicken unit. As a Kentucky Fried Chicken franchisee, he (and a partner) opened 19 units. Later he launched VR Business Brokers, Inc., and Living and Learning Centers, Inc., both of which he sold.

On the other hand, the growth of Fore Systems, Starbucks, America Online, or even Microsoft—during the largest part of what this book defines as the emerging growth years—was mostly internal growth. It seems that first-time businesspeople did quite well in these environments. Another way to characterize these businesses is that they were pioneering new product categories and/or new markets.

And, although the growth of Starbucks was by unit multiplication, still the units were company-owned, and the concept of coffee bars in the United States was new and required major advances characteristic of internal growth. The acquisitions of content providers by AOL were also tuck-in acquisitions—contributing to internal growth—and not synergistic independent businesses. ADP, which was run in the emerging growth years by the original founders, did rely on a large array of acquisitions for growth in the early years—just after it went public, when revenues were only $3 million in 1996 dollars. But those acquisitions were again tuck-in acquisitions—mostly client bases, which were integrated into the company and were transformed to become part of the larger organization.

The only problem with attempting to make a differentiation of management qualities on the basis of business models is that a successful manager of one business model can still grow into becoming a good manager of another business model.

In the case of Paul Kahn, the analysis is somewhat more complex, but still there are definable characteristics. Kahn did grow an independent unit—AT&T Universal Card Services Corporation—from 40 people to 2000. This earned him the label of someone who had a "successful track record in growing companies" when he was recruited to Safeguard Services—the credit card protection company.

But the Ideon Group (formerly Safeguard Services) was quite a different kind of environment—more typical of the classic emerging growth company scenario. First, Kahn's successes at AT&T Universal and Mellon Bank were related to credit card operations. Ideon's failure at the time he was its CEO, is at least partially attributable to the completely new areas that the company was entering. One such failed attempt was the Family Protection Network—a missing-child search service. Other ideas included buying a football stadium for $30 million.

Then, of course, we can stipulate that Kahn's spending pattern might have been OK for a wholly owned subsidiary of the giant AT&T but not for an independent, smaller company (a very questionable explanation because of the relative independence of AT&T Universal Card Services as a profit center). We also mentioned that some attribute the problem to "the reckless action of a poorly supervised executive"—an argument that even with 20-20 hindsight doesn't make sense in light of Kahn's previous, award-winning, high-level positions.

An issue that we feel might be of more relevance is that of big-name prestige, credibility, and (nonfinancial) support systems, which Kahn enjoyed at AT&T and Mellon Bank but not at the Ideon Group. For example, at the point he started building AT&T Universal Card, the promotional and marketing mailings to customers carried the name AT&T, which is not only a recognized brand name but also a symbol of financial strength, and the epitome of a company which can back up its commitments. Furthermore, at the early stages, Kahn was able to draw on a wealth of marketing and other information that a company like AT&T would have. Our experience also shows that it is much easier to generate market interest when representing a big name than when representing a smaller independent and growing outfit.

SMARTS, DISCIPLINE, VISION, AND CHARISMA

Evidently, the distinctions made above can explain some of the facts. But Michael Moe, a principal and emerging growth company analyst with Montgomery Securities in San Francisco, and formerly first vice president and emerging company analyst with Lehman Brothers in New York, articulated the answer to the paradox of the professional manager versus the fresh entrepreneur in a very pragmatic and simple way. He told us in an interview: "Every successful company can't come from someone who has been successful before; it's a combination. Of course it's easier to make the read on someone who did it before. But you can have a gut read on new talent too."

"What you need is visionary leaders who can articulate a vision, and have the type of presence that other people believe in," continues Moe. "Winners win and losers lose and therefore successful people want to be with other successful people." Finally, in the gut read about a manager-leader, according to Moe, people will look for *smarts, discipline, a big vision, and charisma.*

It seems to us that the right formula calls for a mix of the fresh with the seasoned. As the company grows, it has to bring in more and more professional managers, at least for the second layer. Still, the exact level at which those managers come in is not carved in stone, and they don't necessarily have to replace the original, so-called inexperienced managers—who are now in the midst of having their first successful experience at the helm.

As you go further down the ladder, things seem simpler to qualify because the assignments become more and more specific. Still, even in this range you'll find some very interesting new-age approaches. Michael Connors, a senior vice president and divisional president at America Online—the highly celebrated growth story of the 1990s—has been with AOL since 1992 and participated as the company grew through and beyond its emerging growth years. Connors told us in an interview that some of the people hired at AOL are so fresh and young, yet exceptionally intelligent, that they don't have a concept of what they can't do. Experience in a wider context doesn't count when you are inventing the future. What counts is intelligence, drive, and the notion that nothing is impossible.

For the top layer, the exact transition point where large-scale organizational and financial savvy become critical—is not clear. And, perhaps, as in Bill Gates' or Howard Schultz's case there is none. Steve Case of AOL also made a critical transition all in good health. All the above did, however, fortify the management team with professional managers, or, you might say, expert "technicians," in positions such as CFO, director of marketing, and director of overseas operations. And what about Fore Systems and its previously academic team of four top executives? They are doing very well, thank you.

An article in *Network World* (12/26/94–1/2/95) claims that Eric Cooper, Fore's CEO and chairman, was facing the fact that most technologists and startup presidents aren't suited to running big businesses. In the article, a net manager expressed his own worries by saying that the only question he has is whether Eric Cooper can make that transition from technologist to marketing professional as the company grows over $100 million. "There's nothing to say he couldn't, except for all the examples where that's been tried and didn't work," said that manager.

Our response is: And what about all the examples where it has been tried and worked? Besides Microsoft, Starbucks, and Fore, take a look at Vishay Intertechnology, Inc., now a $1.2 billion company—the largest manufacturer of passive electronic components in the United States and Europe, with over 10 plants worldwide. The company was founded by Dr. Felix Zandman—a Ph.D. "technologist" who is still the CEO. Zandman took Vishay, with the help of a talented management team he recruited, from zero revenues in 1962 to the $1.2 billion the company is at today. He definitely had to cross what the net manager called the critical $100 million line.

The story of ADP, the giant payroll and data processing conglomerate—now a $3 billion NYSE company, which in its 1995 annual report declared its 136th consecutive quarterly double-digit increase in earnings per share (136 quarters = 34 years), an unequaled growth record—is different only with regard to its post-emerging growth years. ADP's story started with Henry Taub, a 21-year-old graduate of accounting at NYU, his 19-year-old brother Joe Taub, and the now-famous senator from New Jersey, Frank Lautenberg, an economics major who was in the marketing training program of Prudential Insurance, and who was 26 at that time.

This was a team with no previous track record in the business building sense. Yet when Henry Taub and Frank Lautenberg relinquished their tours of duty as consecutive CEOs to the current CEO Josh Weston, the company's revenues were already multiples above the so-called critical $100 million mark, which in 1981 dollars would be equal to approximately $60 million.

Henry Taub, who's currently a director, an honorary chairman, and chairman of the executive committee of ADP, said to us in an interview: "One man can build a company, two can conquer a nation, three can conquer the world—we were *three* from the start."

Well, Fore Systems had crossed the $100 million barrier—in fact, its FY1996 revenues were over $200 million. And guess what? When we last checked in May 1996 the "four" of Fore were still at the helm: Dr. Eric Cooper—the CEO; Dr. Onat Menzilcioglu, another founder from Carnegie Mellon—the president; and the other two cofounders, Francois J. Bitz and Dr. Robert D. Sansom, who are vice presidents and directors. For how long? We don't know. But is it relevant? Judging by the previous examples, it seems that only 20-20 hindsight can tell whether someone is disqualified from being given the chance to produce in the future what he or she hasn't produced in the past.

John Baker from Baker Capital—the former Patricof & Co. executive who made the initial venture investment in Fore—put it bluntly: People originally branded Fore as a bunch of academics, but the fact is that they were capable of doing things most businesspeople are not capable of doing.

ATTRACTING THE "RIGHT" MANAGEMENT

Now its time to focus on the critical issues related to attracting good people to an emerging growth business. When the Ivy houses Merrill Lynch and Alex Brown took Boston Chicken (now Boston Market) public in November 1993, it had sales of $36.58 million for the previous 12 months (with negative earnings for the same period), and a total of 167 stores, of which 25 were company-operated and the rest franchised. At that time, it set a record on Wall Street for a single-day gain by an IPO. George Naddaff—the man who discovered the original Boston Chicken and its former chairman, who now runs Business Expansion Capital, Inc.—was asked in an *Inc.* magazine interview about potential high barriers to entry for companies in his industry. He named as one of the major factors the ability to attract the right management. Every company has managers or can find managers. But not every company attracts the right people.

Professionals experienced in analyzing growth for investment purposes will unanimously tell you that for a company to be able to grow significantly, it has to be a magnet for top talent. But, of course, attracting good people is only half the equation; keeping them and allowing them to grow is the other half. Keeping the "magnetic field" on, consistently, is essential.

An unusually high turnover rate, even at lower levels, turns the alarm buttons on. For example, Excel Communications, the company we mentioned earlier, which was recently taken public successfully by the Wall Street firm of Donaldson, Lufkin & Jenrette, had an alarming 86 percent turnover rate last year among its independent sales reps. It made many wonder whether the multilevel marketing system on which Excel's excellent emerging growth performance was based can maintain its momentum and performance in the long run with such a turnover rate, besides the legal challenges it is facing.

THE DOUBLE HELIX

Bill Gates believes that companies tend to be caught in a positive or negative spiral. A company in a positive spiral has an air of destiny, while one in a negative spiral is often doomed.

When a company has a hot product, Gates argues, investors pay attention and are willing to put their money into the company. Smart people say: "Look, everybody is talking about this company. I'd like to work there." When one smart person comes to a company, soon another follows, because talented people like to work with each other. A positive spiral draws *good people* into its helix.

Conversely, companies can get caught in a negative spiral. If a company starts to lose market share or delivers a bad product, good people say: "Why should I work there? Why should I trust my future in that company?" A business in a negative spiral will not attract good people and/or will not be able to keep them.

Steve Case, America Online's CEO, feels that fostering the creative spirit is crucial in attracting and keeping top-notch people. He considers one of the major factors in AOL's success to be the creative spirit that the management team has tried to foster. Steve Case confirms that it's "people" who drive his and other creative businesses. It's all about creating products and services that can excite the imagination of millions. That's why attracting the best people and creating an environment in which they can excel and grow is critical.

America Online's management feels that strategic investments and joint ventures help in attracting to a company the best people in the industry. Quoting from AOL's 1995 annual report: "Through a series of strategic investments and joint ventures, AOL has become a *magnet* for the best creative and entrepreneurial talent in the market." This can be explained by the enormous exposure to experienced and talented people with relevant knowledge that a growing company gets when it starts working with other, more established or laterally synergistic companies in the market. The personal contacts and close cooperation are a natural magnet for drawing some of the professionals across the lines to join with the strategic partner.

Sam Walton gives the credit for attracting good managerial people in the emerging growth years of Wal-Mart to the spirit of partnership in the company and its practical manifestations. In his book *Made In America,* Walton claims that in the years after Wal-Mart went public it was the lure of partnership (to buy stock in the company) which helped the company *attract* a lot of good managers.

Walton commented once that as much as people love to talk about all the elements that have gone into Wal-Mart's prosperity—merchandising, distribution, technology, market saturation, real estate strategy—the truth is that none of that is the real secret to its phenomenal success. He feels that what has propelled the company *so far so fast* is the relationship that the managers have been able to foster with the associates. "Associates" refer to those employees in the stores, in the distribution centers, and on the trucks who are usually paid by the hour for their hard work. The relationship with the associates is *"a partnership in the truest sense."* Walton feels that personal partnering is the only reason that Wal-Mart has been able to consistently outperform the competition—and even its own expectations.

George Naddaff, the former chairman of Boston Chicken—now Boston Market, one of the hottest and fastest-growing companies of the first half of the decade—seems to agree about the importance of partnership in attracting, motivating, and keeping good people. Naddaff said in an *Inc.* interview that he finds that more and more businesses seem to be sharing the wealth with employees, and he thinks that it is absolutely essential.

Michael Moe, emerging company analyst and principal at Montgomery Securities, told us in an interview that "to attract good people you must focus on *the future, not the present."* A company whose human and material resources are tied up in handling emergencies doesn't have the platform to attract and keep good people. "Who articulates the company's vision definitely counts," and people will take notice when they consider sharing their professional and economic destinies with an organization.

Giving Up Responsibility

When we spoke with Chip Ottness, manager of a large small-cap fund at J. P. Morgan Investments in New York, he told us that after visiting and studying many emerging growth companies, he has found that "entrepreneurs do not surround themselves with people who can criticize them." As a result, they often can't attract the best people, leading to problems in the transition from the growth stages. Sam Walton, by contrast, looked at every reasonable idea in growing Wal-Mart and hired every good manager he could.

The idea, says Ottness, is "to give up responsibility." Managers and founders who are ready to give up responsibility will eventually attract good people. But those who are not willing to part with some control will not, because good people won't be able to thrive alongside with them. According to Ottness, "often, the company accountant becomes CFO, and the company tends to carry him. But they are wrong. Companies fail because they can't make the transition in the management department."

In the successful growth company, "the CEO, a person with vision, hires the best people to implement that vision, with adequate financial controls to understand where they are, and a long-term plan. *The best people are hired regardless of whether the chairman is out of a job.* Sam Walton hired every good retailer he could find," says Ottness.

One of the "litmus tests" to determine whether the founders are ready to give up responsibility, Ottness continues, is to watch the hired managers when he, as an outsider, asks them questions in front of the chairman or the president as they all sit around the table in the boardroom. A manager who looks him in the eye and doesn't look at the chairman or president is more reliable in Ottness' eyes, because in all probability he or she is the one who makes the decisions in a particular area of expertise. Otherwise the chairman or president makes all the decisions and the others are only puppets. Which reminds us of a wisecrack: Don't be a yes-person—say no when the boss says no.

Of course, people who interact routinely with emerging companies often encounter even extreme cases of founders who are not willing to share responsibility. We once worked with an emerging growth public company that had excellent patents positions, good strategic partners, and a huge market potential, yet for quite a while it didn't attract high-quality investors and top people. This company's stock was in the freezer, when other companies with less going for them were doing much better.

During our experience with the company, only the founder and CEO and an occasional outside consultant or director were present in numerous meetings with investors, and in some major presentations. When some interested investors would wish to talk to other people in the company's management, they were usually blocked from doing so with a multitude of excuses. This is a very unappealing scenario, which is very unattractive to top managerial talent and investors alike.

Thomas Itin, the acclaimed CEO of Williams Controls, puts in other words the capability to give up responsibility—the ability to *delegate* or, should we say, the necessity to delegate. We look at delegating responsibility as a combination of giving up responsibility and keeping a constant line of communication between the delegator and the one to whom responsibility is delegated. Of course, if the CEO keeps a 24-hour watch over the company's managers, the assignment of responsibilities can't be called "delegating."

So we conclude that in order for a company to attract good people to a certain layer of management, and be able to keep it, the layer above must be able to give up enough responsibility to make the managers feel the freedom of creativity and accountability. At the same time, the company must manage to keep tabs on things—gently but firmly.

Victoria Hamilton, executive vice president and COO of General American Investors, a large closed-end investment company, and previously a principal with SRK Management Co., a New York–based private venture capital investment firm, has seen companies when they start, when they grow, and when they are already mature and large. She has a long list of the attributes of top management that will attract and keep good people in all managerial levels:

- Standards of excellence
- Team play
- Sharing reward
- Helping others
- Trusting upper management
- Keeping the company in mind 24 hours a day
- Leadership by example
- Clarity
- Overtime
- Skill at listening
- Humility
- Keeping mistakes in the open
- Rewarding people for daring to point out a mistake

Hamilton considers the last item—rewarding people for pointing out a mistake—one of key importance in attracting and keeping great people.

Moving right on, in an interview with one of ADP's founders, Henry Taub, we asked him how the company was able to attract and keep good people in the emerging growth years of ADP, and what the difference, if any, would be today.

"On the day we went public," says Taub, "we were still a small company of 30 people or so, with $600,000 in revenues based on 1961 dollars, which in today's dollars would amount to $3 million. Still, we made options available to everybody who was off the clock. If you were a manager, and not paid by the hour, you got options from day one. This created a sense of participation." Of course, we can see the same concepts applied by Sam Walton in growing Wal-Mart, and by Starbucks, AOL, and others in the more recent years.

Taub qualifies his previous statement by pointing out that today, with 28,000 employees at ADP, things are evidently different. Yet he would still wager that at least 10 percent of the employees are in some kind of option program. Moreover, stock purchase programs have been part of ADP's hallmark for many years. "We encourage our employees to feel a sense of partnership," Taub says, repeating the core of his philosophy.

And he explains that if a stock purchase program is announced today, an employee can buy the stock at a 15 percent discount off that day's price. In addition, there's built-in protection. For example, if the stock is at $40 on the day the program is announced, the employee buys the stock for $34. If at the end of the program year the stock goes up to $50, the employee still bought it for $34. But if at the end of the program year the stock goes to $20, the employee gets the stock for $17—15 percent off the year-end price. "So no employee loses," concludes Taub.

When we asked Taub whether he saw any difference between building an emerging growth company in the 1960s and 1970s and building one today, Henry Taub drew only one distinction. When you are one company in an exciting growing industry, the competitive environment is of one profile. When the industry has grown, and related industries have sprung up, it's of another.

"Today it's the age of the executive headhunter," he says. "Recently we lost our CFO to Apple Computer. He was well paid, fairly paid, but we could do nothing about it. It was an opportunity he wanted."

We asked Henry Taub to sum up his experience of attracting good people to a growing company. He said: "You've got to create a sense of partnership. You have to demonstrate to an individual that he or she is going to *share the growth prospects* of an organization, that he or she will *have a role to play,* and that he or she *will be rewarded based on his or her contribution.*"

RECRUITING OUTSIDE BOARD MEMBERS

Last but not least, we wish to touch on an issue that is often neglected—attracting and recruiting an effective and helpful board of directors. Chip Ottness, a billion-dollar small-cap fund manager at J. P. Morgan Investments in New York, told us in an interview that "of course a company like J. P. Morgan would be more interested in investing in an emerging growth company if it had Gates, Allen, or Buffet on the board." But according to Ottness, "board members can make a difference only to the extent of complementing a great management team."

In order to get a better understanding of the directions in which a company should look and the tactics it should use to attract and recruit an effective board of directors, we interviewed Bill Green—lawyer, retired congressman, scholar, and investor. Today Green sits on a number of boards, both as a private investor and as someone whom companies and organizations look to for advice.

Bill Green was a lawyer with the prestigious Wall Street firm Cleary, Gottlieb, Steen & Hamilton prior to being elected in 1978 to the U.S. House of Representatives, representing New York's Fifteenth Congressional District (Manhattan's East Side). He served as House chair in the 99th and 100th Congresses, and in 1992 returned to private business. Green manages the Green Fund, a family investment company, and he is an active private investor in emerging growth companies. Formerly on the board of the $2 billion Grand Union, he is currently on the board of directors of two private emerging growth companies, a public NYSE closed-end investment company with over $500 million in assets, two city organizations, and a national government organization.

Specifically, he is a director of ClientSoft—a 5-year-old 50-employee private company which is developing software to preserve legacy systems. He is also a director of Energy Answers Corporation. This private emerging company is a partner in a novel waste processing system and plant. The system first shreds the waste before burning it. This results in higher temperatures, less pollution, and a higher BTU—energy which the company resells. The company started licensing the process to companies like Bechtel, as well as to Japanese and Italian firms.

Green is a director of General American Investors Company, Inc., a New York Stock Exchange closed-end investment company which was established in 1927. The company, with assets exceeding $500 million, states as its objective "long-term capital appreciation through investment in companies with above-average growth potential." He is also a director of the New York City Housing Development Corporation, and is a member and vice chair of the New York City Campaign Finance Board. He is on the Space Studies Board of the National Research Council. The current assignment of the board is to give advice to the federal government concerning the question: What works and what doesn't in international cooperation? Green was also instrumental in arranging $10 million to build the Audubon Center—Columbia University's biotech incubator.

We asked Bill Green: "What should an emerging company look for in outside board members?" He made four points:

- Knowledge of the general field
- Access to lending institutions and sources of capital
- Access to potential customers
- General business experience and acumen—especially important when the original team is young and fresh without significant prior experience in company building

When we asked Green how a company can find and attract good board members, he said that almost invariably the contact comes through personal knowledge—X knows Y and Z. We thought that this was too general and we asked for more specifics. He again made four points:

- Knowing someone with one or more of the qualities listed above
- Making the connection through your area of expertise
- Using people who put up the capital (themselves or their representatives)
- Relying on search firms that specialize in recruiting boards of directors

Finally, one should not completely disregard the motivation factor of the financial rewards a board member may reap. Rewards often include monetary compensation combined with stock options (where applicable). Of course, the financial motivation of investors to become board members is tied to the control over their investments' destiny and the ability to protect their interests.

People in top positions in the industry or the investment community who reach retirement and want to stay involved in business usually make excellent board members. Of course, these people expect to get paid, something companies in the very early stage often can't afford. A business with high growth potential, however, may entice very attractive board members by offering them stock or stock options in the company. Lately, we've encountered a 15-employee computer and internet telephone company that went public with revenues under $1 million, which had on its board a former president of Radio Shack and a former manager of Fidelity's Magellan Fund. And, immediately following its IPO a former vice chairman of Salomon Brothers joined the board. Not bad at all!

Young companies often enlist lawyers and accountants and give them stock in the company, because they need those services and usually can't afford to pay full price for them. As the company grows and nears its IPO, these kinds of board members might, however, be perceived to have a conflict of interest. Bill Green says that, consequently, he sees fewer and fewer lawyers and accountants who are providing services to the company on the board of directors.

In principle, you can use your service providers for information and referral purposes. However, you might find, for example, that a Big Six accounting firm hired by the company when it pursues an IPO may have strict rules about the extent to which it can be involved in recommending and referring board members.

Board members also usually require that a company pay for their liability insurance, which they need because they are part of the management authority. This is a major issue for a public company, in which independent stockholders might sue in case of bad company performance and a significant decline in the value of their holdings. It is less of a problem in closely held private companies. So in order for an advanced-stage emerging growth company, which is already public or contemplating going public, to attract top board members, it must be able to afford the usually costly liability coverage for its board members.

Finally we wanted to know how Bill Green was attracted to becoming a board member of some of the companies he is involved in. In the case of General American Investors, he knew the people, and the monetary compensation was good. At Energy Answers Corporation, he got on the board as part of a private investment he made in the company. And, in the case of ClientSoft, at first he was approached by a friend in the venture capital industry to become an investor. He made an investment in ClientSoft without contemplating being on the board. Later he was asked to become a director, and he agreed.

To sum it up, board members can assist a company's management in navigating the company, and in helping it with the contacts it would need in the industry and in the financial community. A board of directors usually consists of the company founders and members of the management team, industry experts, and investors or representatives of investment companies. The best way to find and attract good board members is through personal contacts and contacts with people who have a vested interest in the company.

THE PRESCRIPTION AT LAST

On the basis of what we gleaned from our informal panel of experts, and in keeping with our tradition of seven, here is the prescription you should follow to attract good people to an emerging growth business:

1. Create a sense of partnership, and share the growth prospects of an organization.
2. Utilize your contacts and constantly develop new ones, to reach and attract the kinds of people you want.

3. Articulate the company's vision clearly—focus on the future, and prove that it is a bright one. Don't allow your company to be perceived as one that is so busy with problems of the present that it might miss the bend in the road and forsake the future. Good people always count on the future. They will be willing to sacrifice the present but not the future.

4. Be fanatical about keeping the company in a positive spiral. The helix of a positive spiral pulls in the good stuff. On the other hand, rumors about problems with product quality, customer satisfaction, or loss of market share usually travel at supersonic speeds and can trigger an avalanche. Good people take notice and do an about-face.

5. Foster the creative spirit, and create an environment in which people can flourish.

6. Delegate responsibility and give others space. Allow people to criticize you fearlessly, and reward people for pointing out mistakes.

7. Establish joint ventures and strategic partnership. You'll naturally encounter successful good people who share your field. They'll get to know you and your staff, and eventually some will join your organization individually or as part of a whole company.

Keep the "magnetic field" on—always. A growing company with an air of destiny needs to continually attract good people. Furthermore, it has to continually do its best to prevent the good people it already has from being tempted by other firms (and executive headhunters) and leaving for greener pastures.

DON'T MAKE TIME—
ALLOT IT

How to Make the Most of Time
in the Poised-for-Growth Business

"Time is money," a metaphor coined by Benjamin Franklin, is one of the most treasured expressions in business. Have you ever stopped to think about the validity of this statement before using it? Here's how we look at it. For those who have already made it big, time is *more important* than money. To quote Queen Elizabeth I: "All my possessions for one moment of time." On the other hand, those who are just starting only *wish* that they could directly translate time into money—"busyness" doesn't always create business. And, how about those in the middle—the emerging growth contingency? Let's face it, *time spent* is never a measure of success among entrepreneurs and managers involved in building emerging growth companies. Granted, at this stage of a company when production and sales are growing, the correlation between time and money is gradually increasing.

Another important observation is that time management extends beyond personal time. *Product* development and manufacturing are subject to similar requirements of proper timing and time allocation. And even a rookie can tell you that *market* timing and time allocation in relation to market development are key ingredients in the making of a successful growing business.

You might have noted that we uttered the concepts of "timing" and time allocation in the same breath. Are they the same? Of, course not. Yet there is more correlation between the two than meets the eye. Timing refers to positioning an activity—personal, product-related, or market-related—in a certain point in time. Time allocation refers to carving out intervals of time—devoting certain periods of time for certain activities related to the above three categories. Both, of course, fall under the category of time management.

We all know the saying "Timing is everything"—and most of us agree. But timing depends also on fluctuating external factors. Therefore, if your time allocation is too rigid and crowded, you might not be able to "time" correctly those activities which are strongly affected by external factors. For example, if you rigidly commit all your company's human and monetary resources to a particular product, and if new technical or market developments or the introduction of major competition indicates a need for a sharp change, then your company will probably suffer a detrimental setback.

This seeming paradox between timing and time allocation is no paradox at all. To be able to time things correctly you must stay flexible with time allocation. And maintaining the correct synergy is, of course, more critical for an emerging growth company trying to scale the mountain than for a large, well-established large business functioning on a relative plateau. Whereas a large corporation can allocate time to a number of parallel efforts, boosting its efforts with the infusion of capital and human resources if it misses the exact timing, an emerging growth business usually must stay focused, and its low budgets rarely allow it to catch up if it happens to miss a major bend in the road.

And for those who still think that time *is* money, to its fullest extent, we would like to quote Edgar Watson Howe ("Communications" by Robert W. Kent in *Money Talks*, 1985): "Half the time when men think they are talking business, they are wasting time." To which should be added Professor C. Northcote Parkinson's famous corollary, first published in *The Economist*: "Work expands to fill the time available for its completion."

(Remember, Parkinson's Laws, as humorous as they sound, are based on extensive research.)

Attractiveness without availability and accessibility is inconsequential. Therefore, time allocation is a crucial component in exposing an emerging growth company to opportunities and new directions. Furthermore, attractiveness combined with accessibility tends to bring in factors that increase attractiveness—in a chain reaction or, if you will, a positive spiral. For example, an attractive emerging growth company that is easily accessible to other synergistic companies will end up creating joint ventures and strategic alliances. These joint ventures will provide the emerging growth company with enhanced products and markets, and possibly with some good people—all to the effect of increasing its attractiveness. Again, these phenomena extend beyond the issue of management's personal availability into areas of accessibility to new products and markets.

So the question we pose and intend to answer is this: How can you, the managers of emerging growth businesses, measure the value of time and allocate it properly—whether it's in your own schedule or otherwise related to products and markets?

MANAGING TIME EFFECTIVELY

Autumn 1973 was a very busy period for U.S. Secretary of State Henry Kissinger. Among other matters, he was facing the start of a major crisis in the Middle East. To epitomize his time constraints at that period, Dr. Kissinger made the following remark in *The New York Times* (October 28, 1973): "Next week there can't be any crisis. My schedule is already full." Does this hit home? Yes, we are sure that every manager can identify with Dr. Kissinger's problem at the time. Some might even say, *C'est la vie!* But let us present two interesting examples—both pointing in another direction.

The Bard Group (not to be confused with C. R. Bard, the large medical devices manufacturer) was founded in the mid-1960s. Bard was in the business of exporting construction materials to the Far East. It was really a more sophisticated operation than it sounds, because the company was competing for entire projects—say a hospital in Korea—to supply all the architectural, electrical, and ventilation materials for the building.

In the 20 years that he owned the company, the president and founder built it up from a handful of people to a sizable organization. Before he sold the company, in the mid-1980s, there were over 100 people at the New Jersey headquarters, and fully functional offices in Japan, Korea, the Philippines, Hong Kong, London, and perhaps more. The size of a typical deal for Bard was in the few millions to the tens-of-millions range.

From the early 1970s until the president and founder sold the business, Bard definitely fit in the emerging growth company category. In one of many conversations with us, the president and founder talked about his time management philosophy in business. We must admit that first we were practically in shock when we heard what he had to say—because it was in direct contradiction to everything we had read and heard up to that time. For the prevailing opinion was that time *is* money, and that people should watch and plan out every minute of their time.

Yet the one-time owner and president of the Bard Group, a very busy person who was building a successful emerging company, told us: "When I go on business trips to visit my offices in the Far East, I plan out only *50 percent* of my time. I found that many great opportunities came to me during *the other 50 percent!*"

In the same period, another person was building a company—this one with a very high visibility. Some called it an empire, but the way we see it, it was an emerging growth company whose "unit of currency" was naturally very high, because it dealt with large real estate deals. Although the sales levels were beyond the traditional limits of emerging growth businesses, all the other parameters fit very well into the emerging growth category. It was, then, a fast-growing, very attractive entrepreneurial firm—The Trump Organization—headed by the charismatic, and some will say enigmatic Donald Trump.

Anyone you ask will probably tell you that Trump must be a workaholic whose calendar is structured around a web of appointments so dense that you can't drop a pin and hit an empty spot. Well, we didn't know it either, but that doesn't seem to be the case. In his book *Surviving at the Top,* Trump talks about his time management technique.

He says that there is a huge difference between working hard and being a crazed workaholic. Then he adds the key ingredient of his "prescription": to work from morning until night, but to try to make sure that there is *plenty of white space* on your appointment calendar. Those empty slots in the schedule don't represent "wasted time." Trump reinforces "his way" with a quote from the English writer Samuel Butler: "To do great work a man must be very idle as well as very industrious."

What things really boil down to is that time is Time, and money is Money. Time is converted into money by creating and selling products and services. Money is turned into (more available) time by buying products and services, which includes hiring people to do certain tasks that otherwise you would have to do yourself. These two processes meet, and feed on each other. The degree to which the two conversions—time into money, and money into time—overlap represents the degree to which *time is money* in a particular scenario.

For example, if there is a buyer for every cabbage-patch doll a company produces—as was the case in the first few months of their introduction to the market—and it takes a certain number of human-hours to produce ten dozen of them, then that time *is* money. But, if the new accounting software you produce doesn't have a well-developed consumer awareness yet, then, while you can turn Time into software packages, you can't turn time into money. Our advice under those circumstances would be that, instead of producing all those software packages, you should spend only part of your company's human-hours on turning out products, and devote the rest of your time to marketing. Figuring out the best balanced strategies, while leaving the door open to changes dictated by external factors, requires time too—which brings us back to the empty white spots on the calendar.

Most emerging growth companies fit into the category of the "accounting software" company, rather than into the class of the cabbage-patch doll manufacturer. This means that only part of the time can be converted into money; the rest of the time is needed to figure out how to convert "the rest of the time" into money.

Still, there are exceptions. And, as they say, the exception proves the rule. Compaq Computers, now a household name, was founded by three engineers who left Texas Instruments. They built hardware compatible with the same accessory cards as the IBM PC. Their computers were also compatible with all the applications that were running on the IBM PC, because they licensed MS-DOS. The machines they produced did everything the IBM PC did with an added bonus—they were more portable. Compaq's annual revenues *exceeded $100 million* in less than two years in business. Now that's called *time is money.*

But usually, even the best emerging growth companies develop at a slower pace—at least 3 to 5 years to maturity, reaching the emerging growth companies' upper limit of $150 million to $200 million. For these companies, a different set of rules apply.

We often hear the expression "Make time for _____." Since even the highest-flying entrepreneur is humble enough to admit that she or he doesn't have the power to *make* time in the literal sense, *making time* refers to pushing whatever is in the schedule out of the way. To make time for something is, therefore, equivalent to making yourself available when, otherwise, there wouldn't have been availability.

PUT FLEXIBILITY IN YOUR SCHEDULE

As noted in our previous discussions, *making time* is not the correct strategy, except when there's no other choice. If you leave enough white spaces in the calendar, you will be able to avoid the familiar neurotic pattern of constant reshuffling. You'll usually be able to allocate time without pushing other things out of the way. When it comes to time, don't *make* it—*allot* it.

There are three areas where this comes into play for the emerging growth company:

1. Allot time for personal flexibility.
2. Allot time for product flexibility.
3. Allot time for market flexibility.

Time allotment for personal flexibility is just what it means—keeping those white spaces on the calendar. Put aside time for evaluation, analysis, and retrospection. And keep the white spaces to allow new ideas and people—and with them opportunities—to reach your company. Again, this is much more crucial at the emerging growth stage than at a point where a company already has ample personnel for strategic planning, and the company has already established a steady, long-term flow of business.

Time allotment for product flexibility means not plugging up all the development and production pipelines of the company with the needs of the next day. Nearsightedness in this respect is like selling extra seats in an otherwise sold-out theater and setting up chairs at the emergency exits. Allot human-hours for product reevaluation, upgrades, improvements of quality, and a possible need to make an 180-degree change in direction. You won't be able to take care of these items if every human-hour is already rigidly committed. Last-minute reshuffling won't help—farsightedness in time allotment will.

Time allotment for market flexibility is probably the most overlooked item among the three. Very few emerging growth companies conduct ongoing market research once they have established a foothold in *a* market. The frustration of years of "waiting for Godot"—in this case, a growing revenue stream—leaves management with a strong desire to breath easier and "take a break." There is a clear tendency to focus the human-hours of the marketing and sales staff, as well as management's attention, on building up sales in that one market segment that already works, and stop worrying about the future for a while.

This tactic might be healthy for a short period of time. But in a highly chaotic marketplace, where customer trends are changing fast and where competition pops up as if from nowhere, you must get vigilant again—sooner than later. Allotting time for constantly evaluating and building new markets, even as the emerging company scales the mountain, is an important part of being *poised for growth*.

To put all the above bluntly: If you talk all the time, you can't listen. If you produce all the time, you can't upgrade and develop. And if you sell all the time, you can't open markets. We are convinced that every competent manager can read a road map of emerging products and markets, except when there is no time left to consider new and different possibilities. Let's look at a few concrete examples.

THE WAL-MART STORY

In 1967, Kmart had 250 stores and a total of $800 million in revenues, compared with Wal-Mart's 19 stores and $9 million in revenues. Wal-Mart was clearly in its early emerging growth stage. Twenty-five years later Wal-Mart became the biggest and most profitable discount retailer in the nation. Now, *your* goal might not be so presumptuous—to build up such a big "empire." Still, you can learn from Sam Walton's time allotment system, which will facilitate healthy growth.

Walton was known to visit various competitors' stores, talk to people, learn their systems, and educate himself on new methods such as using computers. He was also known to frequent his own stores and talk to managers and associates. Whereas other CEOs might have concentrated on directly turning all their time into money, by spending 100 percent of their time on finding cheaper product sources or bargain real estate for new stores, Walton allotted time to learning and experimenting. Eventually, this time paid off and was turned into money—in the long run. In fact, Walton attributes Wal-Mart's growth success to this flexibility and adaptability.

A FEW MISTAKES

Let's look at another example, this time from the financial services sector: D. Blech & Co., a rising-star investment banking boutique of the early 1990s. This story is amazing, because the company, with 200 employees in its New York headquarters, and with offices in a few other states, was wiped off the investment banking map in about a year after it made its first lucrative initial public offering for biotech companies. D. Blech & Co. made many mistakes, but its demise is at least indirectly attributable to the lack of proper time allotment in the product and market categories.

What may sound even more shocking is that at some point during D. Blech & Co.'s last and fastest growth year, the founder and chairman of this emerging growth financial company was listed among *Forbes'* 500 richest people in the nation—primarily on the basis of his stock holdings in the companies he financed. It is also amazing that many of the companies that this firm financed and took public are considered today some of the best in the emerging growth biotech sector. Still, D. Blech & Co. is not around to enjoy the fruit of its early triumphs.

What went wrong at D. Blech & Co.? Probably quite a few things. But from our perspective, we wish to concentrate on the firm's time allotment in terms of products and markets.

D. Blech & Co. was the leading financing boutique for emerging biotech companies. The founder and chairman was actually considered Mr. Biotech. The biotech sector, from an investment banking point of view, is a very exciting, but often volatile sector. It has probably the wildest fluctuations between fat years and lean years. Biotechnological innovations promise unusually high returns, but it takes many years of no-revenue conditions to finish development and obtain regulatory approvals. And the percentage of companies that get to the finish line, with actual marketed drugs, is relatively small.

When a company operates in such a volatile market, it is easy to make mistakes. A lot of time should be devoted to evaluating product and market alternatives. Allotment of time for new products and markets and for reevaluating old strategies is categorically essential. Listening to the market and controlling growth are also critical. No other emerging, aggressive investment banking firm was so exposed in a narrow front as D. Blech & Co.

The rush for gold was on, and the company leveraged itself to do any deal that seemed viable and lucrative. The companies D. Blech & Co. chose were good, but still the pace was extremely fast. No time was allotted for evaluating and considering a change of direction, or any such activity that would slow down the pace.

But this was a "house of cards," and when the wind started blowing, it had to collapse. Once the highly inflated stock market in the biotech sector started correcting itself, D. Blech & Co. had to turn out more deals, faster, allotting even less time to considering different products and markets, or perhaps even to considering a pause. Funds were needed to satisfy NASD basic requirements for IPOs, for rent, and for the payroll—which grew almost tenfold in a little more than a year.

It is clear that trying to turn every minute of time into money is a growth formula that doesn't fit well with an emerging growth business. In the case of D. Blech & Co., the rush for gold didn't allow the company to allot time for checking the road ahead, stopping the wagon, or taking another bend in the road before it abruptly terminated in the abyss.

Another company that made a gross mistake in time allotment in the product and marketing departments is Aldus—the once high-flying innovator of desktop publishing software—which was eventually sold to Adobe. Aldus was so busy focusing its time on squeezing out the maximum profits from its Apple-compatible products that it didn't allot enough time early on to prepare contingencies for the massive invasion of the IBM compatibles and the Windows environment.

Once Aldus realized its mistake and, in 1992, started allotting massive amounts of human-hours to developing new products and markets, it was too late. The company's profits and its stock tumbled 70 and 75 percent respectively, and investors lost confidence and interest. If Aldus had allotted time for alternative products and markets on a routine basis, it might have found the right bend in the road, and its fate would have played out differently.

DIVIDING RESPONSIBILITY AT ADP

In our interview with ADP's founder, honorary chairman, and chairman of the executive committee—Henry Taub—we asked him about the issues of time allotment. Taub feels that with a good cooperative management team, time allotment is not a problem, because responsibilities can be shifted. In the emerging growth years of ADP, if one of the partners wanted to try to build a new segment of business for the company, another would take over some of the partner's current responsibilities.

A good partnership can go even further. At a certain point Frank Lautenberg, a cofounder of ADP who later became a well-known U.S. senator from New Jersey, was offered the leadership of a major charitable organization. They figured that this responsibility would consume up to 50 *percent* of his time. As one of the three top guys in the management of a fast-growing company, what would you say to such an offer? Ask the top managers of any growing organization, and they'll prove to you in a 10-point argument that if they allot 5 *percent* (not 50 percent) of their time to any extracurricular activity, there is a danger that the company won't survive.

Well, Frank Lautenberg did take the philanthropic position. Henry Taub told him: "Let's see how it works. If an urgent need arises to change the time allotment priorities, I'm sure we'll do the right thing." Judging by the results, yes, they did the right thing. ADP continued to grow at a fast pace and with a stellar performance. This part of the ADP example shows that time allotment problems can be eased by sharing and dividing responsibilities.

ADP also managed to develop effective time allotment practices in another area—the product category. When it went public in 1961, half the proceeds were shared by the three partners (who sold some of their shares), and the other half—which would amount to $750,000 in 1996 dollars—went to the company. At that time, the company's sole business was in the employer services category (payroll processing and the like). The company wanted to grow nationally from its New York metropolitan territories.

However, another interesting growth opportunity presented itself in automating the back office ("cage") operations in brokerage houses. In spite of ADP management's awareness of the importance of growing its core employer services business, it

decided to allot a significant amount of time and all the proceeds from the initial public offering to developing the system
for the back office at Oppenheimer—a major Wall Street firm
which was also ADP's lead underwriter.

ADP managed to grow nationally by acquiring around 100
general service bureaus, using its stock as acquisition currency.
Simultaneously, the allotment of time and resources to developing the system for Oppenheimer's "cage" operations, got ADP
into the brokerage-related service industry. This sector represents today 25 percent of ADP's revenues, and in 1995, for
example, it grew internally at an annual rate of 18 percent, and
at a total annual rate (including acquisitions) of 32 percent.

UMBRELLA RULES

We can sum up our umbrella rules for time management in the
poised-for-growth business, as follows:

1. Don't make time—allot time.
2. Leave enough time in its natural form—available time.
3. Let time evolve into money, through other intermediate
   stages.
4. Allow enough time for new opportunities to reach you—
   from the outside and from the inside (your own creative
   ideas). This includes products and markets.
5. Don't be time-frugal, but be time-conscious.
6. Be flexible.
7. Share and delegate responsibilities.

In summary, time management usually becomes a trap for
the emerging growth company. On the one hand, it's the rush to
get ahead and, on the other, the "exhaustion" and "exhilaration"
of getting to first or second base which renders the company
incapable of allotting time—personal, product-related, or market-related—to secure the future. Our rules for time allotment
will solve these problems.

SEVEN RULES FOR ATTRACTING CAPITAL— IN THE FORMAT THAT FITS MOST

MONEY IS AVAILABLE—WHY THE TURMOIL OF FUNDING? VENTURE CAPITAL, LOANS, PRIVATE PLACEMENTS, OFFSHORE MONEY, PUBLIC OFFERINGS

There is much more to financing an emerging growth business than the availability or even the accessibility of capital. Someone once said: "*Quantity* is not important—it's the *quality* that's important, as long as there's a lot." This seemingly funny, paradoxical trade-off between quality and quantity has an important lesson embedded in it.

The founder and CEO of an emerging growth public software company, which has since grown to 150 employees, was trying to raise money in the early years of the business. A friend who worked in the investment community told him that "raising money is easy; what you want is *quality* money." Now, at that time, he would have probably settled for *any* kind of capital—he says. But since then he learned that raising capital and living with its providers takes up time and management's attention. Therefore, the *quality* of the money—that is, the nature of the source—is as important as the *quantity* and availability of the capital.

THE ROAD AHEAD

Once you're on the highway, it's easy to talk about the road ahead." You may wonder how the wealthiest corporate entrepreneur, Bill Gates, obtained his financing. Delving into the initiation rites through which the successful have passed, the emerging growth company might obtain insights into how it could finance its next stage of growth. With all the smarts and with a well-polished business plan buffed to a high shine, the adventuresome capitalists must have greeted Bill Gates with open checkbooks. "Yes, Mr. Gates, and how much will that be today?"

That may have been Bill Gates' fantasy when he was dreaming his dreams in the Harvard dormitory, and it certainly may be your fantasy for obtaining your next round of financing. But in his book *The Road Ahead*, Bill Gates modestly admits that he obtained his initial financing from capitalizing on one of his hidden talents: card playing. Looks can be deceiving. It is hard for us to imagine Gates turning into the Cincinnati Kid, or in his case the Seattle Kid, at the poker table.

Do you think that your emerging growth company can raise additional financing at the gaming tables? Since we do not want to run afoul of the gambling authorities of any state, and since there are other attractive financing alternatives, we suggest you read on for more traditional and more likely methods.

Anyone who has even the slightest doubt about the uniqueness of the financing process for the emerging growth sector should start by taking a close look at a study conducted by Coopers & Lybrand. The study surveys 328 fast-growing small to midsize businesses—basically, the emerging growth constituency of this book. What's very interesting from our perspective is that the study goes back in time to look at the *startup* financing methods of these high-growth companies.

Upon examining the sources that the high-growth businesses used for their primary means of startup financing, Coopers & Lybrand arrived at the following striking, but perhaps expected results.

The vast majority of the companies—73 percent—were primarily funded at startup by the owners, their families, and friends. Of the companies surveyed, 13 percent received their primary startup capital from outside investors, 8 percent from banks, and 6 percent from alliances with other businesses (customers and suppliers).

The study also concluded that the fastest-growing companies were those that managed to get their primary initial funding from banks. The companies that raised the most capital (three times the average) were those that got their funding from outside investors. And the slowest-growing companies were those that relied on customers and suppliers for their initial funding.

It is now obvious why we think that the issues related to financing emerging growth companies are unique. For one, the resource that contributes close to three-quarters of the primary sources for startup financing—owners, friends, and family— does not have the financial capability to contribute sufficient amounts of capital when the same company reaches its emerging growth stage. Indeed, by the time your company gets to the emerging growth stage, your friends may have become your foes and your family members may consider themselves to be only your distant relatives.

Although venture capitalists used to be considered the champions of startups, that has changed drastically. The Coopers & Lybrand study, in fact, indicates that only one in eight high-growth companies received primary startup capital from outside investors—that category of outside investors includes as a *subgroup* the venture capital sector.

In fact, a venture capital fund such as Patricof's Excelsior III, invested *four times* as much money in emerging growth companies as it invested in startups, and the industrywide ratios are growing in favor of the emerging growth sector.

Financing for the emerging growth stage is drastically different not only from that of the earlier startup stage, but also from that of the later stage, when the company has "graduated" and its sales exceed the upper limit for inclusion in the emerging growth category. At this point the company is established. It has assets, a track record, wide analysts' coverage (if public), and ratings. Therefore, debt—either by borrowing directly from banks (or opening lines of credit) or by issuing corporate bonds—becomes a very attractive and practical mode of financing. Having said that, a company that is beyond the emerging growth stage still has the option of financing expansion through large equity offerings.

You see, at this later stage of a company, underwriters with enormous influence, reach, and financial leverage can and are willing to perform almost any acrobatic maneuver and wizardry—to avail the company of the necessary capital, and themselves of the fat commissions that come with large transactions.

A STORY FROM CORPORATE HISTORY

Don't feel that the investment bankers will ignore your firm simply because you haven't graduated to the highest level. A story from the corporate history of one of America's most successful companies—ADP—gives insight into the going public opportunities available to the emerging growth company.

Henry Taub, one of the founders of Automatic Data Processing—the $3 billion New York Stock Exchange company known as ADP—provides keen insights into the importance that "going public" offered his company. ADP operated without the benefit of outside financing for the first decade of its existence. The major source of equity was the sweat of Taub's brow, that of Taub's brother Joe, and that of the now highly regarded senator from New Jersey, Frank Lautenberg. That's a lot of sweat equity even for a company that became as large as ADP.

Since they were young men in the postwar era, when life, as we would all like to believe, was less complicated than it is now, these founders did not need a regular paycheck to take home to their families. Being true entrepreneurs, they made ends meet as they created a market for a service that at that time few companies really believed they needed, and which today no company can live without—payroll processing. Although Automatic Data Processing uses technology in its business, at bottom the company is a service business.

Nonetheless, in spite of the relaxed initial buildup, these young men at ADP were certainly opportunistic. When the over-the-counter (OTC) market took an interest in data service companies, ADP was not to be left behind. In 1961, when the company had reached $600,000 in revenues (in today's dollars, approximately $3 million), an analyst from Oppenheimer who was targeting the industry discovered ADP. At that time Oppenheimer was a prestigious "wholesale" securities firm. Jack Nash, then on the management at Oppenheimer, who has since gone on to venture capital fame at Odyssey Partners, approached the company with the concept of going public. Oppenheimer did not have the distribution capability to sell a retail offering into the OTC market, and suggested another lead underwriter. But ADP did not want to go public with what was then the more established OTC underwriters.

Nonetheless, ADP was astute enough to realize the importance of cementing its good relationship with Oppenheimer and ADP convinced Oppenheimer to be a comanager of the underwriting. Indeed, Oppenheimer was on the "left"; in other words, Oppenheimer was the lead manager. Although 1961 may have been a simpler time than the present times, ADP and its underwriters still recognized the importance of having its financial statements audited by what was then one of the Big Eight accounting firms. Just as important, ADP hired Paul, Weiss, Rifkind, Wharton & Garrison, one of the most prestigious securities law firms in the country, to act as counsel.

As a public company, ADP was able to grow nationally through a unique formula of massive numbers of small acquisitions. Its stock was a highly valued piece of paper which ADP could use to finance its further growth by acquiring smaller firms which were in the same line of business—firms which Henry Taub calls small service bureaus. The IPO proceeds also enabled ADP to enter a new line of business: the automation of the "back office" of Wall Street. Who better than its underwriter, Oppenheimer, to be ADP's first client in this new endeavor? The skills that ADP had developed in payroll processing were equally applicable to the "back office." The stock trades had to be settled in a timely and efficient manner. While payroll processing was a weekly or bimonthly activity, back-office processing was daily. The degree of timeliness needed for the back office required ADP to evolve to the next level.

The ADP situation depicts one facet of the unique financing challenges of this middle range—the emerging growth stage. Before we get into the hows and whens of finding and attracting capital to an emerging growth business, we wish to analyze the financing modalities available to this sector, and how they might fit into the plans of various emerging companies.

Let's not beat around the bush; face it: Most of the influx of money to the emerging growth sector comes through the investment banking community. Domestic (Reg. D) and offshore (Reg. S) private placements and public offerings (initial and secondary) offer a bountiful supply of capital.

The money supply of these sources is bottomless, because the money is not sitting in a finite fund. Each deal of a particular investment banking house will be considered perhaps by different sets of investors—whether high-net-worth individuals or institutional entities—who commit their money case by case and as it's available. The investment banker's game is just-in-time capital. While venture capital funds require a typical 10-year commitment from fund (typically institutional) investors for a total amount that will be apportioned and invested at the discretion of the fund's general partners, investment banking deals are decided case by case and carry a much higher degree of liquidity.

GOING PRIVATE

Although most of the attention usually goes to discussing the complexities of "going public" (and we, too, will spend time on the topic), let's look for a moment at the world of "going private"—that is, making private placements or exempt offerings (meaning offerings exempt from the detailed registration requirements of going public). The rules governing private placements are less complex than those governing public offerings. Nonetheless, neither this book nor, in our opinion, any other book should be used as a substitute for seeking the advice of legal counsel.

Private placements offer new issues that can go directly to one or several major individual or institutional investors. Under this procedure, the securities are not made available to the general public. The advantage of a private placement is that it is not regulated as stringently as a public offering, and is therefore much less costly for the company. It does not have to be registered with the SEC (Securities and Exchange Commission), on the assumption that the private investors are sophisticated and do not need the protection that the general public does. Investors supply an investment letter attesting to their being "sophisticated" investors, i.e., an investor who's capable of evaluating the merits of an investment venture. In addition, a private placement affords the issuing company a great deal more privacy about its finances than a public offering.

It is worthwhile to note that both private and public companies can "float" private placements. Usually they do it through underwriters or placement agents. Some private companies (or rarely even young public ones) find it too expensive to go to an underwriter, or often can't find an underwriter which would be interested or capable to raise the capital at that stage of the company. As a result they would offer a company directed private placement. In this scenario the company retains a lawyer to prepare the document, and then it markets it to people whom the company principals know, or uses finders to recruit additional investors.

Private placements, or as they are also called, exempt offerings, can be used to raise either debt or equity securities. One common private placement, which applies mostly to mature companies, is a Rule 144a offering. The rule permits companies to raise capital by selling either debt or equity securities to "qualified institutional buyers." Those qualified institutional buyers, in turn, can sell the securities to other, similar buyers. In general, a qualified institutional buyer is an entity that manages at least $100 million in assets. Rule 144a is attractive, since it gives institutional buyers a limited degree of liquidity.

For the average emerging growth company, a Regulation D offering, or a Reg. D, provides private placements that are subject to exemptions under Regulation D of the SEC, and in particular Rules 504, 505, and 506. These rules are complex and as of this writing broadly provide as follows:

- *Rule 504* allows an issuer to sell securities totaling up to $1 million over a 12-month period. Such an offering may be made to any number of investors.

- *Rule 505* allows an issuer to sell up to $5 million of securities over a 12-month period. However, the investors must meet restrictions delineated in the regulation. For example, only 35 investors may be "nonaccredited" investors. You are probably asking yourself, "So what is an accredited investor?" An accredited investor is an individual or institution that is knowledgeable and has net worth or annual income which is considered adequate to make such investment decisions.

- *Rule 506* permits the sale of an unlimited amount of securities. For that privilege all nonaccredited investors (maximum of 35) must qualify as "sophisticated" investors. Put simply, a sophisticated investor is one who is capable of evaluating the merits of the investment venture.

By now, all these circular definitions will either have you running to a lawyer or saying to yourself, "Wouldn't it be easier just to go to a bank?" The distinction between various types of investors has probably made you realize the benefit of involving an intermediary who has had some experience in this area and who knows which pools of capital to tap.

It is important to note that although Reg. D offerings—securities which are placed with selected investors and never offered to the public—are exempt from registration and prospectus, they are still subject to the antifraud provisions of the Securities Act, and must meet certain standards. They may not be advertised; there must be disclosure in certain cases; and the price of the securities must be negotiated.

Another frequently used technique is a Regulation A offering, or a Reg. A, which is a far cry from the rhythmic reggae music that comes from the West Indies. An issuer may raise up to $1.5 million per year. However, significant documentation and an offering circular must be filed with the SEC.

A less commonly used exemption from the SEC's registration requirement is Regulation S—an "offshore" offering.

Although less commonly used than domestic exempt offerings, Regulation S can be an attractive alternative if you can find an intermediary that can access non-U.S. investors for your company. Non-U.S. investors may be attracted to your company if a significant percentage of its business is done abroad or for other investment reasons. An issuer is not subject to the complex registration requirements of the SEC if the securities are sold in an "offshore transaction."

Your company can avail itself of the offshore transaction exemption if the buyer is outside the United States when the buy order is originated. In addition, your company and the intermediary used by your company in raising capital must not engage in any "directed selling efforts" in the United States. Directed selling efforts are any activities undertaken for the purpose of "conditioning" the U.S. market for the securities being offered. This includes mailing printed materials to the United States or conducting seminars or other meetings in the United States.

MEZZANINE FINANCING

By now, you probably feel like we have gone through the entire alphabet of regulations of the Securities and Exchange Commission. So...

"Next stop: 'mezzanine.'" Mezzanine financing is one of the modalities of funding that an emerging growth company should first consider. It is a type of financing that is between senior debt financing that you would get from a bank and common equity that you might raise by going public. Since it is a hybrid type of financing, the varieties and possibilities are greater than those for the other sources of financing. The flexibility of this type of financing makes it one of the most attractive means of raising capital for the emerging growth company.

Mezzanine financing can take the form of preferred stock, which can be redeemable, but according to most sources, mezzanine financing is subordinated debt, which carries in the parlance of the financial trade an "equity kicker." Fortunately, "equity kicker" is less harmless than appears from the sound of the term. It means the debt either has a conversion feature into common stock or carries "warrants" for the company's common stock.

Let's take a break for a definition of a word you may have encountered before, but not in the context of corporate finance: warrant. A warrant is a security issued with a bond or stock that entitles the investor to buy, during a set period of time, a certain amount of common stock at a specified price that is usually higher than the market price at the time of the issuance of the warrant. You should also be aware that "warrants" are transferable and usually can be sold separately from the security to which they are attached.

Since much of the mezzanine financing available is debt (in the form of subordinated debt with those warrants attached), it has the disadvantages of any other debt financing. Interest and principal are payable when due, unless the holder converts the instrument to equity, in the case of a convertible subordinated debenture. As such, mezzanine financing presents financial constraints to an emerging growth company.

THE MILESTONE PHENOMENON

Now that we got you out of the basement and up to the mezzanine, we wanted to conclude with a few more observations about the private world of venture capital in which you may be pursing these types of financing. That people like Bill Gates do not rush to the adventuresome capitalists should actually come as no surprise and has even been borne out by academic studies about the relationship between venture capitalists and the entrepreneurs whom they back.

In a *Journal of Management Studies* article, Steier and Greenwood delineate the reason that entrepreneurs may be turning to the gaming tables or the public markets, rather than the venture funds. First, penetrating the venture network requires relationships, which may be even be more important than a business plan.

In fairness to our friends who get to play *Let's Make a Deal* every day, the venture capitalists no longer live in a shadowy world akin to the gnomes of Zurich. They all have listed phone numbers, and the directories listing venture capital firms have proliferated faster than the number of venture capital firms. Computer software exists that can track them down. Put quite succinctly, they are overwhelmed with schemes and need a filter to separate the "not so real" from the "truly unreal." Thus, enter the necessity for a well-timed, well-connected, and hopefully well-regarded "intermediary" to introduce the founders or company managers to the venture capitalist.

The drawbacks of taking advantage of venture capital do not end with the entrepreneur's difficulty in finding the right button to push. Once entrepreneurs have gotten through the door, many of them begin to look for the exit. Venture capitalists establish "milestones," which as Steier and Greenwood point out, actually may undermine the flexibility that a firm needs to operate. Certainly, every business needs focus, and milestones or benchmarks are highly reliable means for objectively determining whether you are moving in the right direction. Nonetheless, if you are putting in 18 hours a day into your business, it is difficult to find the time to sit down frequently with your favorite financial backer and talk about how things are going.

Finally, the corollary of the "milestone" issue is that venture capital firms have become institutionalized and hierarchical organizations. Thus, venture capital firms have become the epitome of the organization with which an entrepreneur may have difficulty working.

GOING PUBLIC

That may be part of the reason that "going public" has such a prominent role in every book and magazine you have picked up before. Going public is the corporate world's equivalent of becoming a celebrity. You have arrived. It may not get you one of the best tables at a restaurant in Hollywood or New York, but it changes your corporate status in a unique way. The change is the same kind of one that occurs in the life of an individual who becomes a celebrity, at least an individual who is a celebrity for more than the Andy Warhol 15-minute time slot. One can quietly negotiate equity financing from venture capitalists, and admittedly the ongoing relationship with the venture financier changes the way in which your company operates, but going public is different. When your company is publicly held, the whole world is watching, or the whole world can be watching, what you are doing.

If you listen to Henry Taub, the act of going public sounds simple: Take two investment bankers, add an accountant, and stir with a prestigious securities law firm. Instant IPO success. Before you pick up the phone to call your neighborhood investment banker for an instant IPO, let's have a look at the pros and cons of taking the public plunge.

First, the bad news. You lose your operating freedom by becoming subject to the myriad disclosure requirements of federal and state securities laws. As we mentioned before, you are in the public eye, a corporate celebrity. Sometimes your shareholders demand dividends, even when it may make more sense to plow the earnings back into the business. In addition, a recent phenomenon that has received a great deal of press is the "bear raid" by short sellers who may consider your stock to be overvalued. Finally, the one aspect that has received the most criticism: the "short-termism" and fickleness of the 1990s shareholders. Overnight, you can go from a shining star to a shooting star that breaks up in the atmosphere and falls to earth as so many forlorn pebbles on the beach.

We saved the good news to help you recover from the delusions that may have just set in. Going public does provide continued access to long-term financing. You no longer have to look at your credit card statement to ascertain your available balance for future financing alternatives. With stock incentive programs, you can attract better-quality professionals. Moreover, as noted in our interview with Henry Taub, your company now has a "currency" with which it can acquire other companies. Your growth prospects are no longer limited by your ability to generate growth from your own resources or from resources that want to keep a tight control on your actions.

Reaching Critical Mass

Now that we have dispelled the bad news about going public, you should ask yourself if you are really ready. In the Coopers & Lybrand study mentioned previously, the accounting firm discovered that companies considered going public once they reached a certain "critical mass." The companies that were "somewhat likely" to go public had an average of $13 million in annual revenues and 107 employees. Companies "highly likely" to go public had an average of $21 million in annual revenues and 186 employees.

We do note, however, that the actual threshold for going public may be lower, as in the case of ADP, which had only $600,000 in revenues in 1961 or about $3 million in current dollar terms. Furthermore, there are numerous companies that went public in the 1990s with zero or minimal revenues and fewer than 50 employees. Hey, that's the nature of averaging. It reminds us of the story about the 6-foot guy who almost drowned in a pool which had an average depth of 5 feet. Of course, the incident took place near the 9-foot end.

Although your company may have reached the critical mass needed to go public, the Coopers survey found significant deficiencies in the ability of a company to go public. Would you believe almost a quarter (23 percent) of the companies surveyed lacked a business plan? This is a simple deficiency that would also preclude a company from tapping other sources of financing. About a third had not even established a board of directors that met regularly. Add to the previous list a lack of audited financial statements and an inability to prepare quarterly financial statements and you walk away from the study wondering how the companies surveyed had ever gotten out of the basement or the garage.

To our mind, however, the study really highlights the different perspectives of the entrepreneur and the financier. After weighing the pros and cons of going public and having taken your "weight" to determine if you have reached the "critical mass," you still have to decide if you want to make the lifestyle change of being a public company. If you want the cachet of saying you are public, it does require that you add a new suit to your corporate wardrobe : the public company persona.

Deciding whether going public is for you can be easier if you know more about the process. It is critical to choose the right underwriter. The managing underwriter sells securities to individual and institutional investors alone or through a syndicate of other securities firms. Most important, the underwriter should advise your company on the timing and pricing of a stock offering.

Timing of a public offering can be crucial, as demonstrated by a 1996 public offering of the northeast-based coffee bar chain New World. So what's so new about New World? Unfortunately, for its shareholders, not enough.

In one of the cruelest New York winters, New World decided in December 1995 to go public with a New York–based underwriter that had experience in IPO offerings. Perhaps, the cold weather dampened the ardor of the New York underwriter and the underwriter sought to postpone the offering.

Rather than taking a coffee break at one of its ritzy locations, the founders of New World headed west. What better place to find an underwriter for a coffee bar than the home state of Starbucks and countless other coffee bars—Seattle?

The offering was for 2.5 million shares priced at slightly more than a double mocha latte—$5.25. By the end of its first day of trading New World was selling at a discount of 18 percent, or $4.25.

What happened? On the face of it, New World has the cachet of Starbucks, and the stores are in some of the best locations in Manhattan. The service of the people at New World is as efficient and congenial as any young eager person at Starbucks renders. Yet the winter timing was truly cruel to New World. In an interview with *The Wall Street Journal*, Ryan Jacob of the IPO Value Monitor said: "The timing was kind of weird....Coffee is kind of a story that's played out."

IS COFFEE PLAYED OUT?

In a wide-ranging interview with *Inc.* in November 1995, before New World went public, George Naddaff, one of the founders of Boston Chicken and its former chairman—who visited restaurants for a year looking for a very desirable, franchisable concept—stated that even Starbucks may be played out. Naddaff suggests that we watch and see what happens in 3 or 4 years. He claims that it will be hard for Starbucks to maintain the same store sales, and suggests that (if they're smart) they sell it to somebody and go off. Well, you be the judge. The fact is that after decades of success, the leading chains of name-brand burgers and fried chickens are still around. But, hey, anything is possible.

From New World back to your world—from having coffee in public back to going public. In addition to managing the distribution and timing of going public, the underwriter prepares the prospectus or offering document. The prospectus is a legal document which must comply with the federal and state rules and regulations regarding disclosure, but a good underwriter knows how to sprinkle a dash of marketing flavor into the otherwise prosaic document.

As Henry Taub noted, the selection of an independent auditor may be the next most important decision. The SEC requires that the company prepare 3 years of audited financial statements. There is discretion in determining accounting policies, and those policies impact significantly the financial presentation of the company's performance. Moreover, you should be aware that many underwriters request that companies use one of the Big Six accounting firms. By no means should you rush out and select a new accounting firm simply since you're not with one of the Big Six, but you should be aware that the national standing of your accounting firm may be a point of negotiation between you and the underwriter.

The next person you will find on your payroll is "issuer's counsel." True, you may have been working with one highly competent corporate attorney who has guided you through many of the difficulties of becoming an emerging growth company. Nonetheless, unless that attorney has special expertise in securities matters, you may have to supplement the attorney with an outside securities specialist. As we said, your traditional lawyer should merely be supplemented by a securities counsel, since the knowledge that your traditional counsel has is invaluable and that attorney must stay involved in the process.

You will see another person in the room who, at least, indirectly will be on your payroll and that is the underwriter's counsel. This counsel will also focus on the legality of the public offering process, but is clearly representing the interests of the underwriter in the process. Underwriter's counsel will also help negotiate the underwriting agreement and other legal documents related to the underwriting process.

THE SHELL GAME

For those of you who may now be saying that there must be another way of going public, we do have an answer: the shell game. Well, not exactly the same shell game you see magicians play; rather, the merger of a private company into an existing public company that is usually an "empty shell"—in other words, it has no current business. This might be viewed as a "poor person's" alternative to going public, or perhaps as a premature entry to the public markets for a company that's not fully ready for prime time yet. It does allow, however, for faster liquidity, which might tempt some investors who would otherwise wait a few more years before they invested in such a company. In fact, merging into a shell is often referred to as a *reverse* acquisition transaction because the private company acquires the whole shell, but instead of merging the shell into the company, the *shell* acquires all the company's shares and thus the company merges into the shell, takes over it, and becomes a public entity.

STRATEGIC PARTNERING

Another important option that becomes viable for some companies as they grow is a major investment by a large strategic partner. Although this modality is much less prevalent than the investment banking and venture capital options, it's nevertheless the preferred and most profitable route for companies whose need for funding is only part of the need for a complete support system. Funding for emerging growth businesses is also provided through mergers and acquisitions, one form of which—the leveraged buyout—has become quite popular and effective.

The public offering process sounds like a lot, but don't think that you can simply go running into the arms of the venture capitalists. Venture capital funds impose numerous selection barriers to entry, and offer usually little money for a large control and percentage of the company. Another rarely mentioned malaise of the VC funds, except perhaps the largest ones, is that they have "dead" periods. This happens when a fund is largely invested, and before raising the money to open a new fund it tries to reserve the leftover monies for the frequently needed follow-up infusion of capital to its existing portfolio companies. There is no equivalent to this phenomenon in the investment banking sector's just-in-time system.

For the sake of fairness, however, it should be mentioned that investment banking deal-flow is sensitive to stock market performance, the so-called window of opportunity. (After Netscape went public, other firms tried to tap the market by adding the suffix -*scape* to their name.) By contrast, a sitting venture capital fund *theoretically* shouldn't be sensitive to market performance. But realistically, that's not the case either. A long-lasting bearish stock market causes venture capitalists to retrench, because, on the one hand, they cannot turn their investments liquid at a fair profit and, on the other hand, the institutions, whose money creates new funds, turn bearish on investing in developing companies and redirect part of their money to other financial markets.

The good news for the emerging growth sector is, as we stated previously, that the venture capital community has been gradually shifting its resources from funding startups to financing emerging growth businesses (mostly second- and mezzanine-stage financing). By nature of the relatively larger, often multistage investments required by the fast-growth sector, the larger funds such as Patricof, Warburg Pincus, Summit, Sprout, TA Associates, New Enterprise Associates, Frontenac, the Harvard funds, and venture capital arms of major banks dominate the more lucrative deals involving fast growing emerging companies.

If we take the Patricof & Co. Ventures model as an approximation, we may conclude that more than $3.7 billion of the $6 billion annual venture capital financing goes to fund emerging growth companies, while less than $800 million finds its way to fund startups. The balance of approximately $1.5 billion is allocated for buyouts and restructuring.

THE FUNDING GRAND SLAM

Some companies are lucky enough to win a funding "grand slam." They finance their startup by the ever-so-popular owners, friends, and family resources plus possible contributions from local state, city, or federal sources. Then they attract capital from the venture capital community, and finish with an IPO through the investment banking and securities industry—all in just a few years.

Case in point. Fore Systems, Inc. was in fourth place on *Business Week's* 1995 Hot Growth Companies list. Its $235 million in revenues in its fiscal year ending March 31, 1996, put Fore beyond *Business Week's* upper limit of $150 million. Fore was launched in April 1990 by four researchers from Carnegie Mellon University. The startup capital: $100,000 from savings, and an almost immediate infusion of $2 million from the U.S. Navy. The premise was simple. The high-speed networking switches developed for telephone companies could also be used to up the capacity of smaller computer networks that link workstations and PCs.

The $2 million Navy contract, and the start of sales in November 1991, carried the company comfortably until December 1992. When Fore's sales were already at an annualized level of over $4 million, Patricof & Co. Ventures (PCV) injected $4 million in venture financing at 62 cents per share, for a third of the company—according to PCV's former senior partner John Baker, who initiated the funding.

Less than 18 months after the venture capital funding, in May 1994, the company went public with net proceeds of $35.5

million from the IPO. The company's growth has been phenomenal. For the 1992 fiscal year sales were only around $1 million, whereas for FY1995 sales had leapt to over $75 million; as we mentioned, revenues for FY1996 were $235 million, a figure that in all fairness does include the revenues from a major acquisition. Market capitalization exceeded $2.5 billion. Fore Systems, Inc. definitely attracted capital—in the right format for its various stages.

Another grand-slam story, but one in which the founders didn't have to go it alone even for a day, is that of Mentor Graphics. This story is not as contemporary as the story of Fore Systems, and dates back to the early 1980s—perhaps not coincidentally. Back then, venture capitalists were still excited about funding companies from their seed stage all the way through their exit strategy. In all fairness, some still do, but less frequently and perhaps with less enthusiasm. Well, "the times they are a changin'" indeed, Dylan.

In a fairly typical multistage financing of the times, Mentor Graphics was founded in the early 1980s by three major VC funds: Venrock, Greylock, and Sutter Hill. At the company's incorporation it received $1 million. Thirteen months later, when it had a product prototype, it received an additional infusion of $2 million. Then, 9 months after the second round when the company had a product and had entered the market, it received $7 million for market expansion in a third and final round of private financing. Twelve months after the final round of private funding, Mentor Graphics went public to the tune of a $55 million IPO. Grand slam.

OTHER FINANCING SOURCES

Thus far, most of the ink in this chapter has been spilled on the two most likely areas for emerging growth companies to obtain financing: going private or public with the investment banker and going to the venture capital funds. However, other, less well-known sources are also available. For example, small business investment companies (SBICs) run regular funds that are backed by various government perks. These funds leverage the capital they raise with debt. There are limitations on the size of companies that SBICs are allowed to invest in, but a wide range of emerging growth businesses would be included. A catch: SBICs are usually run by VC firms.

Vankirk, which published a guide to venture capital firms, also published the *Guide to New Small Business Investment Companies.* The statistics gleaned by that guide demonstrate the attractiveness for the emerging growth company seriously pursuing the SBIC route. SBICs have almost $1 billion under management. More interestingly than the amount the SBICs have under management is that when asked by Vankirk about which stage of development they prefer to finance, 76 percent of the SBICs said second stage, 70 percent said mezzanine, and only 21 percent said seed, which puts us back again in the emerging growth sector. Vankirk's venture capital guides have since been acquired by Asset Alternative and are published as *Galante's Complete Venture Capital and Private Equity Directory.*

Before leaving the topic, we want to sprinkle in a little international flavoring touted by the Coopers & Lybrand's *Financing Source Guide:* the U.K. offering. London is an international financial capital and the emerging growth company should not rule out crossing the pond. There are two main advantages, especially of a listing on the Unlisted Securities Market in the United Kingdom, as detailed by Coopers & Lybrand: (1) smaller offerings are more accepted by overseas investors, and (2) less financial information is required to be disclosed in an overseas registration and the continuing financial reporting is less demanding.

The costs associated with the U.K. offering can be lower than those in the United States. Finally, and hopefully for your company, offering prices may be higher than in the United States, since U.K. underwriters often use forecasted results instead of historical results as the basis on which they price the shares.

Another international vehicle with less cachet than the United Kingdom is to be found north of the border, if you are in the United States—in Canada. A listing on the Vancouver Stock Exchange is easier than a similar listing in the United States; you may try Toronto too. Even the "shell games" might be less costly. As your company evolves, it could then pursue a listing on the NASDAQ or other organized markets in the United States.

TAP A GLUT OF CAPITAL

So the way we see it, there is a glut of capital or, if you will, an abundance of money available to fund emerging growth businesses. The high-growth companies, or those that *promise* fast growth, *can* pick and choose their sources of financing, if they follow the unwritten rules of the industry. Even those emerging companies that show a slower, but steady growth or potential growth can obtain financing without major obstacles.

The turmoil associated with attracting capital is not the result of the lack of it, but is rather related to the emerging growth company's ability to master the following seven rules:

1. Know what type of capital is most appropriate for your company—the stage you are at, the market you are in, the owners' goals, and the investors' goals. This is what we call *quality capital.*

2. Know whom to approach, and use the right contacts and pipeline.

3. Assemble the right management team that will attract capital.

4. Do not tie yourself up in the wrong route. Major delays, excess dilution, and even litigation can arise from mistakes related to ignorance in this respect.

5. Be realistic about valuation and control, and understand the dilution process.

6. Promote your case and your company through a public relations (PR) process.

7. Act like a "public company," even if you decide not to file a registration statement and actually go public for the time being.

LEVERAGING THE FUTURE

If by the time you enter the emerging growth stage, your business is not exciting and it's not promising a high growth potential, no knowledge and accessibility will help you excite those who can infuse capital in the form of equity. You could still be running a business that's self-sustaining, and that will grow slowly by recycling sales profits. Or, if your business has meaningful assets, you could finance growth by borrowing. Those are legitimate methods that apply to certain companies.

But to finance fast growth, you must leverage the future. You must get more money than you currently "deserve"—on the basis of future expectations. To achieve this kind of growth, backed by the appropriate capital, you must know and apply the seven rules stated above. Let's look at them in more detail.

A PRACTICAL FRAMEWORK FOR OBTAINING FINANCING

1. *To know what type of capital is most appropriate for your company.*   You must define the company's goals, as well as the personal goals of its founders, owners, and previous investors. If you go to an investment banking firm for a *major* transaction into the public markets, you want to ascertain whether the firm has a research department which covers your industry. Has the firm underwritten similar offerings previously? You should always have a business plan on hand—it crystallizes the overall picture and helps in the evaluation. Study industry directories, get brochures from the various funding sources, and look at their typical investments. Talk to capital sources from the various categories, talk to people you know or companies like yours that did it before, and hire financial consultants if you can afford it.

When you receive capital, there are always strings attached. You must, therefore, make sure that these strings have enough flexibility and won't choke you. Bottom-line considerations of investors are often asynchronous with the needs of a fast-growing enterprise. Jack Meyer, the CEO of Urologix, who received $5 million from Patricof & Co. Ventures (PCV), admitted to a little nervousness about the timing. As Meyer explained in *Financial Week* (September 13, 1994), his nervousness stems from the notion that PCV runs these 10-year funds, and Urologix is already 5 years into it.

To underscore the different timetables of investors and investees, we should note that investment in new-product development, for example, erodes the bottom line, which affects *short-term* investors' equity. But it is crucial to the company's future growth—and hence to *long-term* shareholders' equity. Being a public company, for example, puts extra burden on management and increases administrative costs. The company and its management have to spend *time* and *money* to comply with SEC filings and other regulations. The company has to be careful with projections, to avoid getting sued in case it can't meet the set goals, and it also has to control the flow of information—to avoid being blamed for insider trading.

Nonetheless, the wish of a company to postpone going public might be in conflict with the wish of certain early investors to cash in. The larger early investors usually have board seats and other means to influence the choices the company makes in providing liquidity to its investments.

At the bottom line, you might say, every type of financing source has the same goals: to generate the largest ROI (return on investment) in the shortest time, and to be able to exit (cash in) as soon as its financial target is met. This generalized view, which happens to be microscopically correct, might lead you to believe that every investor will look at you—the emerging company—in the same way, and therefore, you'll get the same deal. Consequently, you may conclude that you might as well approach everyone you can homogeneously—sort of blanketing the industry. Well, this sounds like a simplification, and indeed it is. There are major differences in the cost of money, sharing of control, and owner-management equity. Take, for example, the issue of time frame. Usually, the more an investor has to wait to cash in, the more expensive that capital will be for the company.

The following is a description of the practical time frame that different investors aim at in the various financing modalities. Since there are many detailed legal issues involved, you should seek legal counsel for the specifics.

Generally, investors in the registered securities of a public offering, such as in an IPO, can exit the fastest. But not everyone can get a cut of hot public issues. Offshore Reg. S private placement investors can also exit quickly. Of course, this is practical only when the company is public and there is a market for its securities. For private companies a Reg. S investor will likely hold the securities for a longer period if for no other reason than the lack of liquidity. Some U.S. *public* companies are concerned with the Reg. S scenario, because of the possible dumping of a large number of shares by speculators.

Investment banking deals such as Reg. D private placements usually restrict the resale of securities for over 1 year. Once again this becomes especially relevant for public companies, where the securities have a market. Private companies normally do not offer liquidity unless they are acquired. Sometimes though, even in a private company, an investor may be able to sell a large block to another investor or group of investors. Venture capital exits after even a longer period, except for mezzanine financing, which is a very late stage of financing that takes place not far ahead of the IPO or the acquisition exit strategies. Early-stage investors (friends and family) who finance private placements wait still longer—because it will take time until there is a market for the securities—but their investments usually appreciate the most. Debt financing, which carries monthly returns for the financing entity, will generally be the most patient capital and is governed by the terms of the debt offering.

Patricof's fund, for example, exited its $488,000 investment in America Online before the company made it big, or as Patricia Cloherty, president of PCV, put it: "Before AOL became America's biggest lonely hearts club." It was a seven-bagger for PCV, that is, it returned seven times the investment, which isn't much in light of the meteoric levitation of AOL's stock some years later. PCV also sold out its $315,000 investment in Apple Computer *before* Apple went public. It still became a 50-bagger for PCV.

2. *To know whom to approach is critical.*   You have to find out who in a particular company does this stage and size of deals in the particular industry you are in (communication, retail, health care, and so on) and would potentially be interested in a business like yours. To put it in other words, you need to find someone who would be your potential "champion" in a particular investment firm. First get the firm's brochures. Then call the firm or the companies it financed to find out who does and who did the particular type of deals which are similar to what your company would represent. Some industry directories or write-ups in magazines could help. Search databases by the funding or the funded company names. Finally, people you know in the industry may have the information.

Most important of all, seek personal introductions. This is where well-connected friends, business associates, or board members can play a vital role. Good intermediaries may also help you get to the right people.

Yes, even when you're apparently dealing directly with an investment group, you are actually competing with other companies—because only a few will reach the finish line with a particular investor. And, only infrequently will an investor who receives an over-the-transom business plan take it seriously. It's not out of laziness or snobbishness; it's because experience shows that most of the goodies come either when the investor seeks them out or when they are obtained through referral or intermediaries the investor knows or has heard of—in short, through a "filter."

Granted, it happens that an exquisite opportunity lands on an investor's desk from nowhere, but that would be like waiting for Godot. Yet it's very common for young and immature companies to use directories and blanket the investment community with business plans.

Let's not fool ourselves. Even if you produce a good business plan, it doesn't guarantee that you'll receive a fair hearing. Sorry, business is not a system of civic justice. It's a system of interests and priorities. Fair business practice doesn't include the obligation to do business in the first place.

You've probably heard this at least 100 times, so here it is once more. Investors receive hundreds of business plans per year, of which they can fund, and nurture in the long run, only a few. Even if you argue that there are hundreds if not thousands of potential sources, the statistics are still in favor of the source of money. And then there's the herd effect—when investors smell a good deal, they all flock to participate in it and leave the others hanging.

So the bottom line is something very familiar. It's often more important *whom* you know than *what* you know. In other words, the pipeline through which the deal arrives at the investor's desk—whether it's a venture, investment banking, corporate, or even private source—is at least as important as the quality of the deal.

The pipeline becomes a filter for the investor. The investor's or investment group's logic is simple: "If I can do only 1 or 2 percent of the deals that arrive on my desk, and if my pipeline—someone I know, someone with a reputation, or my own scouting—provides a screening filter for those deals that are probably the more viable ones, then, by ignoring the over-the-transom deals, I can save a lot of time, yet lose very little in unexplored opportunities." In fact, the Sprout Group, one of the largest New York–based investment firms, has established close relationships with a network of intermediaries—the agents of the investment banking industry.

These phenomena apply to the corporate partnering process, as well. We have, for example, forged a relationship with Ciba-Corning (now part of Novartis)—the giant pharmaceuticals concern—in order to explore the possibility of a strategic partnering (and investment) in one of our client companies. Brenda Manning, manager of licensing and acquisitions, explained to us that, as you would expect, Ciba receives hundreds of applications every year—and guess what? It can execute only a few. We managed to get a half-day meeting for our client with the key marketing, development, and licensing people of the appropriate division at Ciba—and an extensive follow-up. Still, many wouldn't even manage to get through the door.

Approaching the right type and size of investors and investment companies, finding the right person in the investment firm, and if possible being introduced by the right contact are crucial. Contacts become even more powerful if they invested their own money in your company. For example, from our experience, JAFCO America Ventures, the U.S. venture capital arm of a large Japanese investment company, usually wouldn't consider a company someone brings to its attention unless the referring party or a major investment firm has already invested, or to say the least is planning to coinvest with JAFCO in the company.

3. *Assembling the right management team to attract capital is essential.*   In some instances, the key people might be a CEO and CFO who had previously tapped the capital markets and who know how to do it again. In other instances, it may boil down to putting together the kind of management team that will project to prospective investors that your company is ready and able to climb to the next level of growth. It's a favorite saying of investors that the three most important things they look for in a company are: management, management, and...management. And, for the icing on the cake, assembling an influential board of directors with wide industry contacts will definitely enhance your company's investment "magnetic field."

As a caveat we may note that the Sprout Group—the large venture capital affiliate of the Wall Street investment banking firm of Donaldson, Lufkin & Jenrette—will not entertain an investment in a company unless its CEO previously ran a successful company in a related market segment. It follows that Apple Computer, Microsoft, and ADP could have knocked on Sprout's doors in their early to middle emerging growth years, but probably wouldn't have been able to get an investment.

George Naddaff played on both sides of the game—the receiving end and the giving end. As the person who discovered Boston Chicken and as its former chairman, he was one of those who had to persuade investors to trust their money in the hands of his management team. Now at the helm of Business Expansion Capital Corp. and Food Trends Acquisitions Corp., *he* makes the judgment about the management team in whose hands he'll trust his firms' money.

Defining his unique skill in his team as "the visionary," he puts a high emphasis on passion, commitment, and the capacity to put up with trauma as the criteria for a management that would attract his attention and, now as an investor, his monetary support. But Naddaff, the visionary "street fighter," found another quality in the company in which he entrusted his group's latest investment. He felt that the company was very unusual in the sophistication of the management and the technology it utilizes, the up-to-date reporting system, and the way it captures information about its customers.

Naddaff is looking for management teams which, you might say, *have everything.* They are passionate, visionary, committed, up to date, and sophisticated in technology that can help the business, and they have some of the street fighter qualities. Such people attract his attention and investment capital.

To be more realistic, we suggest that you refer to Chapter 2 in this book, which gives you a wider range of views concerning those management qualities which investors consider crucial, and those which they would prefer but not demand.

4. *Do not tie yourself up in the wrong financing route.*   If you do, you may produce major disruptions in the progress of your growing company—which in turn can be detrimental because competitors might catch up, crucial personnel might flee, and investors might lose confidence and move their resources to the next opportunity.

The number-one rule is do your homework, and when possible stay flexible. But beware not to be perceived either as flaky—someone who jumps from tree to tree—or as a perennial fence sitter. If you are perceived as one of those, nobody would want to invest time in you just to find out that it may take forever for you to make a definitive decision or that, conversely, tomorrow you'll be gone somewhere else. The right consultants and advisers can help in doing some groundwork. But, of course, if you are *desperate* for capital, mistakes are inevitable. Refer to the old advice—always stay overcapitalized.

5. *To be realistic about valuation and control is tricky.*   Often valuation is based on projections and naturally it is subjective. You can learn about your realistic valuation by looking at other companies in your market sector, talking to experts, and floating some "trial balloons" with investors. Since valuation also determines retained control and the level of equity dilution, the valuation in one round will strongly affect the prospects of future rounds of financing. In multistage financing—which is the typical scenario—if, for example, 50 percent of your company is already owned by a third party, you'll have a problem attracting a major venture capital player, but you can still attract some investment banking sources. This is only the tip of the iceberg. A whole chapter in this book—Chapter 7—sheds light on the issues of valuation—capital, control, and dilution. All in all, issues relating to valuation require careful long-term planning as well as a lot of flexibility.

In this vein, we recall our interview with Michael Moe—an emerging growth company analyst and principal with Montgomery Securities in San Francisco and formerly with Lehman Brothers in New York—who cautioned entrepreneurs against trying to maximize the amount raised in a particular round of financing. It would be better to be less aggressive in the initial valuation of your company in order to build goodwill that will give your company further financing options in the future.

"People get too cute on price," says Moe. "Every emerging company wants to take every last dime when it gets its capital. It is a shortsighted view," cautions Moe. "What's more important is that the company sets expectations with investors which it can comfortably meet or exceed, that it builds up goodwill with corporate partners or investors, and that over time it has a ready supply of funds." "As you know, the stumbling block a lot of the time for the emerging company is that availability of capital," concludes Michael Moe. How about creating the possibility of rewarding your investors with a "happy surprise"? We recommend that you try it.

6. *Promoting your company through a public relations* (PR) *process is crucial.* This is true whether you hire a PR firm, launch your own networking campaign (if you know how to do so), utilize the connections of your board members, accountant, lawyer, and other early investors—or do all the above. It's like launching a political campaign. Compare the styles of two Southern governors who campaigned for the White House. Remember when Jimmy Carter ran for office? Most of America asked "Jimmy, who?" Well, he was eventually elected because of effective PR. When Bill Clinton, the governor from Arkansas, ran he was quite well known and in fact, at times, he would have preferred to be less well known. Still, an effective PR campaign defused the problems.

You want to minimize the occasions when one investor will tell another when asked about your company: "Never heard of it." Even if you are not a public company, gain public recognition. It opens up financing possibilities and can even attract new business.

And the best PR you can get is by gaining the reputation of someone who delivers more than promises. As Michael Moe from Montgomery Securities told us: "Building goodwill and a reputation in the investment banking community that you deliver more than you promise can pay long-term benefits." If you received funding and you delivered more than you were supposed to, it makes it much easier to obtain future rounds of financing, whether from the same or from new investors. News travels fast.

7. *Acting like a public company even if you are not one gives you credibility.*   For example, simply produce a brochure for public consumption on a par with a marketing document that a public company might produce for prospective shareholders. We appreciate that you don't want to disclose detailed financial information to outsiders, but the brochure should still give the reader an idea of the size and reach of your business. We are personally leery about companies that hide behind a shroud of secrecy, and use the fact that they are private as a justification for an excessive degree of evasiveness.

More important than producing information for third parties is producing internal financial information in a format that would be used in the event that you decide to "go public." For example, prepare quarterly and annual financial information on a timely basis, as if you were a public company. Some of these informal exercises may also determine whether you have the internal makeup to become a public company and eventually enjoy the bounty of public capital.

But first and foremost, compiling and presenting information like a public company will enhance the internal communication between people in the company and among the various departments. When everyone can see the total picture and work within a well-understood framework, companywide effectiveness and attractiveness increase.

To sum it up, the emerging growth sector has the most and the widest financing options. It is the most exciting area for growth-oriented investors. However, to know how to attract capital, pay the right price for it, and live in peace and harmony with its providers, you have to know a lot, and use other people's expertise and contacts—which means that you have to excite them. Learning how to play the game is somewhere between learning to drive a car and learning to fly a jet. Then again, the other alternative is to follow in the deep footprint of Bill Gates and learn to play cards really well. Maybe you can break Vegas and not have to be accountable to any third-party backer. (Only joking?!)

Once you apply the seven rules of this chapter, you will draw capital—and the right kind for your business. If you get good at it, you might even want to try a flirting approach—spread the rumor that you are looking, and let the right capital source allure you.

FIVE GUIDELINES FOR INFORMATION CONTROL

You Have to Be Well Informed to Be Attractive, But the Information Revolution Is a Double-Edged Sword

The days when the crucial information to a company's survival and growth was exchanged at the water cooler or the local watering hole are over. The web at the water cooler has been replaced by the World Wide Web, and today, more than ever, information is the lifeline of a successful enterprise.

No company operates in a vacuum, and no individual or department within a company can be detached from the rest of the company. Like players in a team, all have a certain freedom in carrying out the details, as long as they stay coordinated with the rest of the team and carry out the coach's strategy. On the "microscopic" scale, individuals and departments in a company must stay coordinated with each other and follow the management's strategy. On the "macroscopic" scale, the company as a whole, must stay coordinated with the marketplace, the competition, and new developments in their products and services. It's usually a give-and-take game—you're both a trendsetter and a trend follower.

What keeps the individual or the department coordinated with the rest of the company, and the company coordinated with the outside world? Information. Or, to be more precise, the gathering, processing, and exchanging of information.

Ask any investor, large corporation, Wall Street analyst, or prospective key employee or director to give an impression of an emerging company he or she has visited. Those who are attracted to the company will often say: "These folks really *know* what they are doing." Those who are not attracted will often sum it up with: "I *don't* think these folks *know* what they are doing." Of course, knowledge is directly correlated to information—whether of internal or external origins.

INFORMATION AND PERFORMANCE

There are five levels in which information critically correlates with performance. (In this context, knowing means also analyzing and understanding.)

- Knowing everything about your own organization
- Knowing everything about your market—globally
- Knowing everything about your competitors—globally
- Knowing everything about your products, their proprietariness, and new developments in the industry pipeline
- Knowing the rules and regulations—how to navigate within the law, the culture, and the bureaucracy (e.g., patents, exports, SEC filings)

If prospective investors, large potential corporate partners, key people, or Wall Street analysts and fund managers are convinced that your emerging growth company is well informed in those areas, and that it can interpret the information correctly, they gain the confidence that, barring unexpected developments, your arrow will be pointed in the right direction and you'll be able to react to the necessary changes along the way. They will be *attracted* to your company.

Sam Walton was famous in understanding the role of information in growing Wal-Mart, especially in its emerging growth years; he would go out and perform his own research and information gathering. In Walton's biography *Made in America,* Don

Soderquist, the former president of Ben Franklin who eventually became the vice chairman and chief operating officer of Wal-Mart, describes one of his first meetings with Walton. In 1964, Walton was one of the largest franchisees of Ben Franklin, a discount retail chain. On a visit to Ben Franklin's headquarters in Chicago, Walton had presented to Ben Franklin executives the concept of franchising Walton's discount stores in small towns. The answer from the management of Ben Franklin was a flat no, but Walton still turned his visit to Ben Franklin's headquarters into a productive mission. First, he visited the office of Soderquist, who was then in charge of data processing. Walton wanted to know everything about computers and how they were being used. As was Walton's style, he took everything down on a yellow legal pad.

Walton's research did not end at the offices of Ben Franklin; he also engaged in a field visit. The following Saturday, Soderquist was shopping at a Kmart near his home. Walton was there too, but he wasn't shopping; he was gathering information. Walton was quizzing the salesclerk about the frequency with which the store ordered merchandise. He also asked how long it took for ordered merchandise to be delivered, and on and on. Yes, Walton was taking everything down on his yellow legal pad. There's no substitute for doing your own information gathering and doing it firsthand.

Bill Gates, the cofounder and chairman of Microsoft, is definitely an expert and industry insider when it comes to information technology (IT). In his book *The Road Ahead,* he paints a picture of an explosive penetration of IT in all facets of our lives—a revolution in every way. From our point of view, we find Gates' analysis in the chapter titled "Implications for Business" especially interesting.

He points out, for example, the different ways in which large and small businesses benefited from the introduction of the PC. Gates feels that small businesses have gained the most, because low-cost hardware and software permit small outfits to compete better with large multinational corporations.

He feels that for large companies the biggest benefit of PCs comes from improving the process of *sharing information* and avoiding the large overhead of meetings and other internal processes—all aimed at staying coordinated. Financial planning and management software, such as the type provided by Hyperion, a company mentioned earlier in this book, allow the various departments in a large organization to look at the information from various angles—sales, marketing, manufacturing, accounting, and so on. At Microsoft there are no printed computer reports. All the information is available only on a computer screen. All the departments can examine the data from the various points that would affect their contribution to overall company performance.

For smaller companies, on the other hand, the PC opened a whole new world. The different software applications on their PCs can replace the need to hire a specialist in each discipline—such as financial analysis (and we don't mean accounting) and creation of promotional and marketing materials.

You might argue that this aspect of the difference between large and small business diminishes gradually as the company climbs up the emerging growth ladder, when it starts hiring more and more specialists in various fields. But that's not completely the case, because there are certain factors that have to do with the culture of a company rather than its financial condition.

Emerging growth companies are still not free from the behavioral patterns of their early years. In many ways this is very good, because they manage to keep their vigilance and pioneering spirit. But often, even when the company gets to the level of 100 or more employees, the clear tendency is to concentrate humanpower in the departments that are short-term and directly associated with growth and revenues, such as R&D, manufacturing, and sales. You'll still find that the president, senior management personnel, and even department heads wear many hats. Therefore, even in the emerging growth business, wherever a software package can to a certain extent replace a specialist—it will.

But, of course, the internal IT needs of a company are only a small part of the total picture. Many aspects of information gathering, interpretation, and management, especially for the emerging growth company, have to do with the outside world—markets, competition, patents, new technology, potential sources of capital, potential strategic partners, original equipment manufacturers (large-volume buyers)—the list goes on. The business flow of a large corporation—which usually has established name brands, patents, marketing channels, and pipelines for new products—is less sensitive to short-term outside fluctuations, and hence the internal IT becomes somehow more emphasized.

We are not trying to say that large corporations are not vigilant with respect to keeping a close look at what's happening in the areas of new markets, new technologies, competition, and so on. After all, as we are writing these lines, Apple Computer finds itself fighting for its life in the PC market, Microsoft is fighting for an appropriate share of the Internet browser market, and many large retailers face fierce competition from more agile specialty chains—the same way that Wal-Mart in the 1970s beat many of the large discounters in America's heartland. Still, it is generally true that the emphasis on outside information versus inside information is significantly higher in the emerging growth sector.

Industries vary in their levels of commitment to IT. A Coopers & Lybrand (C&L) study about the role of IT in the chemical process industries found that managing and controlling information is becoming the most important factor in increasing productivity and reducing costs in this sector. Yet, at the same time, the chemical processing industry is resisting a commitment to global implementation. Since we believe that this phenomenon is prevalent in other industries too, it might be interesting to elaborate on C&L's findings.

The key IT factors identified by the 31 respondent firms as crucial to their success were improving internal communication, controlling information, and obtaining information about the marketplace and the competition. The most critical area needing IT support was identified to be sales, while other areas such as marketing, manufacturing, distribution, safety, and managing supplies were also mentioned. It is interesting to note that almost half the companies surveyed spend less than $10 million annually on IT—in spite of the firms having between $1 and $5 billion in annual revenues.

THE INFORMATION MARKETPLACE

We hold C&L and their study in the highest regard. Still, we wanted to do our own homework: Is there something else going on in the IT nooks and crannies of corporate America? Peter Lynch, in his book *Beating the Street,* taught us that if you want to measure how well a retailer chain's stock should be doing, you should visit a couple of its stores and check the traffic—a simple and effective starting point. Then, you can do the rest of your analysis.

We didn't go to the suburban shopping mall to see what corporate America is doing for its information needs. We did, however, go to the mall where corporate America tells us how it is looking to beef up its personnel, and right now that is through the newspapers (someday it will just be the Internet). If you look at the end of the business sections of the major newspapers, you'll notice a fairly clear trend. Many of the available middle-management job positions relate in one way or another to information technology. This, of course, doesn't necessarily indicate a lack of available positions in other sectors. Yet, in an era of downsizing and consolidation, it clearly means that companies are significantly expanding their IT capabilities—and that their needs exceed the normal supply of such professionals from internal sources, or other means of recruiting.

You'll also notice that all the big accounting and consulting firms—Coopers & Lybrand, Deloitte & Touche, Price Waterhouse, and others—have constant demand for more and more IT professionals. Since these firms are service companies, there must be a huge demand from their client bases.

THE INTERNET CRAZE

And, the latest Internet craze is no more an illusion, but a dazzling reality. In early 1996 there were an estimated 13.5 million users of the Internet. *The Wall Street Journal* (March 13, 1996) also concluded that currently and in the near future the Internet's number-one use is for information and not, as some people envisioned years ago, as a cyberspace mall where people could buy and sell on-line 24 hours a day. In fact the "battle for the Internet" among the various software developers and on-line providers was described by Dataquest's Allen Weiner as one of the greatest and most exciting marketplace battles of the last 30 or 40 years.

The premier warrior in the information marketplace battle may be America Online. Its name is more than a corporate logo, it's a description of where America is heading with the information revolution: America is on-line. Until a few years ago, "on-line" was usually something that you had to get into on a Saturday night to see the latest Hollywood blockbuster. Has Steve Case, CEO of AOL, replaced Steven Speilberg? Not yet, but even the legalistic document known as the 10-K Annual Report of AOL reads more like a marketing brochure for the twenty-first century than a filing with the U.S. Securities and Exchange Commission.

Let's point and click at AOL's menu of features: Online Community, Computing, Education and Reference, News and Personal Finance, Travel and Shopping, and Entertainment and Children's Programming. Let's click on the first icon: Online Community. AOL promotes real-time communication by scheduling conferences or discussions on specific topics. By now, we are all familiar with some of the public chat rooms or lobbies where fellow surfers can exchange information on the latest whatever. But AOL also promotes its private rooms for teleconferencing. We are assured that AOL takes extensive precautions to ensure the privacy of member communications, subject to its compliance with laws governing the storage and transmission of illegal information. AOL's teleconferencing features may not yet be replacing Ma Bell, but if the price is right and if people learn to type fast enough, having a conference call through AOL could be a cost-effective way of multinational communication, and of course exchange of information.

An on-line service such as AOL or CompuServe can, of course, provide the emerging growth business with more than a means to communicate. It can provide "hard core" information—reports, stock quotes, financial data, and more. It also provides easy access to the Internet.

When you get tired of brainstorming, you can take a rest by clicking on the Entertainment icon. AOL offers multiplayer games and "other related content" for both children and adults. Examples include Nintendo Power Source and Kids Only, but don't worry there's also Baby Boomer Forum.

Granted, there are many issues to be pondered and solved about information services, especially the Internet. For on-line services the issues include the large defection rate of initial subscribers and questions like where the core revenues will come from to sustain a "rich in content" operation: subscriber fees (as it is today) or advertising revenues and royalties from retailers, as AOL's CEO Steve Case projects. For the Internet there are other poignant questions that need attention: Will the increased number of Web sites make the navigation impractically slow when users want to get to specific packets of information? Will the hardware be available and affordable on a mass scale to allow practical usage in multimedia formats? Will it allow for practical commerce to take place in cyberspace? Will the issues of security and confidentiality be fully solved? How can piracy be prevented in cyberspace? And, of course, a more indirect question arises—whether the huge valuation placed today on Internet companies will not backfire in what George Soros called a boom-bust cycle, and bring the industry down, at least temporarily.

Most of those Internet-related problems are being addressed by key industry players like Microsoft, Sun Microsystems, and Netscape (which owns 85 percent of the browser market), and each new month brings expansion and improvements much like the strides made with a variety of applications software in the 1980s.

A UNIQUE CULTURE

There's definitely a unique culture that's being developed, and as Bill Gates puts it in his book, our children and grandchildren will find the IT world and conducting their dealings in cyberspace as natural as our revolutionizing our own system in one decade since the arrival of the PC. We are already hearing about the Wild West of cyberspace—Internet bounty hunters like Tsutomu Shinomura, the Internet security expert who is credited with catching fugitive hacker Kevin Mitnick. (See *The Wall Street Journal*, February 9, 1996.)

Let your interest in the Internet extend beyond the hack-ers—and the sleuths hunting for them—and you will find the Net much more valuable than watching a bounty hunt unfold. Many large corporations, including AT&T and American Express, are setting up Web sites targeted to the emerging growth companies. Some of the Web sites offer more than just information. For example, the International Business Exchange (IBEX) matches buyers and sellers from around the world and gives them the opportunity to negotiate on-line. The service even provides the credit and bank references for its clients.

IBEX will search its database for potential partners using information received from you. The buyer or seller then receives by fax or e-mail a notice summarizing the offers and how those offers may differ.

Commerce Clearing House (CCH) is one of the oldest com-panies providing services to the legal community. That service has been reoriented to the business community. Although you may still want to consult a lawyer for your financial needs, many legal forms and contracts may be obtained through the CCH site, which is currently available either through the Microsoft network or the AT&T service.

Not to steal from the excitement of what on-line services and the Internet have to offer, but we would like to point out that these services cost money. They may be priced on per item or per entry basis, and there may also be one-time or annual membership fees. Internet service only is the cheapest, but then again on-line services offer more features, and, as of today, in a more organized format.

But, from our perspective, the real question is whether the small-cap emerging growth sector would, in the short run, reap all the benefits from the information revolution, or whether it will remain a "rich kid's" privilege for the near future—a miracle worker for the large corporation. If we wish to use the Peter Lynch litmus test, it is definitely apparent that most of the IT positions in *The New York Times* or *The Wall Street Journal* are directly related to large corporations, or indirectly to the same, via the services that are being provided by large consulting firms to large companies.

TRADITIONAL SOURCES OF INFORMATION

You see, today the "cheap" Internet is still not the main source of all the categories and disciplines of information needed by a typical emerging growth business. Most information still lies in reports, SEC disclosures (some of which you may find on the Internet), company brochures, investor packages, private information bureaus, expensive industry/market research reports, seminars and conferences, and what you may call legitimate (and legal) industrial "spying." Accessing the variety of information resources, and setting up the mechanisms to collect, classify, digest, analyze, and assimilate the information, still requires significant labor and monetary resources.

The Information Revolution Task Force of the White House Conference on Small Business tried to address some of the government-related concerns in terms of the accessibility of information for the small business sector. Later in this chapter we'll dwell on this important forum in some more detail.

One major stride was widely publicized in early 1996 when the Vice President of the United States unveiled a new Internet service called U.S. Business Advisor. The service permits business owners to call up on their computers economic reports and journals and recent news from many federal agencies. It also enables businesses to obtain guides and forms for complying with regulations or applying for government-backed loans or other federal assistance. U.S. Business Advisor provides "one-stop access to federal agencies that regulate and assist businesses," said the Vice President.

But the IT trickle-down problems are really not as poignant as they sound. In fact, you might even find some apparently paradoxical trends, whereby large companies are moving away from their centralized mainframe systems to client-server PC-based networks. And many (small) software companies capitalize on this trend and provide migration software and reengineering from legacy applications to the client-server environment. Therefore, you might say that almost paradoxically the large companies are the ones acquiring the tools and systems of smaller firms. Or, putting it more succinctly, there's a decentralization trend and a migration toward systems that can be easily duplicated by smaller firms. The great success of Windows NT just confirms the validity of this scenario.

What's more acute, however, are the problems faced by emerging companies in the areas of information cost and control. Granted, you have to be *well informed* to be "attractive." However, the information revolution is a double-edged sword—it helps you and at the same time it helps your competitors. It can also become a time and cost trap—you can drown in information. You have to know what kind of information you *need,* and how much time and money it's worth. We'll present five guidelines for information cost and time control later in this chapter.

Then, you must remember that since so much information is available about you, you must control your own intellectual property—trade secrets, patents, proprietary information—and understand the importance and the traps of too much confidentiality.

The confidentiality considerations can become quite tricky for an emerging growth company. When we approached a potential large strategic corporate partner for an emerging growth company that we represented, we were told clear and loud that the company was not interested at the initial stages to see any information that would require signing a confidentiality agreement. We know of a large venture fund which would send back business plans that carried a "confidentiality" stamp—unread.

THE CONFIDENTIALITY ISSUE

So how should you handle this damned-if-you-do and damned-if-you-don't situation? On the one hand, you need to protect your confidential information; on the other, you must provide enough information to attract investors or corporate partners. Of course, those things that can be patented should. But most types of information fall into different categories: strategic, marketing and financial plans, proprietary processes, and other such quanta of information.

An investor or potential corporate partner will have far fewer confidentiality issues to iron out with a public company, by the nature of the disclosures and filings required by the SEC. Private companies, on the other hand, keep all their information under lock and key. Still investors or corporate partners might find an opportunity for a higher return if they established a relationship with a company during the years prior to its IPO. Therefore, they will still be attracted to this kind of company even though the confidentiality arrangements might turn out to be more elaborate.

Our analysis and pointers in this book do not intend to replace detailed legal advice that each company must seek according to its specific situation. Whether you seek legal advice or not, consider the following. You must evaluate the issue from a risk-reward perspective. Evidently, you would not disclose any information to your competitor. On the other hand, you would have no problem disclosing most information to a partner. Well, in the gray, in-between areas, you have to make a judgment and balance the risk with the potential reward.

You may go about it along the following lines. If you absolutely need financing, and if your best financing options are reluctant to sign confidentiality agreements, you may ask yourself what *part* of the information you should disclose anyway. If the financing source doesn't have a potentially competing company in its portfolio, what is the chance that your information will get into the wrong hands? Perhaps, it is low enough to warrant taking the risk. Now, if there are certain pieces of information that can be detrimental to your company's well-being if they leaked out in any shape and form, you must hold back on them until enough interest is generated, and the proper confidentiality arrangements can be made.

Very often, and this is especially true for the more advanced emerging growth stages, confidentiality problems tend to diminish in time. First, if product proprietariness applies, it may have already been taken care of by patents. As far as the marketplace is considered, since the company's foothold in the market has already been established, there is less that needs to be hidden. Finally, at a relatively advanced emerging growth stage, potential investors and large corporate partners will find it worthwhile to iron out an appropriate confidentiality arrangement, something they might not have been willing to do for a startup or a very early-stage emerging growth business.

PATENTED TECHNOLOGY

Patent issues also belong to the information category. It is perhaps the ultimate way of securing information advantage. But the various industries differ in the relevance of patent issuance. Most investors will tell you that an attractive company should have product differentiation that's protectable—meaning that the product differentiation should not erode once other companies become aware of the product. Yet there are evidently many ways to skin a cat. Major industrial success stories such as Starbucks, Staples, and America Online did not have patent protection while growing the business throughout the explosive emerging growth years. Yes, they had and have proprietary trade secrets, but that's not the same as massive patent protection.

Did patented technology bring in the bucks to Starbucks? Not quite. Starbucks has over 100 trademarks registered around the world. Neither the name Starbucks nor the star-struck mermaid corporate logo sell the coffee. Yes, Starbucks does have a patent on a coffee-on-tap system, but how does that affect the business? Very little. The cachet of Starbucks and the flavor of its beans are all fair game for competitors. Still, nobody does it better.

Did investors shy away from these companies? To the contrary. Starbucks et al. were built by investor enthusiasm. On the other hand, a biotechnology company like Amgen or Genentech could not have grown without patents, because the only way to recoup the huge expenses required for development and regulatory approval is to have a window of years when the company can build its market without interruption from other, mainly large competitors.

Can we generalize and say that high-tech companies are built around patents, while low-tech or no-tech are not? Not necessarily. Case in point. There was no patent on the PC; otherwise one company would have been the primary player for many years. Much of the software written in the 1980s was not patented, although it did have a much weaker kind of protection—copyright. Only recently has the interpretation of the patent law begun to lean toward allowing the issuance of more software patents.

Granted, in the emerging growth sector, which is built mostly around high-tech, health-care, and retailing companies, retailing is a fairly patentless area, while the other two are relatively patent-rich areas.

It is easy to fathom that having patents—a powerful kind of information protection—will make an emerging company more attractive. While many other kinds of information protection are subject to, say, industrial spying—a patent is not. Once you are protected, it doesn't matter how the other side obtains the information. Competitors are not allowed to infringe on your patent. Sound like an ideal situation? Well, if you think so, you are subject to a rude awakening. Being protected by a patent is like saying that no person, corporation, or organization can ever harm you, physically, emotionally, or financially because you are protected by the law. And, if others do harm you, you can always sue them—a practically impractical piece of truth.

The patent-related issues faced by a small emerging growth company are monumental—and we don't use superlatives lightly. The legal costs involved in processing and filing inventions— especially to obtain international protection—often put a staggering burden on an emerging growth company. And, then, if a large company chooses to infringe on the patents, the company will need a small fortune, not to mention time, to try to defend its rights.

The United States, perhaps more than other nations, depends upon the creativity of small companies for the pioneering development of new products. When original technology is pirated, despite intellectual property laws, small business innovators lose the opportunity to earn a reasonable return on investment. According to government estimates, U.S. industries lose as much as $60 billion in annual revenues because of intellectual property theft.

A U.S. Small Business Administration study found that the costs of intellectual property infringements are especially burdensome to small, emerging companies. These companies must choose between absorbing the financial and competitive losses of intellectual property piracy and paying the enormous legal fees required for court battles.

Now, some may think that most of the problems related to protecting patent rights will revolve around infringements by foreign entities. It is easy to envision that the smaller firms are more likely to have problems in securing proprietary protection overseas, because of the significant added monetary burden involved. Well that's not the case. According to the U.S. Small Business Administration (SBA), approximately 80 percent of infringement disputes—for both small and large company patents—are with *domestic-owned* organizations. This is a truly surprising but very revealing piece of information.

So one thing is for sure. We can't blame the patent piracy on other countries, because most of it happens in our backyards. Furthermore, even though the percentage of domestic infringement disputes is the same for small and large companies, the available recourse definitely discriminates against the emerging growth company. Besides the obvious time and monetary factors, there is the crucial point of the roadblocks that infringement can cause in the growth of a company, especially if that company relies on one or a narrow set of patents.

In our attempts to pitch a particular emerging growth company to investors, we encountered difficulties while the company had a pending legal patent battle with a subsidiary of a large corporation, B. F. Goodrich. Some investors, justifiably, were worried about the potential monetary disaster of litigating against a deep-pocket foe like that. But when that battle was settled, much to the advantage of the small, emerging company, the investors were much more willing to invest in the company.

Now, imagine that the battle would have been drawn out further. Not only would it impose a short-term financial difficulty on the company, but it would drain the company's resources and divert the attention of its management away from a full focus on growth. And, obviously, potential investors who would otherwise invest to replenish the dwindling resources of the company would have been further intimidated. Such a disastrous roller-coaster ride could have led to the company's demise.

The front end of patent protection is as difficult and controversial as the back end, if not more. At the back end, we are talking about measures that have to be taken upon infringement. Our previous discussion dealt with some of these issues. At the front end, we are talking about creating an environment which (1) makes the filing expedient and affordable to "all," (2) is strong enough to prevent infringement, and (3) can provide the opportunity for a company to earn a reasonable return on its significant effort.

FIRST TO INVENT...

During the preparations for the 1995 White House Conference on Small Business, one of us sat on a task force that debated the problems of patent protection for small emerging businesses. A background article titled "Reinventing Patents," by W. John Moore, published in the *National Journal* (March 20, 1993), offers an amazing tale of the labyrinth of political and business interests that are involved. When the Senate, the House of Representatives, and the White House become players, you know that the stakes are high—in fact, very high. Balancing the politics and economics of the present versus the future of national innovation is not an easy task, even for the Washington wizards.

Under the existing *first-to-invent* system in the United States, inventors can obtain a patent if they can prove that they had the idea first, regardless of when the patent application was filed. In the rest of the world the patent goes to the party who is the *first to file,* regardless of successful litigation.

In a fairly well-publicized battle in the 1980s, Gordon Gould managed to prove that he was the *first to invent* some crucial aspects related to lasers. After fighting for many years, he won a case in court. But actually Gould didn't have the resources to handle the legal battle. Much of the funds were put up by a third party, who in exchange was due to share in the pay-off of a successful litigation.

Still, when it came to fighting an all-out battle to force the many industry players into royalty agreements, a new company named Patlex took care of business. Patlex structured a deal with the inventor and the first backer, and proceeded to successfully litigate and force most industry players to enter into royalty arrangements for the laser patents. The first lesson we learned is that if the potential rewards are high, you may be able to find someone to finance the battle for protecting your patent rights. The second lesson is that, had the U.S. law followed the *first-to-file* strategy, Gordon Gould and his backers wouldn't have been able to achieve such a breakthrough success, more than 20 years after the invention of the laser.

...FIRST TO FILE

But exactly this difference in the filing law between the United States and the rest of the world is a source of major debates in the Senate and the House of Representatives. It's called patent system harmonization. In short, the idea is to harmonize the U.S. patent laws with those of the rest of the world, or in plain language, switch to the first-to-file system.

Small companies and their political proponents are extremely concerned with this system. They say that emerging growth companies can't beat corporate America—the large corporations—in the rush to the patent office. The first-to-file system will not permit a smaller company to test and fully develop its proprietary products, before committing the time and expense required to obtain a patent. Furthermore, large companies have the resources and the mechanisms in place to respond to a first-to-file system by submitting applications, even if the patent never produces a worthwhile marketable product.

Large companies need only score "statistically"—in x number of products. For an emerging growth company, the whole future depends on one or two proprietary products. We can also assume that a first-to-file system is more susceptible to the perils of industrial spying (someone finds out about the essence of the invention and rushes to the patent office), an area where large companies have much more muscle than their emerging growth counterparts.

The proponents of the first-to-file system claim that the "harmonization" will help Americans get patent protection abroad and will speed technological innovation. And, what about the small business sector's concerns? Well, some of the suggestions on the agenda in the White House conference task force were a requirement for binding arbitration, a relaxation of the burden-of-proof test to make it easier to prove infringements, and the possible establishment of a mechanism for providing financial assistance to defray legal costs incurred by small companies engaged in litigation against infringers.

While the debate rages, we would like to finish the chapter. By this point, it is patently clear that you have all the knowledge you need on patents short of retaining a high-priced patent attorney or representative.

MORE INFORMATION ON INFORMATION

An emerging growth company doesn't usually have information positions on its payroll. We are talking here not about people who handle the computer systems of the company, but about dedicated information gathering, analysis, and distribution. Every department and every individual become part-time information officers.

Where would those people go for information? Your natural tendency to review the business publications in your industry—general and specific—will provide you with a good starting point. You can call editors or authors of articles for additional information. Trade associations release detailed information about the industry, and if you become a member you can get the addresses and phone numbers of other members—competitors and potential partners.

Libraries, especially in major cities or academic institutions, can become your best and cheapest source for information. Besides various industry publications, libraries stock an array of reference material, forecasts, and reports. Librarians are usually excellent in directing you to the proper sources. And many large libraries have complete databases on CD-ROM which can allow you to search in a multitude of criteria, almost about any subject. You can usually get an article abstract, and often the article itself.

ON-LINE SERVICES

On-line services (America Online, CompuServe, and others) will avail you of all the types of information you ever dreamed of (some more than others), and it's at your fingertips, on your desktop, with no need to go to the library and often wait in line. Except, it costs money by the hour—for most specialized data. Overall, for extensive searches it can cost a lot of money. For example, you can obtain general company profiles in Compu-Serve for no extra charge (the service is included in the month-ly fee) or S&P company summaries for a couple of dollars each. Access to more detailed sources, which the on-line provider contracts with, can bring your bill up to hundreds or many thousands of dollars if searches are used companywide.

The Internet is the new kid on the block. The price is right, but finding information is still not as easy as it is, for example, with the on-line services. Also, the Internet doesn't yet carry all the sources which are still pondering how to make a profit by providing information on the Internet. Some companies have stopped pondering, such as Sun Microsystems. The Sun has shined on Java. Java is a programming language that is hotter than any scalding cup of coffee you can serve up, and Sun is now embedding the program in the operating systems of Microsoft and Apple. Java is more than just a programming lan-guage; from Java you can download bits of programs from the Internet that can assist you in your business. For example, you can download a spell checker, instead of buying a somewhat costly multifeatured word processing program. When you are writing a business plan, a spell checker can come in quite hand-ily. It certainly helped when we were writing this book.

Nonetheless, while doing research for this book, we encountered some of the limitations of the Net. The Securities and Exchange Commission (SEC) operates EDGAR, through Lexis/Nexis as the dissemination service, which enables investors to retrieve corporate filings, such as annual and quarterly financial reports. There were several companies whose information we wanted to retrieve—for example, Starbucks. The problem is if a company doesn't file certain forms on EDGAR, those data are not available via the Internet from EDGAR. Although, as of May 6, 1996, all public domestic companies are required to make their filings on EDGAR, there are many exceptions, including a hardship exemption. By contrast, one of the pay-as-you-go on-line services will give you that information. In addition, there are vendors who will provide you with a hard copy of the most recent corporate filings, once again for a price. In a sense, since most of the information on the Web is free, you do get what you are paying for—then again, sometimes you may get more than you are paying for.

OTHER MODALITIES

A few other modalities of information gathering come to mind. Some of the large consulting firms like Coopers & Lybrand, Deloitte & Touche, Ernst & Young, and many smaller entities sell an array of industry reports, which usually are not cheap. Private information bureaus, such as Find/SVP, will research any subject for you for a relatively hefty fee. And, if you are looking for information on public companies, you can always call up their investor relations department for a kit containing their most recent annual report, various press releases, sales brochure, and latest SEC filing. If you prefer, you can obtain many of the documents directly from the SEC.

But there is an untapped wealth of resources in an area that's usually looked down upon—the network of government information resources. The simplest form of resource is the U.S. Census Bureau, which publishes guides, catalogs, indexes, a newsletter, and other aids.

The most neglected resources are those provided *for free* by the U.S. Small Business Administration. We already mentioned the U.S. Business Advisor Internet service that was unveiled by the Vice President. But that's only the tip of the iceberg. Since the early 1990s some powerful mechanisms were established by the SBA in the area of information access for small business.

Paradoxically perhaps, but in line with typical consumerist phenomena, there is no rush for the "gold" for free SBA information—at least not within the emerging growth sector. The only explanation we have is that these services carry the stigma of poor person's tools that are adequate perhaps for *startup* companies, but not "grownups"—a totally misleading perception. Some striking information, from the Information Revolution Task Force of the 1995 White House Conference on Small Business, shows that many emerging growth companies (at least those with fewer than 500 employees) could benefit in a cost-effective way, from the bounty of free government-provided information resources.

Take for example two major programs that the U.S. government offers: business information centers (BICs) and small business development centers (SBDCs). The BICs are public facilities designed to assist the entrepreneur with information for business planning—in the early or later stage. By contrast the SBDCs are oriented to management assistance and counseling, mostly applicable for early-stage companies. Another significant program that is coordinated with the SBDC program is the well-known SCORE—the Service Corps of Retired Executives. The SCORE program matches retired executives with business owners seeking advice on how to operate their businesses more effectively.

We think one of the more important services offered by the SBA is the user-friendly BIC. The BIC enables the entrepreneur to engage in research with "friendly computer software." The custom-designed software guides you through the business planning process. In addition, separate software entitled Small Business Expert and Insight help the entrepreneur understand industry standards and regulations.

If you need to talk to an accountant, one is available; at least, the accountant is available on an interactive business video. On a video simulation entitled Business Disc, Harrison "Harry" Fields, a dynamic accountant, will guide you through issues on cashflow and taxes. If there's a Harry video, then there must be a Sam as well. Yes, Ask Sam is a computer locator that helps you find publications and select reading resources.

Want to sell overseas? That's available, too. CORE II is a computer survey that tests your company's readiness to export. In addition, if you want to test the waters before you plunge in, you can play a computer simulation game called Export to Win.

Finally, one of the best features of the BIC is its electronic library, which allows you to access information around the clock from your office or home computer. Users can electronically transfer information from the BIC to their own computers via a telephone modem. As the SBA says, you can "borrow" materials from the electronic library, but you don't have to worry about returning them.

FIVE KEY GUIDELINES

So, now that we have identified places where you can obtain more information than you could use during your business lifetime, here is our guide for information time and cost control for the emerging growth business. We classify it into the following five categories, and each one has its own guideline.

1. Obtaining or gathering information
2. Analyzing information
3. Distributing information
4. Developing information
5. Protecting information

Obtaining or gathering information is the number-one priority of a company. Without that you have no anchor and no frame of reference; you can do some great stuff but it can be completely irrelevant or inconsequential. You must be an expert about your market. You must know exactly what the competition is doing. You must understand your product's or service's advantages and disadvantages compared with other products and services in the market. And you must be knowledgeable about the processes you need to deploy in your business, such as how to finance your operations, how to access global markets, the rules that apply to your workforce, government regulations, if applicable, and many other such disciplines. Gathering information is an ongoing process, but at the early stages of an emerging company it can become a monumental burden.

Theoretically, you can't measure the importance of the above information base in terms of time or money. These are issues related to corporate survival. But, in reality, there are some very useful trade-offs. First, you and your staff want to access those sources of information which cost the least and which take you away from the office as little as possible. Downloading information from the SBA, using the Internet, and obtaining free annual reports and brochures by mail all seem to fall into this category. Showing up personally at a library or BIC will consume more of your time, but will allow you to research further select issues in trade publications, databases, and reference sourcebooks.

In the early stages of an emerging growth company, cost is usually a significant factor. At a later stage, you may find that using on-line services extensively, joining trade association, and buying various industry reports definitely make a valid trade-off between cost and time savings. And we would not underestimate the usefulness of hiring away experienced staff from competitors or large corporations, a method which Sam Walton used unabashedly when growing Wal-Mart.

Obtaining information alone will not allow you to see the picture clearly and act on every necessary front. The information must be analyzed. *Analyzing information* takes time, but the time can be spent whenever you have an opening in your schedule, or over the weekend. You are usually not tied to a location. Various people on your team can attack different aspects—markets, competition, products, regulations, financing. At a later stage of a company, you can hire consultants or junior staff to help make sense of the information and present it in a concise and useful form.

Distributing information among your management team, different departments, and outside sales networks is crucial to a harmonious, coherent, synchronized, and efficient operation. All departments must communicate with one another and understand their place in the total picture. As Bill Gates noted, distributing reports or holding constant meetings is often cumbersome and time-consuming. In an early-stage emerging growth company, cost constraints might dictate having only one central location where all the information is available; hence the old-fashioned method might turn out to be the most cost-effective. But in a fairly advanced emerging growth company, tying a bunch of computers to a local network will allow people to access companywide information and communicate and exchange information via e-mail. Whether the company would be able to afford extending this internal network to its sales offices around the globe will depend on its cash position at that particular juncture in its growth. And, with all the electronic hoopla, sometimes you may still prefer the "personal touch" of a face-to-face meeting.

Developing information can fall into a number of different categories. For example, designing a new product or service, developing alternative business models, developing new marketing strategies, or studying multiyear financial performance as a function of variable business parameters. We believe that there is no way that a company can succeed without *developing* information.

Therefore, the time and cost that should be allocated to these areas depend only on the maximum a company can afford. Although it might seem that the time factor is more critical than the cost factor in developing information, this kind of distinction cannot be made. If the company can afford the cost, it can translate money into additional employees or consultants, both of which will effectively contribute to the availability of time to develop information.

Finally, we move to the time and cost control issues of *protecting information*. To be attractive, a company must demonstrate product or service differentiation. For some companies, especially in certain high-technology or medical sectors, obtaining patents is a matter of survival. The modus operandi of many of these companies is based on a long cycle of product development, and without protection they might lose everything to larger competitors before they are able to generate revenues. These problems are especially poignant in the pharmaceuticals and biotechnology industries, which are subject to development and regulatory approval cycles of 5 to 10 years.

In areas such as retailing—for example, Boston Chicken, Staples, and Starbucks—there is no meaning to patents. Although these companies might have some proprietary processes, the main differentiation lies in the basic concept, and the ability of a visionary management to translate this concept into business reality faster than everybody else. Other service areas, such as clinics, nursing homes, and other companies involved in health-care administration, are subject to similar rules.

Software companies do have many proprietary intellectual properties which are essential to their success. But again, during the growth years of many of today's household names, the primary official mode of protection for software prodigies such as Windows, Quicken, and WordPerfect was copyright protection—which as we know is much weaker in nature than an equivalent patent protection would be. One of the reasons for the success of copyright in the software industry is the cumbersome tens of thousands of programming steps that make up a complete application program. This complexity effectively becomes a proprietary barrier—a process hard to duplicate.

Therefore, we conclude that protecting information through government filings, such as patents, trademarks, or copyrights, can be worth all the time and money to one company, and can be only moderately important to the other. Since trademarking and copyrighting usually do not impose a large demand on time and other resources, the real issue of the cost-effectiveness of protecting information becomes poignant primarily in the case of patent filing. Consulting a lawyer in such matters is essential.

ISSUES OF DISCLOSURE

There are two other aspects to protecting information—both relate to confidentiality arrangements. One is when you want to disclose information to a potential investor, large potential corporate partner, or key candidate who is considering joining the company or the board. The other is when you want to prevent industrial spying or the disclosure of information by disenchanted employees who leave the company.

We believe that confidentiality agreements are more a deterrent than a real effective means to protect information. Of course, you must sign your key employees to confidentiality agreements, the ability to enforce those is another issue. But since such a procedure is usually routine and doesn't carry any major price tag or time expenditure, there is no need to elaborate on it. To prevent industrial spying, a larger company should hire security consultants, and a small company should run background checks when hiring employees and should institute access procedures to information that is highly confidential. Still, there is no reason to get paranoid and carry this matter too far. Often, even information that you would not volunteer to disclose would not cause much damage if it fell into other hands.

Protecting information through confidentiality agreements with potential investors, corporate partners, or key future personnel can sometimes turn into a double-edged sword. It's actually a Catch-22. In order to become *interested* enough to sign a meaningful confidentiality agreement, one that offers real protection, key players must first know enough about your company to make a determination as to their *level of interest*. We find the practices in this field often exaggerated and impractical. Sometimes companies spend too much on legal fees and waste precious time on drawn-out confidentiality agreement negotiations. Granted, there are cases where those are needed, for example, when one company is evaluating a joint venture with another company, which is in a similar or related business—but before you go too far, think about the following guidelines related to confidentiality:

- Are you blanketing the industry with your search for funding or corporate partners? Or are you focusing on carefully selected areas where you believe there's a strong strategic fit, and/or where you have contacts?

- Are you in a strong enough position to hold back information and provide only an executive summary with general data, until you elicit enough interest so that you can get confidentiality arrangements? Or will prospective investors or partners pass because you haven't whet their appetite enough?

- What is the worst that can happen if some information that you consider borderline confidential falls into a few hands? Eliminating confidentiality requirements with borderline cases can give you a lot of leeway.

- What is the danger, case by case, or category by category? For example, most investors will not do anything with the information, unless they have a similar portfolio company. A large potential partner might still prefer to do a deal with you than steal your information and start from the beginning, unless of course it already has a group working in the same area.

Finally, if you have serious doubts in any of the above areas, consult a lawyer. In some cases, taking the proper precautions is essential for the survival and growth of your emerging growth business.

EIGHT RULES FOR ATTRACTING THE RIGHT CORPORATE PARTNERS

WHAT LARGE CORPORATIONS LOOK FOR IN AN EMERGING GROWTH BUSINESS, AND WHAT MAKES AN EMERGING COMPANY AN ATTRACTIVE CANDIDATE FOR STRATEGIC PARTNERING

A "scoop" has a way of making a point by exaggeration. Often we are led to believe that a poignant example represents a widely encountered phenomenon—which is usually not the case. The media, for example have been continuously blamed for presenting only (or mostly) the catastrophic aberrations of society— such as the clear bias toward stories about disaster versus those that can be billed "positive" parables. But, even if a poignant example is just what it is, a singular case, the general conclusions drawn from it can be meaningful, once we learn to discount the sensationalistic part and focus on the moral of the story.

A BUSINESS PARABLE

The following anecdote, which opens our discussion about attracting large corporate strategic partners, bears no stigma of disaster. On the contrary, it's a story of triumph. Yet you'll agree that it is quite interesting and to the point.

In the late 1980s, we were consulting to a Mitsubishi Group company to position a new business in the United States, preferably through strategic alliances. That particular group is one of the 50 or so in one of Japan's largest conglomerates. The product line of the business had applications in the field of industrial quality control as well as in medicine. One main direction for Mitsubishi was to create strategic partnering with original equipment manufacturers (OEMs) in the United States—companies that would use the products in *their* product lines. This way, Mitsubishi expected, once the functional relationship was in place, there would be a constant flow of business.

A segment of Mitsubishi's product line was targeted at the medical market. An upcoming opportunity presented itself in a pioneering field at that time—photodynamic therapy (PDT) of cancer. In this modality, the patient is injected with a particular dye, which after a few hours would leave most of the body's cells, accumulating only in the cancerous cells. Then, a catheter with a fiber-optic cable would be inserted into the body, and the tumor would be illuminated with a weak laser light which would be strongly absorbed by the injected dye. This process would leave the healthy tissues unharmed, but would destroy the cancerous cells that contained the dye. From the point of view of Mitsubishi, it would have been a great business because, in an era of significant AIDS awareness, the fiber-optic cables would become disposable, and hence provide a constant flow of revenue.

THE ROSTER OF PLAYERS

From the business point of view, we soon discovered an interesting set of players. First, the leading group in the field of PDT consisted of a Johnson & Johnson (J&J) affiliate named Photomedica. This J&J unit bought the original rights from the inventor. But around the time that we started discussions with the J&J group, a decision had been made at a high corporate level to divest this business unit—it simply didn't fit into J&J's long-term strategic goals.

Who was the would-be buyer? Well, it depends how you look at it. American Cyanamid, another industry giant, was interested in developing the J&J photodynamic therapy business— funding the development, and reserving the worldwide rights for the marketing. However, there was a caveat. American Cyanamid didn't want to bring the business unit into the company (in contrast to what J&J did, or perhaps learning from the J&J case).

Enter QLT (Quadra Logic Technologies), a small emerging growth biotechnology company, then traded only on the Toronto and Vancouver, B.C., stock exchanges. At that time, in 1987, QLT was doing research, among many other areas, on a second-generation drug to improve on J&J's lead compound. American Cyanamid negotiated a strategic alliance with QLT— and what a quantum leap for QLT. Its stock doubled soon after the deal with American Cyanamid was announced.

American Cyanamid acquired a 19 percent equity interest in the company for Can$6.5 million, and was granted warrants to acquire additional common shares for the equivalent of US$10 million. It allowed QLT to buy the J&J technology. American Cyanamid reserved the right for worldwide marketing. It committed to participate in funding further development, and to be a significant resource in obtaining domestic and international regulatory approvals.

American Cyanamid got what it wanted. Without committing to establish a group within its own corporate structure, American Cyanamid established a presence in an area that still had some question marks, at that time, as far as the large-scale business viability of the therapy. QLT got a major boost, you might say because of its capabilities, but also by being in the right place at the right time, and playing out its hand well.

That transaction gives us an interesting perspective. What looked to many like a deal between two giants, J&J and American Cyanamid, was actually a transaction divided into two transactions; each transaction was between a large corporate entity and a small emerging growth company. QLT acquired J&J's technology and at the same time it established a strategic partnering relationship with American Cyanamid. It became a crucial link between a giant who didn't want to be in that market and another giant who did, but who didn't want to commit to it internally and expose itself to the uncertainties of this new market.

THE ALLIANCE IS FORGED

Today, QLT's flagship PDT product, Photofrin—the one it bought from J&J some 9 years before—is approaching final approvals from the U.S. Food and Drug Administration in a variety of medical indications. And, perhaps, by the time this book hits the market, some approvals would already be granted. American Cyanamid, which has been taken over by American Home Products (AHP), is currently holding a 10 percent equity stake in QLT, compared with 19 percent in 1987. But, considering the dilution of more than 2.5 times in QLT's shares since 1988, these holdings still indicate a significant stake in the company. Looking at it another way, the marriage is holding up and it will soon be entering its tenth year.

The role of the American Cyanamid/AHP alliance is still strong in a number of areas: international marketing, product development, and clinical trials. QLT, since, has entered into marketing alliances with Ciba Vision and some foreign companies. It is also pursuing the further development of the next-generation drug, BPD. But the company admits in its 1994 annual report that its top priority in the near term is securing solid commitment to Photofrin—the original product that was acquired from J&J.

A lot of credit goes to the management of QLT. But the pragmatists would say, and as some people articulated at that time, that QLT was an attractive candidate for strategic partnering because it didn't have that much to lose by becoming the "scapegoat" if the market viability of photodynamic therapy failed—but it had a lot to gain. Having American Cyanamid as a major shareholder, corporate investor, and marketing partner boosted QLT financially, strategically, and in the prestige and reliability department, not to mention in gaining a potential deep pocket and experienced source for the expensive and tedious product development and regulatory approval cycles.

Now, before you blame us for being a little too pragmatic in our portrayal of the QLT story—in putting so much of the credit on the American Cyanamid strategic alliance—let's look at the company some 9 years later. If you browse through the 1986–1988 annual reports, you will find that QLT is involved in the development of a vast array of products. In the recent annual report, you'll notice that the company is practically focused on photodynamic therapy—the activity that was launched in a meaningful way upon the J&J/Photomedica acquisition and the Cyanamid alliance. In fact, to reflect this focus, the company changed its name to QLT PhotoTherapeutic, Inc. And, even within the PDT field, where the company is developing a second-generation compound, currently most of the advanced activity is related to Photofrin, the compound acquired from J&J—which the company calls the Gold Standard.

The prestige and reliability, and the expedited development and regulatory progress gained by the American Cyanamid relationship, were no doubt also contributing factors to the two very successful secondary offerings of the company in 1992 and 1993, which raised a total of $39 million. Indeed, by 1996 QLT reentered the market. This time the company engaged in a joint Canadian and American underwriting in which the well-known Canadian investment bank of Nesbitt Burns joined with the prestigious Dillon Read and UBS Securities to raise a total of over $73 million for QLT. The company's improved financial position during the early 1990s also allowed it to be listed on the NASDAQ National Market System. And, just for the sake of completeness, we wish to mention a US $1.68 million loan to QLT from American Cyanamid in 1991, and an aggregate $11 million contribution to development costs in 1992, 1993, and 1994.

There is no question that the QLT PhotoTherapeutic of today was built on the American Cyanamid strategic corporate partnering and the J&J Photofrin technology. Having said that, we wish to emphasize that the above wouldn't have worked, and American Cyanamid wouldn't have been there, if the company didn't have a capable management team and staff to engineer the alliance, nourish it, and capitalize on it.

We asked Michael Moe, a principal and emerging growth company analyst at Montgomery Securities, to sum up what the emerging growth company's motivation should be for corporate partnering (besides direct cash infusion). He articulated three reasons:

1. It provides the emerging company with a leverage for growth (mainly markets).
2. The emerging company gains much enhanced exposure and credibility.
3. The association with larger quality companies improves the emerging company's own quality. In other words—quality rubs off.

When the motivation of the large company and that of the emerging growth company can work in unison, you've got an *attractive* platform for a strategic alliance that will happen and work.

Moving from the pristine shores of Vancouver to Seattle, we decided to find out what some of QLT's American cousins have been up to. Let's pick one of your favorites—Starbucks, a maker of a different "drug." Starbucks must have been listening to Michael Moe, since it has attracted—through its emerging growth years—Holland American Cruise Lines, Barnes & Noble, Delta Airlines, Crate & Barrel, and ITT Sheraton. Whether you are taking a leisurely cruise, flying across the globe, or just heading over to the bookstore to buy this book, you can drink the brew of choice. It is easy to see that the same top growth companies that manage to attract people, capital, and the attention of Wall Street are also a magnet for strategic alliances with large companies—again, the chain reaction of attractiveness is at work.

EIGHT DYNAMIC RULES

To find out what other factors persuade a large corporation to establish a corporate partnering relationship with an emerging growth company, we interviewed Brenda Manning, manager of licensing and acquisitions at Ciba Corning (now part of the Sandoz-Ciba merged entity, Novartis). Ciba Corning usually does 20 or 30 strategic alliances per year, 10 to 20 percent of which are full acquisitions. Among other topics we discussed with Brenda Manning were the rules that a large company follows when it considers an emerging growth company for strategic partnering—including perhaps (but not necessarily) a potential equity investment. There are eight:

1. The major purpose of a large corporation seeking strategic partners and acquisitions within the emerging company sector, is growth—faster and cheaper growth than the large corporation could achieve internally. The candidate company must satisfy this axiom.

2. The candidate company has to fit perfectly in terms of *strategic focus*.

3. The large company has to be convinced that the candidate company has a strong and unique (preferably proprietary) position in its market.

4. The candidate company should not be one in real financial trouble, so that it will not become a financial drain.

5. If monetary investment is involved, the investment risk has to be well balanced by the potential reward. The large company recognizes that if it were to develop the product and the market itself, it would cost money—and so it is prepared to invest. But it will conduct a strict risk-reward analysis.

6. Large corporations prefer to exchange technology and services rather than cash. If an emerging company can utilize such a scheme, whereby the large company can provide marketing networks, regulatory assistance, production expertise, and such other in-kind services, it would be easier to attract the larger company. A relationship that starts without cash infusion might easily lead to investment by the larger company down the road.

7. If the large company buys a stake in the emerging growth company, it would prefer situations in which it can pay with stock, or a mixture of cash and stock. The less cash that is needed, the more attractive the transaction, provided that the other components are in place.

8. The large company has to feel comfortable with management's competence.

Finally, Brenda Manning noted that a large company gets an enormous number of strategic partnering proposals annually, all across the board from pure exchange of technology, services, and marketing expertise to outright acquisition. The percentage of companies that it would finally associate with is comparatively low. The cash amounts that a large company might invest in an emerging growth strategic partner would run the gamut from zero to many millions of dollars. The emerging growth company manager might find that the licensing and acquisitions people will try to avoid investing cash, even if the company is rich in cash.

But, with all these stipulations, there are significant opportunities for emerging companies in the area of large corporate partnering. The most important factor to attract a large strategic partner is to first *find a strategic fit*. Who starts the ball rolling? Well, a candidate company that has something that's really worth something should contact all the big players in the market. It might sound like a contrarian approach, but Brenda Manning believes that if the emerging growth company can do the job itself, and the word gets out about this wonderful new thing that actually works, it will probably be courted by large corporations to share in the opportunity and can then demand a very high price for a slice of the pie.

If we look at the QLT/Cyanamid deal in terms of those criteria, a question arises: Didn't American Cyanamid realize that a small and fragile company, as QLT was at that time, could become a financial drain? You might say it's 20-20 hindsight, but if you look at how things developed, it's obvious that as a public company, and with the American Cyanamid prestige as a booster, QLT managed to raise *over $110 million* from outside sources. If American Cyanamid wanted to develop the technology itself, this money would have had to come from its internal development budgets. So it again comes to the old question of seeing the glass half full or half empty. In this case, American Cyanamid saw it half full.

EMERGING-WITH-LARGE MATCHES

Every day that you open the financial newspapers, you read about a new strategic partnering or acquisition arrangement between an emerging growth company and a large corporation. Although you can often read about strategic alliances and even full mergers among large equals, sheer numbers and economics make the emerging-with-large match much more frequent and interesting.

In some cases, you might even find that a large corporation would rather partner with an emerging growth company than with a large corporation that can offer a similar product or service. Case in point: H&R Block's well-established CompuServe on-line services recently went public in an underwriting led by Goldman, Sachs & Co. CompuServe chose the emerging growth company Netscape over the giant Microsoft in a broad licensing and marketing pact, allowing CompuServe's more than 4 million subscribers to use Netscape's widely distributed software to surf the Internet's World Wide Web.

In fact, Netscape's strategic attractiveness was so high that in 1996 Microsoft with 100 times Netscape's revenues had to battle for every inch of territory. In a battle over America Online (AOL), the largest on-line service with more than 5 million subscribers in early 1996, Microsoft had to agree to bundle AOL software with Windows 95, in order to get a broad partnership with AOL which will make Microsoft's World Wide Web browser an integral part of AOL's software. Still, this didn't prevent AOL from establishing a more limited, but still lucrative agreement with Netscape.

The majority of strategic partnering deals are not full acquisition deals, but as we gleaned from the QLT case, they can still be extremely lucrative for the emerging growth company. Take for example i-Stat of Princeton, New Jersey. The company, with FY1995 revenues of $20 million and revenues of $13 million for the first 6 months of FY1996, makes a hand-held device that allows blood to be analyzed at a patient's bedside in under 2 minutes, down from the 20 minutes or more it takes a hospital to get results from a lab. Some critics, however, say that the i-Stat system is more expensive than using a lab.

Nevertheless, this didn't prevent the prestigious giant Hewlett-Packard's $1.4 billion medical equipment division from announcing a strategic alliance with i-Stat to expand the development and the distribution of i-Stat's products for world-wide markets. This division of the $25 billion in revenue and 100,000 employee Hewlett-Packard (HP) made a whopping $61 million equity investment for 14 percent of i-Stat—placing a $436 million valuation on the company—a sales multiple of 22 when averaged over FY 1995. The news caused i-Stat shares to soar in mid-1995 to $43.75, a figure that later, in mid-1996, settled under $20. i-Stat still hadn't turned a profit when these lines were written in the fourth quarter of 1996.

Although there were many naysayers who found it more attractive to "short" the stock, in early 1996 one of the Ivy houses, Fidelity Investments (through one of its mutual funds), became the largest shareholder in i-Stat. It seems that by attracting a large strategic partner, i-Stat managed to attract a large investor—a confirmation of what we call the chain reaction theory of attractiveness. Or, as Michael Moe, emerging growth company analyst and principal at Montgomery Securities, put it to us: "Winners win and losers lose."

What attracted HP to i-Stat to make such a huge investment for a relatively minority stake of one-seventh of the company? Well, the strategic market fit, which will allow HP to generate immediate sales results, was definitely the determining factor.

HP's OmniCare patient-monitoring system is installed at more than 70,000 bedsides around the world. Integrating into it i-Stat's instant, electronic blood-monitoring module, fits naturally into the scheme. Access to blood chemistry test results through patient monitors is expected to significantly enhance the productivity of care providers, giving them critical information where and when they need it most. And hospitals will be willing to pay for it—increasing HP's business.

Other, future synergistic applications could include an interface with HP's new PalmVue system, a wireless communications system that sends bedside patient data directly to physicians carrying an HP200LX palmtop computer.

Certainly, many reasons abound for strategic marriages. When we interviewed Mike Connors, senior vice president and divisional president of America Online, he enunciated that AOL engages in strategic alliances "to expedite the time which it takes to bring a service or product to the market," or as it is usually called "time to market." AOL has brought itself to the market very quickly. From 1992, when it was at the threshold of high-growth, it has become a $1 billion enterprise.

Chip Ottness, a small-capitalization fund manager responsible for a substantial portfolio at J. P. Morgan Investment, cites two pragmatic reasons that a large corporation has for making strategic alliances with emerging growth companies:

1. Strategic partnering is another form of R&D for the large corporation—one with reduced risk.
2. Since a large corporation usually has a massive marketing capability, strategic partnering provides it with exposure to new markets.

FOOD FOR THOUGHT

His comments gave us some "food for thought," and to prevent you from hitting the fridge for a snack, we thought we'd give you some too. We are going to discuss a company dedicated to producing food for thought—Martek, which has recently entered the food business.

Martek has created a baby formula which has been shown to enhance the mental development of infants—Formulaid. Not only does Formulaid boost the IQ of infants, it has also boosted the attraction quotient of Martek, which has strategic partners lined up around the maternity ward. Sandoz, Mead Johnson, a subsidiary of Bristol-Myers Squibb (BMS), Wyeth-Ayerst, Nutricia, and Maabarot want to partake of this formula for success. Those leading companies manufacture close to half the baby formula for the U.S. and worldwide markets.

Why are the strategic partners lining up? For one, Martek saves them many years of risky R&D, and they can now get the same results by buying Martek's know-how. Is that all? Do the alliances open new markets as well for those established companies—after all they're already selling the baby formulas?

Well, think about it this way. A baby's mother might opt to prepare her own food if all there is to it is *food*. But if the food she can buy would also increase her child's IQ—then by preparing her own food she might deprive her baby of something important. It's reasonable to assume that under those circumstances, many mothers who didn't use baby formulas before will now use them. So, Martek does open new markets (not Marteks) for Sandoz, Mead-Johnson, BMS, Nutricia, and others.

But there could be other, less obvious motivations for lucrative strategic partnering arrangements or outright acquisitions. The large Medtronic acquired the tiny InStent, Inc., for stock that was valued at $215 million at the time of the transaction. InStent had less than $3 million in revenues, and fewer than 75 employees. So, what clinched the deal with such a high valuation?

Kurt Krueger, a Montgomery securities analyst, pointed out that InStent's products may allow Medtronic to circumvent the strong patents that Johnson & Johnson has established in the market. The transaction offers the large corporate partner—in this case, Medtronic—a way to hedge its bets in a very lucrative business, which otherwise would be partially or totally closed to it because of existing proprietary positions of other companies.

If that story made your heart beat faster, just think how Geoworks must have felt. A much earlier stage emerging growth company that demonstrates significant growth in revenues and consistent reduction of losses is Geoworks of Alameda, California. Geoworks bills itself as a leading developer of operating systems for the emerging consumer computing device

(CCD) market. This includes providing operating systems for smart cellular phones, organizers, and other items. Although company sales for the June 30, 1996, quarter were only $2,429,000, its market valuation in early September 1996 was more than $280 million.

And, talk about attracting capital and large corporate partners. Geoworks' corporate partners run the gamut of the "who's who" in the industry—the likes of Toshiba, Hewlett-Packard, Novell, Nokia, and Ericsson. All the above except Ericsson are also *equity investors* in Geoworks. Furthermore, just 18 months after the company went public, it completed a secondary public offering (in November 1995) to the tune of $40 million. Not bad at all!

Emerging-with-large strategic partnering is a wide-open field with a large multitude of variations. On the lower end of the dollar spectrum, Fred Wilson of Euclid Partners—a New York venture capital fund—engineered a unique strategic alliance pact between his brainchild, Multex Systems, and Automatic Data Processing.

Isaak Karaev, Multex's CEO, was a senior software developer at the $3 billion Roseland, New Jersey, giant known as ADP. Interestingly he was developing an investment research service which ADP wasn't interested in marketing widely. Enter Wilson and Euclid Partners. Euclid managed to convince R. R. Donnelley & Sons Co. (large strategic partner number one) to cofinance with Euclid the start of Multex Systems. Multex now runs Karaev's project (formerly at ADP), an on-line service that distributes brokerage house research. Multex also lured from ADP 20 employees who were working on the project.

Since our focus is on the emerging growth stage, here is what's interesting. Karaev kept his immediate former superiors at ADP informed of his activities. He also convinced them that ADP could retain access to the Multex technology, and ADP's divisional president of information and processing services agreed to be on the board. Lo and behold, soon thereafter ADP became a strategic partner in Multex to the tune of $2 million. But why did ADP let Karaev's group leave, and then try to get hold of the same products? Sounds confusing, doesn't it?

Understanding the above paradox will bring you one step closer to comprehending the line of thought of large corporations vis-à-vis strategic partnering, and ultimately will lead you to position your company to attract those valuable giants.

Ralph Koehrer, ADP's divisional president, clarified the situation (to *The Wall Street Journal*). He said that ADP was interested in the products and services that Multex was developing, but didn't want to fund them entirely on its own. Koehrer explained that his division at ADP will fund and license interesting products, but for many of them, 100 percent ownership doesn't make sense.

As you already gleaned from the examples we presented up to this point, and from Brenda Manning's guidelines of corporate attractiveness, there's a clear thread that runs through the corporate thinking of major companies when it comes to strategic partnering with emerging growth companies.

The large corporation is attracted to situations where there is a clear strategic fit—but it wishes to keep its options widely open. To grow, a large corporation needs a wide array of new products and services. However, it doesn't wish to take the risk of funding internally the development of each potentially lucrative route. Strategic partnering and acquisitions are part of the lifeline of large corporations. So why aren't they chasing after the emerging growth companies? Because they have a wide array of choices, and because small companies are usually hungrier and more cash-starved than large ones.

To attract large corporate partners, assuming that there's a strategic fit, you have to show them that by *gradual* commitment, they can avail themselves of a product and market they need, and split the risk with others. *Gradual* is the key word in the equation, unless there's an interest in an outright acquisition. Large corporations also want to see that the strategic partner involves them in the crucial decisions. And, of course, they must believe in the ability of the company's management team to achieve the results.

But never fool yourself into thinking that these deep pockets will just open their wallets and let the dough flow. Rather, approach the strategically fit potential partners, and position yourself carefully on the basis of the instructions we described above.

HYBRID PARTNERSHIPS

Not all strategic alliances are created equal. Partnering or conducting an acquisition transaction between equals is very different from partnering with large corporations. In the case of Williams Controls, a company we feature in this book, growth by acquisition of "equals" seems to work. We believe that it is significantly correlated with the astute management of Tom Itin, Williams' CEO, and with the relatively good cash positions of the acquired companies.

In the early 1980s, we witnessed a different kind of acquisition, at the lower end of the emerging growth sector. For various reasons we will not mention the names of the companies involved. The stock of a microcap public company (company A) was boosted to around $9 (from close to $1) by the development of a new product and a strategic agreement with a large distributor. With this expensive "paper," it acquired another small company (company B) with which it had a good strategic fit. But lo and behold, because of regulatory approval problems, company A's marketing agreement with the large distributor fell apart, and its stock dived almost back to its initial value of $1. The original owners of the acquired company (company B) found themselves with some worthless paper, and the loss of control of the company they founded. It seems that there are some alliances that perhaps you don't want to get into. (But remember: The acquiring company was itself an early-stage emerging company.)

There are some innovative corporate partnering formats that are probably not that widely known. An interesting one, which is effectively a hybrid venture capital/corporate partnering setup, is Edelson Technology Partners (ETP) of Saddle Brook, New Jersey. ETP manages more than $70 million and invested in more than 60 companies in a variety of stages, but mostly emerging growth ones.

ETP was formed and operates by investments from large corporations such as ABB (Asea Brown Boveri), AT&T, Cincinnati Bell, Ford Motor Company, 3M, and Paramount Communications. The large corporations are corporate limited partners, and ETP is the general partner. All investment decisions are made autonomously by the general partner.

Up to this point you might argue that the above arrangement has nothing to do with corporate partnering. It simply represents investments made by large corporations in a venture capital fund—a common practice in the industry.

But that's not the case. All the corporate partners in ETP have made a *strategic investment* decision by investing *corporate funds,* rather than pension funds. It is usually pension funds and not corporate funds that are invested in the venture capital industry. By investing *corporate funds* in ETP, the large corporation is using the same source of capital it would use to invest directly in a strategic partner. In fact, when appropriate, ETP introduces its portfolio companies to their corporate partners for potential business liaisons.

By attracting an organization like ETP, you can achieve, if you will, multiple goals by drawing on the experience and resources of a financial and corporate partnering organization. You can get funded, and you may also get corporate strategic partners. But, remember, the cost of money in a venture shop like ETP will be higher in terms of the equity you'll have to part with, compared with what it would cost you if you were to strike a deal directly with a large company. Another disadvantage of the hybrid formula is that you have someone between you and the corporate partner. That someone in many ways controls the relationship.

As always, if you have the experience and wherewithal to explore the stratosphere of large corporate inhabitants on your own and have the right expertise and contacts to attract a large corporate partner to sit down with you and negotiate a serious deal, do it. Even if you don't have the experience in house, you can obtain the help of intermediaries and other consultants.

The rules articulated by Brenda Manning, a corporate part-nering expert from the large Ciba Corning (now Novartis)—rules for what attracts a large corporate partner to a particular emerging growth company and what doesn't—represent only that part of the picture which can be put on the table, openly. But then there are those things that, so to speak, "they don't teach you at Harvard Business School." That is, the *hidden agenda*—which you must add to your knowledge base, if you want to position yourself to attract large corporate partners.

First you must remember that corporate partnering is a clash of two very different cultures. And since these cultures are represented by people, it is a clash between very different peo-ple—from the professional and business points of view, at least. The corporate types advance and climb up the ladder of very structured organizations. The policies are well developed, and the hierarchy is clear. Decisions are made in a very systematic manner, usually subject to the verifications of many layers. Plans are long term—with a relatively stable platform for exe-cution. Money is usually no object—when it comes to embark-ing on an important project.

Although "lifetime employment" is not an American expres-sion, especially in light of some massive layoffs in corporate America, the majority of the large corporate workforce starts in an organization at a relatively early age, and then progresses within that organization or moves to a similar one to continue their career. After 15 or 20 years in such organizations, these are the people who now decide on a corporate strategic part-nership with your emerging growth company.

Whom are they facing across the table? Usually entrepre-neurial pioneers (even if those entrepreneurs have done it before). People who learned how to build things, sometimes on a shoestring. People who had to beat the system to gain a com-petitive edge in the land of the giants. People who make deci-sions fast, and sometime gamble everything. These are gazelles who hop and jump—free-spirited "savages."

If you grew up in the first group, wouldn't you be afraid of the second? Wouldn't you be leery of a close relationship that might turn your world upside down, and perhaps interfere with your company's harmony? Wouldn't you be afraid that the partnership would fail, and then you might lose your job—because you "dragged" the corporation into this relationship? You probably would.

Convincing the management and executives of a large corporation to expose themselves and their company to the perils of a smaller enterprise—and possibly jeopardize the position they worked for, for so many years—is not for the faint-hearted. These folks will pull the plug on any negotiation if they discover an area of imminent danger. Because of the vast number of opportunities each large corporation has in the field of corporate partnering, saying no is safer and easier than saying yes. If they smell danger, they won't face, sit, and study it, but will move to the next opportunity.

A good strategic fit can't compensate for the lack of full trust, when someone's job is on the line. To attract a large corporate partner, you must tone down your entrepreneurial ego, and show the ability to work with a "big brother or sister." This requires that you present to the partner an astute team of managers who will serve as the corporate liaison committee. Having among those someone who worked within a large corporation, preferably one well known to the potential corporate partner, can increase the level of trust and feeling of safety. Board members who are closely involved with the company, and who were in a fairly senior position with a large corporation, should be brought into the discussions right from the start. The management of the emerging company must impress the large corporation not only with its experience and operational capabilities, but also with its adaptable, flexible personality.

It may sound at first like a Catch-22. Here is a corporation that wants you in the first place because of the results you have achieved, predominantly via an entrepreneurial and pioneering aptitude and vehicle. At the same time, this cute giant watches to see whether you are "conservative" enough to be a team player with your partner. In truth, there is no paradox here. Once the strategic partnering is implemented, the financial, marketing, product development, and other potential support that you'll get from the partner will alleviate the need to do some of the things in your old-fashioned, guerrilla warfare style. This will in some way bring you closer to the partner's corporate culture. Big brothers or sisters need to see that you can make the transition and meet them halfway.

MEASURING BENEFITS

There is another seemingly paradoxical issue which you must realize and turn to your advantage when wooing a large corporate partner. This is how it goes. Large corporations have deep pockets—it is well known and usually true. But since this money is earmarked for business and not for philanthropy, no *unnecessary* penny will be spent, except, maybe, for specific charity projects that the company is involved in. If a large corporation feels that it can achieve the *same benefits* from a strategic partnering arrangement, without investing cash, it will usually do so. The crucial point here is to define the term: the *same benefits*.

If the large company measures only the services it receives as the benefit, then indeed, as Brenda Manning put it, the corporation will attempt to get away with providing only services in exchange, or when necessary it will make an equity purchase for which it will pay with stock.

But, then, there's another area of potential benefit for the large corporate partner—the increased valuation of the emerging company resulting from the collaboration. It happened for QLT with American Cyanamid, and for i-Stat with Hewlett-Packard: Upon the announcement of the strategic alliance, the smaller partner's valuation increased in a quantum leap.

By making a cash equity investment in the emerging growth corporate partner, the large corporation can share in the financial profits associated with the increased valuation of their partner—an augmentation for which the corporation is largely responsible, but the benefits of which will elude it without an equity investment. So, in addition to the benefit that the large corporate partner can gain by putting equity investment money to work within the emerging company in developing joint products and markets, the large corporation earns an investment banking kind of financial return on its investment—a double whammy, if everything goes well.

What does this mean to the emerging company? A lot. In trying to attract a corporate partner, you must realize that you can be a very juicy fruit. Not only are you saving large corporations years of development, and not only are you providing them with access to growth without taking the full risk or paying the full bill for it, but you can also give them a simple financial return on investment by increasing the market value of their holdings in your growing company.

DESIGNING YOURSELF TO FIT

If you approach large potential corporate partners from this kind of position of strength, and manage to convey to them the full message of the scope of benefits that this cooperation can bring for them, in a convincing way, then your attractiveness is guaranteed. The design-to-fit approach, which we advocated in Chapter 1, can be a wise formula to set the stage for becoming an attractive emerging growth corporate partner down the road.

In the design-to-fit strategy, you build your company with corporate partnering in mind. For example, we know that one of the strong "commodities" of large corporations is marketing and distribution networks. Since you envision yourself as a company that will eventually join forces with a larger corporation, the design-to-fit strategy would mean that you should concentrate on developing the best product, get the maximum proprietary protection for it, and demonstrate its salability and its wide market potential. You shouldn't spend your limited financial and human resources on what would be an extensive marketing and distribution system—which you expect to secure through your future corporate partner.

In the early emerging growth years of ADP, after the company went public, it decided to expand across the United States, from what was before a local operation in the New York metropolitan area. Henry Taub, a founder, whom we interviewed for this book, described ADP's strategy at that time: "We were finding partners that we understood, operating general service bureaus, which are small service operations that do some payroll, some receivables, and some punched-card operations." Taub adds: "These general service bureaus were dealing with the marketplace on a random basis, and victimizing themselves in the process because they were everything to everybody, and didn't specialize in anything."

Then, Taub explains, "the technology started to change." In the early 1960s payroll operations were moving from punched cards to the IBM System/360 family of computers. Small bureau operators couldn't catch up, and they started depending on software and hardware specialists. ADP management successfully convinced around 100 of these service bureaus across the nation to enter into a partnership whereby ADP would acquire the companies and support them in the areas of software, hardware, and marketing. This way, they could concentrate on servicing the clients. Of course, the "currency" ADP used to acquire the companies was mostly its stock.

ADP today is a multibillion-dollar corporation, and a would-be ideal large corporate partner for emerging growth businesses in a variety of areas related to its core businesses—employer services (payroll and tax), brokerage services, and dealer services. It focuses on acquisitions much more than on strategic partnering arrangements. This has not, however, prevented ADP from making the $2 million strategic investment in Multex, which we described earlier in the chapter.

Henry Taub explains why ADP has always had more need for acquisitions than for strategic partnerships (joint development, and such): "We are a service company. We are not developing basic technology. Therefore, we never had to be vanguard, but in performance."

Let's look at some of ADP's acquisitions in the past years. In 1995, it acquired WTR, a benefits consulting and 401(k) plan processor. Another 1995 acquisition was Turbodata, a leading European auto dealer computer service company, with 3000 clients in Belgium, France, Germany, and the Netherlands. In 1994 ADP acquired Computer Care, a leading provider of customer service reminder programs to auto dealers. In the same year, it acquired National Bio Systems, a company that helps auto insurers control the costs of accident-related medical expenses. And in 1994 it also acquired Peachtree Software, a vendor of accounting and payroll software products.

You can see that ADP concentrates on acquiring companies that fulfill some or all of the following three requirements:

- Control territories, in payroll and various other areas of application.
- Allow ADP to enter new areas of applications.
- Contribute to global expansion (i.e., in foreign countries).

So an emerging growth company that wants to attract ADP has to know first that ADP is interested mainly in acquiring companies, and not so much in joint development or joint marketing efforts (and we are not talking here about such arrangements with large companies of equal size). Then the emerging company has to analyze ADP's past acquisitions and see whether they fall into one of those categories.

How can you find those things out in your particular situation, for a number of large corporations you'd be interested to approach? Well, the majority of large corporations are public. Public companies will furnish you with detailed annual reports and SEC filings. Those document not only will enlighten you about strategy, but will offer specific information on past acquisitions. You may want to start with a company snapshot in the Standard & Poor's stock reports. The next step would be to call the department of the director of new business development, and the manager of licensing and acquisitions, and ask for the company guidelines.

Sometimes you are lucky and find other clues. *The Wall Street Journal* of March 8, 1996, discussed the then-upcoming merger between the two giant Swiss pharmaceuticals companies—Ciba-Geigy and Sandoz—to create the second largest drug maker in the world: Novartis. In evaluating the strategies of other giants, the *Journal* noted that Johnson & Johnson is a gigantic, diversified health-care company that tends to *buy up-*

and-coming, smaller companies and turn them into operating units. What an interesting way to be informed that J&J is naturally attracted to the emerging growth sector. And, if you have a strategic fit with its needs, the corporate strategy is already in your favor. Note that J&J, like ADP, emphasizes full acquisition—a most valuable piece of information.

Whatever the channel is, finding out the kind of information indicated in this chapter about your prospective large corporate target for strategic venturing or acquisition allows you to pull in the right partner, and do it faster.

Henry Taub enlightened us about what will attract a large corporation, such as ADP, to join forces with an emerging growth company. Here are the central factors:

- There is that unavoidable *strategic fit.*
- The management team can get along with the corporate partner.
- Since many companies will sell out because of financial problems, lack of profitability is not a deterrent. But the potential for improving profitability under the large corporate umbrella has to be evident. This means that the company's financial problems are not caused by an inherent flaw in the products, the nonexistence of a clear market, or across-the-board human problems.
- The company *can be built up* by providing it with the tools of the larger corporation.

PARTING WORDS

For just a dab of icing on the cake, we wanted to finish off with some advice from two venture capital professionals, Mark Radtke and George McKinney. But first you should know that venture capitalists are fond of corporate partnering because it helps their portfolio companies grow with less investment from their side, and because it allows them to exit—to cash in at least on part of their investment (if the large corporation makes an equity investment).

In their opinion, which they express in an article titled "Corporate Strategic Partnerships" in Pratt's *Guide to Venture Capital,* what takes place after the agreement is as important as the dance before the agreement. First, there is the issue of "unpleasant" surprises; they can be avoided if the emerging growth company partner communicates openly and frequently with the larger corporate partner. It is good to remember that while an emerging growth company may communicate important information at the water cooler, larger firms communicate by electronic or typed memorandum. Microsoft, for example, prefers the all-electronic, paperless system; others still use both.

In addition, you must continually "sell" the strategic logic of the relationship within the large corporate partner. Once again, in the fluid environment of corporate America, the players may be shifting and a new manager needs to be educated about the value of the relationship. Finally, and this is a corollary to the previous point, be willing to change the agreement or plan as objectives or circumstances dictate. Even though you are now associated with or part of a larger organization, the benefit of an emerging growth company to the larger corporate partner is your firm's agility and nimbleness.

VALUATION: THIRTEEN RULES FOR THE RIGHT SELF-APPRAISAL

KNOW THE TRUE VALUE OF YOUR EMERGING COMPANY—INVESTORS AND CORPORATE PARTNERS WILL TEST YOU

Although value is no joke, it may be best to start this serious discussion with a bit of humor that will add some perspective. A joke tells the story of three executives who are flying back on a chartered plane from a corporate retreat weekend in the Pacific. Suddenly the pilot notices that they have major engine trouble, and informs the executives that he must perform an emergency landing. The plane lands in a small clearing in the middle of the jungle on one of the islands. The executives ask the pilot to guard the plane as they embark on a journey into the jungle to see if they can find help or another way off the island.

It is too late when their eyes catch the unmistakable symbols of a cannibal tribe. A few moments later they are surrounded and captured. The next morning, the tribesmen lead one of the executives to the middle of the square, where a big pot of water is boiling. He immediately realizes what it means. He runs to the person who looks like the chief, gets down on his knees, and presents him with a gold watch, a gold chain, and a gold ring. "There is much more where these came from," he says. "If you let me live, you'll become rich." The chief consults with his council, and in a couple of minutes comes back with the decision. "Food has much more value here," he says, and the poor executive becomes the tribe's breakfast.

Around lunchtime the second executive is brought to the square, and she too sees the big pot of boiling water. She kneels in front of the chief and pulls out, from a hidden compartment in her briefcase, a diamond, a ruby, and an emerald. "There are much more where these came from," she says. "If you let me live, you'll become very rich." This time, the chief consults feverishly with his council, but again he comes back with the same horrifying verdict: "Food has more value here," he says, and the executive becomes lunch.

When the third executive is brought to the square at twilight time, he already knows what's waiting for him. As the senior of the three, he approaches the chief and, without kneeling, hands him his business card and says: "If you let me live, I'll give you 1 million shares of this company. These shares are worth a lot now, but in a couple of years, their projected value will enable you to buy all your neighboring islands and become the king of this part of the Pacific."

The chief, who seems impressed, takes his council aside and after what seems to be an unusually lengthy and feverish debate, turns to the executive and says: "Convertible preferred, or you are dinner!"

The story of the cannibals is intended to be taken lightly as a humorous example of value being relative. We move now from the dark world of the rain forest, which at times appears to be a lot like the corporate jungle, to the mysterious world of Wall Street.

For those who have not been admitted to the inner sanctum of the Temple of Finance, the value placed on "castles in the sky" like Netscape or Spyglass seems confusing. To put it succinctly, when Netscape was priced in the summer of 1995, the company had only $17 million in revenues for the 6 months ended June 30. Nonetheless, the market valued Netscape as if it were a seasoned, blue-chip company, turning the shares over until the company's total valuation settled in at billions of dollars. If you are the manager of an emerging growth company, you are not only confused about the valuation process, but you are perplexed over how best to take advantage of your options for raising capital. Where will you get the best value for your company? And, just as important, you are asking yourself: "What is the best fit for me?" Generally speaking, there are several avenues available to the emerging growth company manager for unlocking the value of the business: private market versus public offering, and financial investor versus strategic investor.

In this chapter, we will not attempt to rival the many great works on valuation used by the financial types you may encounter when bargaining over what percentage of your company you must give up for what particular amount of money they are putting on the table. Many of those books on the shelves already offer details on various valuation techniques and models. We would, however, be doing you a disservice unless we exposed you to some of the rudimentary concepts in those financial books. We also might be forcing you to go out and buy another book—and we would like this to be the only book you will need for the time being on these topics. For those of you who have already had more than enough exposure to the issue of valuation, please skip over the next few pages and tune in for the rest of the story.

VALUATION METHODS

There is no single approach when it comes to valuation. The best value you can obtain for your business may come through your own negotiating skills—sitting down with a prospective investor to convince the investor of the underlying value of your business. However, before sitting down with that prospective investor, or if you do not have the opportunity for a one-to-one meeting, you should be aware of the generally accepted methods for valuation: balance sheet valuation, income statement valuation, and discounted cashflow valuation. Later, we will discuss those unwritten methods, which are based on less analytical and more intuitive considerations.

THE BALANCE SHEET

In the case of balance sheet valuation, most people value the business on the basis of its "book value" as presented by the audited, historical balance sheet. The formula is simple: "Total assets less total liabilities less the liquidation price of preferred stock equals book value." In a sense, people are paying only for what they see. Although such a formula can be used as a starting point, in most instances, people who use this method adjust "book value" for factors not reflected on the balance sheet. The classical example is real estate that is accounted for at a low historical cost, but that is now by prevailing market conditions appraised at a considerably higher value.

For an emerging growth company, the balance sheet does not reflect the intangible value of the business: its "goodwill." Since the goodwill that your business has developed is not readily quantified by the balance sheet valuation technique, this approach is the least attractive method to utilize in evaluating your business. Furthermore, the balance sheet valuation technique does not take into account the future *growth prospects* for your business.

On the whole, the balance valuation can be more appropriately used when determining how much a bank might lend against your balance sheet. It is not a viable approach for evaluating the equity of your business. In the final analysis, you might view this technique simply as a minimum valuation for which you could readily sell your business. If, let's say, you wanted to retire early and quickly, this could be the approach for you.

Before leaving the topic of balance sheet valuation or leaving you on the beach to luxuriate in retirement, there is one other balance sheet valuation technique you should know: liquidation value. This approach estimates the worth of the company if its assets were sold immediately at an auction. It is sometimes known as a "fire sale" valuation. If someone approaches you with this techniques, we suggest you smile and quietly walk out of the room (unless, of course, your business truly has had a fire). You have not found your valuation soulmate.

The Income Statement

The income statement valuation technique is probably the most widely used of all valuation methods. Even the most sophisticated of financial investors will utilize this method, and it is an effort to persuade the investor to stray far afield from the value that this technique yields. Under the income statement valuation technique, the most commonly used approach is the application of a multiple to EBIT: earnings before interest and taxes. EBIT measures the "earning power" of the underlying business without the impact of the capital or tax structure of the business. It is preferable to use earnings before tax and interest, rather than aftertax profits, since the potential buyer or investor may have a different capital structure that can be utilized or may be subject to a different tax bracket from the one to which your company is subject.

If your company decides to utilize this technique, or if in your discussion with potential investors this technique arises, most of the discussion will surround the appropriate "multiple" that should be applied to the EBIT results. There are many rules of thumb. One that we encountered in *Managing the Small to Midsized Company,* by Collins and Lazier, suggests that 4 is a suitable multiple for companies with an "unglamorous" product line, slow or no growth, and low market share. Since the audience of this book is the emerging growth company, we hope that you do not encounter an investor who wishes to put a multiple of 4 on your EBIT results.

A multiple of 5 or 6 EBIT is a typical range within which "a majority of private companies trade." Put another way, it is a range in which private companies are bought and sold in arm's-length transactions. Rather than viewing book value as the low end of your valuation range, it would be more appropriate to view applying a multiple of 5 or 6 to your EBIT as the low end of the valuation range.

A multiple of 7 times EBIT (or higher) is appropriate for a "growth" company, and a buyer who sees the true future prospects of your business should be willing to apply this higher multiple to your EBIT. The question is how high a multiple is appropriate. In that regard, we recollect a jocular anecdote that Henry Taub, cofounder of ADP, made about the thinking on valuation at the time that ADP went public. He recalled a much-quoted saying in the investment community that if the P/E is less than 100, it's cheap, meaning that valuing a company at 100 times earnings wouldn't necessarily be considered an inflated valuation. It's possible that those analysts were forecasting the multiples that would be placed on the stock market in Japan; if so, they were among the first to realize the hidden value of that emerging growth market.

Yes, 100 times earnings can be viewed as "cheap," depending upon the stage at which the company is being valued. For example, a company with a huge growth potential that just broke even can be given a multiple higher than 100, and it would still be considered cheap. When investors consider the appropriate multiple for either a public or a private company, they turn their attention to multiples of publicly traded companies to obtain an appropriate range for valuation. In these instances, you should come in armed with publicly traded companies that you believe to be comparable to your business and that are demonstrating high growth and have been accorded high multiples by the market. You should be able to articulate why your company should be accorded even a higher multiple than the comparably traded public companies. When it comes to your company, you are the expert as to why a particular company is comparable to your own, and you should also be able to convince a potential investor of what makes your company unique and distinguishes it from the competition.

In the case of publicly traded emerging growth companies, the most common rule is that the multiple applied to the company's earnings should be lower than the rate of growth in that company's earnings. Most investors in public companies focus on the price-earnings (P/E) ratio, since that ratio is the most widely circulated. The same concept, however, would apply to the appropriate EBIT multiple.

An example from the May 1996 issue of *Worth* magazine will put in context the meaning of this rule of thumb. If an investor bought a $30 stock with earnings of $1 a share—in other words, a P/E ratio of 30—and that company had a growth rate of 30 percent a year, it would take 9 years for the stock to generate earnings that add up to $30. Thus, in order to command a high multiple of either aftertax profits or EBIT, you must be able to convince a prospective investor of the long-term—indeed, 5- to 10-year term—growth potential of your company.

Discounted Cashflow

The third most commonly used technique is discounted cashflow valuation. Under this technique, "free cashflow" is projected 5 or 10 years into the future, and those cashflow streams are discounted to present value. First, a definition of free cashflow. Free cashflow is net income (profit after taxes) *less* the increase in assets from the prior year *plus* the increase in liabilities from the prior year *plus* depreciation and amortization for the year.

Deriving free cashflow is time-consuming, but it is the easiest part of the discounted cashflow valuation process. Determining the appropriate discount rate requires a great deal of research and creative financial acumen. The discount rate should capture a "required rate of return" that the investor feels makes the risk associated with the investment worthwhile. It is at this juncture where the buyer's and seller's views begin to diverge. Since you know the risks associated with your business better than the investor, and feel more comfortable with them, you have a completely different view of risk. You also have a much more optimistic view of the future growth prospects for your business.

Of the methods discussed so far, the discounted cashflow technique places the greatest emphasis on future earnings performance and is one of the most attractive approaches from your standpoint as an emerging growth company. There are two other approaches worth mentioning that we characterize as "cashless" flow methods of valuation.

There actually is no method called the cashless flow method, but there are times when a company neither has positive cashflow nor significant revenues. In some situations, the company has just begun to generate revenues and still is burdened with high buildup costs. Although owners have yet to generate profits or cashflow, they still need an outside infusion of capital to grow the business to the next stage of development. In this instance, the outside investor would be valuing the company on the basis of a multiple of revenues. That multiple will be derived after an analysis of comparable companies and the multiple of revenues placed on those similar growth businesses.

In still other cases, the company has yet to generate any revenues, let alone profits or positive cashflow. In these cases, the value of a company can still be significant, especially if either the research it is performing or a patent that it possesses has significant future value to a prospective strategic partner. Virtually all the value is based on distant projections of revenues and other possibilities. More important, the value in this situation is the value of the business to the company making the investment.

Another factor that you should be aware of that typically affects the valuation of the company is the percentage of ownership or voting interest that is being sold. The sale of an ownership interest of less than 20 percent of the company will be subject to a "minority shareholder discount." That minority shareholder discount could be around 10 to 20 percent of the full value of the company, although there are some investors who will claim that it should be higher than 20 percent. For example, a prospective investor acquiring 10 percent of the voting shares would not be willing to pay a full 10 percent of the total value assigned to the company, regardless of the technique used to derive that value. This minority shareholder discount reflects the lack of influence that the investor has over the business, as opposed to an investor who bought a significant minority stake—let's say, one-third, or a controlling stake. Conversely, in those situations where you are selling a controlling interest, you can and should ask for a premium to the total value of the business.

STAGES OF FUNDING

Now, often the funding stages are determined by the investment sources. This is especially true when a company needs significant support from a very early stage, and naturally those early investors have a significant influence on the affairs of the business. In many instances the contributions of investors such as experienced venture capitalists, in terms of marketing and business development expertise, outweighs for the entrepreneur the drawbacks of relinquishing some control.

Here is an example of the evolution of valuation for a company from its inception until, and slightly after, going public. Mentor Graphics was founded in the early 1980s and was seed-funded by three major venture capital firms. At this point it sold 1 million shares at $1 per share. The development stage, which lasted 13 months, produced a product prototype, at which point the company was ready for market entry and product finalization. The company then sold another million shares in a private round, now doubling the price per share to $2. Eight months after this second financing, the company was ready for the third stage—market expansion—and sold 1.4 million shares in a third private round at 2.5 times the price per share of the second financing and 5 times the price of the initial funding—that is, at $5 per share.

Eight months after receiving the third stage of financing, the company became profitable, and 4 months thereafter it went public (IPO), issuing about 3 million shares at $18.5 per share—close to 4 times the value of the shares 12 months earlier. Finally, 3 months after the IPO the market valued the shares of Mentor Graphics at $23 per share. We didn't expect you to keep track of all the months, but if you did, you'd realize that the whole story took place within exactly 3 years. In these 3 years the company went from nonexistence to become a growing *public* company. The value of its shares increased 23 fold, in stages—from $1 to $2, then to $5, then to $18.5, and in the thirty-sixth month to $23—a return of 2200 percent for the initial investors.

In the previous example, the steps of the multistage financing were mostly dictated by the milestones that the company had to go through, to prove to investors its viability as a business. But, in other cases, by the nature of entrepreneurs being taught to find ways to gain advantage even when they are the underdog, they come up with schemes in selling minority interests which don't necessarily work to their advantage in the long run.

We have encountered emerging growth companies—and there are many of them—that do not need the hand-holding of a venture capitalist and that try to raise capital in too many consecutive stages, each time issuing shares amounting to a relatively small percentage of the company. The logic behind this system is that as the company grows, its valuation would increase; thus each consecutive stage will command a higher valuation. So, for example, if the company needs $6 million for the next 24 months, it will try to raise $2 million first at one valuation, then 8 months later raise another $2 million, hopefully at a higher valuation, and finish 8 months later with issuing shares for the last $2 million at an even higher valuation.

What's wrong with this picture? Quite a lot. First, there's a waste of time and effort involved in closing financing deals, and it usually takes the top management's attention away from growing the business. There are also significant legal and accounting expenses involved.

Then, investors are never sure how the products and markets of the company will develop in the short run, and when new problems will pop up. If you have a chance to raise a larger sum when investors have a very favorable assessment of your company, you should seriously consider doing so. Experts will tell you that an emerging growth company should always be overcapitalized. If you don't accept a sum that will carry you safely to the next level, because you want to increase your valuation by the time you need the second half of the money, it might not be available when you need it. Or you will end up going through the whole process for the same or even lower valuation. We have seen it happen.

There is another important issue that you should know when you are dealing with prestigious investors. Trying to sell the lowest possible percentage interest in your company for the highest possible valuation and then returning periodically to the table for yet more capital to seek a yet higher valuation will not work with an investment house like the Chatterjee Group, which is an investment arm of the Soros Funds. You see, an investment by such a group immediately raises a company's valuation.

In our dealings with the folks at Chatterjee on behalf of an emerging growth company seeking short- and long-term financing, they made it clear that they would not make split investments on the basis of higher and higher valuations that have been achieved in the first place, because of the original investment which they made in the business. For this and time cost-effectiveness reasons, such a group will insist on making a larger, lump-sum investment at the current valuation, and perhaps return to the table when the company makes a major stride forward. Investors, generally, will be reluctant to pay for value that they have brought to your business, in the short run.

But, of course, if development or growing marketing costs are not burdening your company and you expect to break even or even turn a profit soon, or if you already did, take less money at low valuation and keep more of the company. Microsoft, for example, was quite self-supportive in the early emerging growth years, and it didn't need to raise any significant sums of money until the IPO, when it got a good valuation. The rule is of course to plan long term and try to stay overcapitalized. The underlying principle is simple. If your company grows and succeeds you'll be rich anyway, because even 10 percent of $100 million is $10 million. But 100 percent of zero is always zero—no matter how you cut it.

To sum up, liquidation or book valuation techniques yield the lowest possible valuations that could be accorded your business. If the discussions begin at this point, it's better to part company amicably. The most commonly used technique is the EBIT valuation method, which values your business on the basis of its current earnings. This technique could yield an attractive valuation for your business if the multiple applied to the EBIT results is attractive. Next, and hopefully the technique that you will be able to employ in valuing your business, is the discounted cashflow method. Although preparing a cogent cashflow presentation can be time-consuming, since it requires you to project your business's earnings many years into the future, it has the potential for yielding the highest value for your business.

Finally, there are two approaches that are applied to businesses that have yet to generate any significant cashflow. In these situations, if a company is generating revenues, that company will be valued on a multiple of its revenues. If the company has yet to even generate revenues, then the business might be valued on the basis of a patent the company possesses or, most frequently, by the future market potential of a technology under development. The biotech industry is rich with such situations.

DETERMINING FAIR MARKET VALUE

As we stated, this chapter is not intended to be the definitive guide to financial techniques for valuation. Rather, we would like to assist you in demystifying the valuation process and discussing how to position your firm to obtain fair value and, equally important, to attract high-quality sources of capital, even if fair value might not be the highest possible value you can obtain. Value should be viewed in the broader context of your overall corporate development.

This discussion of value brings us back to one of the knowledge points we addressed in Chapter 1: Your *perceived* value is your value. Value is a topic which, like beauty, is in the eyes of the beholder. As we have previously stated, to be taken seriously, you will have to distance yourself from your feelings about your company and project that you can objectively think about your company's perceived value.

One of the first issues you must address is where to seek a fair value for your business. Should you go to the venture capitalists or merchant bankers to articulate the merits of your firm? This approach has the benefit of presenting to the potential investor the future prospects that you envision for the company. On the other hand, a financial investor in the venture capital venue is looking for significant double-digit returns—let's say, a 25 percent annual rate of return or better.

A rule of thumb which is often used is that at the seed stage a venture capital firm may offer $1 to $3 million for 40 to 60 percent of the company. At those valuation levels, the incentive of management may be so sapped that the "seedling" never makes it to a "sprout." A more seasoned company in the emerg-

ing growth category which has demonstrated its earnings potential can obtain greater sums of capital and will be able to give
up less control of the company.

FORE SYSTEMS

Fore Systems presents an example of the valuation of an emerging growth company as it underwent financings at different
stages of its development. As it entered the realm of emerging
growth status, it was able to obtain very attractive terms from a
venture capitalist. When we encountered John Baker, a former
Patricof & Co. Ventures (PCV) senior partner, he explained to
us the process he went through in courting Fore Systems. In
December 1992, PCV, under the aegis of Baker, invested $4
million in Fore Systems, which at that time had about $4 to $5
million in annualized revenues. For this investment, Patricof
received a minority stake of one-third of the company. In other
words, Baker valued the entire business at $12 million and paid
about 3 times revenues. This is admittedly not the stratospher-
ic heights you might like to see, but still a fair valuation at a relatively early stage. Nonetheless be assured that Baker still went
away happy, since the investment for him was a "70 bagger."

By the time Goldman Sachs took Fore Systems public in
May 1994, some 17 months after Patricof & Co.'s investment,
the perception of the company's value by the marketplace was
dramatically different from that offered by the venture capitalists. In its initial public offering, Fore sold 2 million shares for
net proceeds of $35,450,000; another 1 million shares were
sold by the shareholders. The 2 million shares sold by the company represented 18.9 percent of the total outstanding common
shares after the conversion of the preferred shares into common shares. With revenues of $23,506,000 for the fiscal year
ended March 31, 1994, Fore had a value of approximately $197
million, or more than 8 times its 23.5 million in revenues.
(These data are based on the number of shares outstanding in
1994, before the company split its stock 2 for 1 in 1995.) This
valuation represented an earnings multiple of approximately 95,
not far from the old saying of 100 times earnings being "cheap."

It is interesting to note that when Fore returned to the market with a second offering of stock in October 1995, demand was still strong for the company. At that time, Fore sold 4 million shares at $32.50 for 12.3 percent of the company, which put on Fore a valuation of close to 9 times the most recent 12 months' revenues of approximately $120 million. The earnings multiple for this secondary offering was 93.

The high and similar multiples of earnings and revenues placed on the company's valuation in May 1994 and October 1995—revenue multiples of 8 and 9 and earnings multiples of 93 and 95—show clearly that people still see a lot of growth potential in Fore.

As a caveat, we should note that the high valuations that Fore enjoys still don't come close to the valuations placed on companies like Netscape and Spyglass in the relatively recent Internet craze. At a certain point, both Netscape and Spyglass reached market valuations that exceeded *100 times revenues* and 200 times earnings. This happened while Netscape's revenues were only around $40 million and Spyglass' revenues were less than $4 million!

FUTURE VALUE AT ADP

The value accorded Fore and other more recent IPOs stands in contrast to our discussions with Henry Taub and his IPO experience of 1961. When his company went public in what at that time was perceived as a *strong* IPO market, the market valued ADP's shares at only $1.2 million—2 times its $600,000 in revenues, a valuation that might be placed on a company by an astute venture capitalist, rather than by a buoyant IPO market. (In 1996 dollars, the above would correspond to $3 million in revenues and a company valuation of $6 million.)

But then, Henry Taub has never been too concerned about *current* valuation. He would rather focus his efforts on growth—which means *future* value—than spend his time shopping around for the best deal. He also knows that "who" makes the deal is often as important as or more important than the numbers, because the quality and stature of your investor in the current round will strongly affect your attractiveness in the next round.

In his interview with us, Taub explained how ADP persuaded Oppenheimer to become the lead underwriter for its IPO, even though at that time Oppenheimer didn't have the distribution capability to sell a retail offering into the over-the-counter (OTC) market. Taub told Oppenheimer that if it refused to put its name on the prospectus, preferably as the lead underwriter (on the left side), he would start shopping around to get the best deal he could get. Well, Oppenheimer agreed, and judging by the meteoric growth of ADP, be assured that when it came time for the founders to cash in, ADP's valuation was high up there. Still, in the short term, ADP sacrificed valuation to gain a specific underwriter, and dedicated the time it would have taken to shop for another deal to grow the company. Thinking in terms of growth and future valuation, instead of current valuation, definitely paid off.

But still, times have changed and the high priests of higher valuation preaching the merits of selling stock at much higher multiples of revenues, not to mention very high multiples of earnings, might find more disciples now than in 1961. In addition, part of the reason people may be willing to pay more for IPOs these days is the greater interest in IPOs, especially for companies that have the ability to dominate a market, and the amount of money flooding into the equity markets.

As adventure capital funds have become less adventuresome, the private market has begun to yield some alternative sources of capital and an alternative method for unlocking the value of a business with which you may be associated. For example, you may be a frustrated corporate executive (sometimes that may seem like a definition, rather than a description) who sees the opportunity to buy a product or idea from the company for which you are working. The product or idea could ultimately achieve growth company status, but it does not fit the corporate strategy of your employer. As we said, value is in the eyes of the beholder; that value is something your corporate employer may not be able to behold. It is still possible to unlock the value of that idea.

EUCLID PARTNERS

Euclid Partners, a New York–based firm, has little to do with geometry and a lot to do with seizing on the opportunities being ignored by the new, more focused companies of corporate America. It has been the key in some instances to unlocking the value trapped in the coffers of corporate America. Fred Wilson, the founder of Euclid whose exploits were praised in a *Wall Street Journal* article, seeks out projects or ideas that have been developed in the bosom of corporate America, but that the parent company no longer wants to fund. Using relatively small sums of money, Wilson is investing in businesses which have the potential to be the emerging growth companies of the future. And his efforts have not gone overlooked or unrewarded.

In one instance, Wilson invested in a group of Ingram Industries executives, part of a conglomerate with large publishing interests. The company, Upgrade Corporation of America, a provider of automated computer help services for high-technology companies, received a $1.5 million investment from Euclid. In a short period of time, the investment increased in "geometric" proportions. One day not so long into the corporate existence of the company, a Japanese software company "upgraded" Wilson's investment: It bought the company for $7 million. And that's during an era when Japanese investors were having very little to do with investment in America or elsewhere.

FINDING A STRATEGIC FIT

Another possible venue in which a company can obtain fair value for its business is through an alignment with a strategic partner. Perhaps you feel that working with the financial types might undermine your freedom. Quarter by quarter, you have to hit your numbers. So you begin to think that a strategic partner might place the greatest value on your firm. Rather than seeking double-digit returns, the strategic investor will focus on the overall value of your company to its own business. True, this may yield a higher possible valuation than might be obtained from a financial investor. But if the "strategic fit" doesn't work, you might end up being jettisoned in the latest corporate reengineering.

Of course, running the risk of being jettisoned might well be worth it, if as they say the "price is right." When we read in *The Wall Street Journal* the headline "Big Blue Opts to Pay Steep Price to Fill Hole in Software Strategy," we thought we were reading another article about the acquisition of Lotus by IBM. Instead, for a mere $743 million IBM bought Tivoli, a software firm that allows companies to manage networks composed of different brands of computers.

The price paid by IBM equals about 15 times Tivoli's 1995 revenues and 135 times its earnings. By contrast, IBM paid about 3.5 times revenues for Lotus. However, in fairness to the number crunchers at IBM, the price paid for Tivoli was only about 25 percent over Tivoli's stock price, compared with a near 100 percent premium paid for Lotus. Perhaps the average of the two transactions would represent fair value to IBM.

Another possibility for unlocking the value in your business is to sell a minority stake to a corporate partner. An example is i-Stat, which makes a hand-held device that allows blood to be analyzed at a patient's bedside. With FY1995 revenues of $20 million and first half of FY1996 revenues of $13 million, i-Stat still drew the attention of the multibillion-dollar Hewlett-Packard. In exchange for $61 million, Hewlett-Packard received 14 percent of i-Stat; that deal placed a $436 million valuation on the company, or a multiple of 22 times revenue. For those of you who are looking for a multiple of earnings (P/E ratio) or of EBIT for i-Stat, you will find it listed as "N.A.," or "not applicable." The earnings per share of i-Stat at the time the Hewlett-Packard investment was made was negative $1.90 per share, and the cost of sales was almost $2 million greater than i-Stat's revenues. As we said before, there is such a thing as the "cashless" flow valuation, especially when a company has a product that is strategically important to a large corporate partner.

Strategic importance can sometimes go beyond the simple notion of contributing in terms of improved or somewhat different products. Recently we heard about a medical device company, Medtronic, paying $214.6 million in stock (10 million shares for $21.46 per share) for a small emerging growth company called InStent. InStent went public only in mid-1995 at $13 per share and closed 1995 at $15 per share. The valuation placed on InStent by Medtronic was 65 percent higher than the IPO valuation—not a bad gain for a company which finished last year with only $2.4 million in revenues.

What's even more interesting is that the valuation placed on InStent was almost 90 times its revenues, compared with the 22 times revenues that HP placed on i-Stat—a company in the same general market sector. But here is the scoop. Medtronic bought InStent mainly because the acquisition might allow it to circumvent some Johnson & Johnson (J&J) patents in the very lucrative stents market that Medtronic wishes to play a major role in. (Stents are minute sleeve-like tubes that are implanted by surgeons in arteries treated in angioplasty procedures to prevent reclosing.) So Medtronic's executives are actually hedging their bets—and they are ready to pay a higher than usual price.

If you cannot find an adventure capitalist, a deep pocket like Hewlett-Packard, or if your luck at "geometry" isn't as good as that of the executives at Upgrade, another possibility for unlocking the value of your business is to turn to the somewhat more mysterious public offering market to which we have alluded previously. Should you seize the moment, when it appears that the initial public offering market is frothy? It's always nice to have your company valued by the market at a level that will make you wealthier than you ever dreamed. The IPO market, however, is subject to the vagaries of what is called the "window of opportunity." That window can be affected either by overall market conditions or by industry-specific trends.

In 1993 and 1994, there was a "window of opportunity" for biotechnology stocks, but that window was temporarily bolted shut when one of the key underwriting firms, D. Blech & Co., collapsed. Alas, nothing is forever and there is now revived interest in the biotechnology sector.

Just a short word of caution. When tapping the IPO market, remember that high-fliers like Netscape are walking a very high tightrope of expectations from the public market investors, especially institutional investors, and there is no "net" under

Netscape if it disappoints. So far, Netscape has gone from over $100 a share down to more than half of its all-time high. One indicator of disenchantment with the valuation placed on Netscape occurred on March 5, 1996, when the Times Mirror, seeking to lock in some gains on its investment in Netscape, sold an innovative "derivative security" through Morgan Stanley. The derivative security was called a PEP—Premium Equity Participating securities. But it was not such a pep for Netscape, since in the process it lost the interest and backing of a very important strategic partner. As the newspapers reported, the Times Mirror's Netscape stake "is, a leftover of a now rejected strategy that was to take the newspaper...into elaborate investments in emerging multimedia technology."

TAPPING THE IPO MARKET

Now that we have gotten caution out of the way, let's get back to what you really want to hear and what we really want to talk about: how to become rich, if not famous, by tapping the IPO market for higher valuations. In a *Wall Street Journal* article (February 9, 1996) entitled "Fortune Smiles on Some Entrepreneurs Who Held Large Stakes in Firms at IPO," several significant observations are made about the buoyant IPO of 1995. The article observes that the percentage ownership interest in a company that the founder is able to retain is "directly related to the stage at which a company receives its initial funding." Yes, you might have suspected as much.

Furthermore, as we all can appreciate, companies that need financing before they have any revenue often must give up a majority percentage to their investors. Yes, but the IPO market of 1995 made a difference, because public investors were willing to "generously value companies that don't have any profits or sales, entrepreneurs got to keep more of their ventures," according to Charles Federman, managing partner of Broadview Associates. Good news, if you are able to sneak through that "window of opportunity."

Before we finish with the frothy IPO market of 1995, we do not want to leave you with the impression that only the technology stocks participated and only the young hotshots made out like bandits. According to the *WSJ* article, the oldest entre- preneur to hit the big time was Alfred Mann, a youngster of 69. Mann is the founder of a provider of infusion systems for dia- betics. The value of his stake at the time the company went public was a mere $89 million. Admittedly, it's not quite the $262 million that Jim Clark of Netscape was able to garner. But we are sure that Mann is enjoying his newfound wealth.

BOSTON CHICKEN GOES PUBLIC

It may seem that 1995 was a unique year for IPOs, or that the IPO market favors only dazzling technology. There is franchise value in other things, and in fact there is franchise value in fran- chises in years other than 1995: Enter Boston Chicken, which tapped the frothy IPO market of 1993. 1993 was also consid- ered to be a frothy year for IPOs; in fact, whenever you read a story about the IPO market, it seems to be called frothy.

Boston Chicken, an operator and franchiser of food service stores that specialize in (yes) chicken, is noteworthy for many things. In our opinion, it would be noteworthy alone for the management which the company has attracted. In its earliest stages, from 1988 to mid-1992, the company was under the management of George Naddaff, a successful operator of Kentucky Fried Chicken franchises. After a change in the own- ership structure, Naddaff left and Scott Beck entered. As described in the public offering prospectus, Scott Beck and his father, Lawrence Beck, are the founders and the driving forces behind several businesses, including Blockbuster Video. Lawrence Beck is billed as a cofounder of Waste Management Inc., the current WMX Technologies.

When the Becks decided to take Boston Chicken public in 1993, it was a well-established growth story. In 1990, Boston Chicken had slightly less than $3.5 million in revenues and had established 14 outlets; by the end of 1993, the company was generating over 10 times that amount of revenues and estab- lished 167 outlets. In November 1993, with the assistance of the "thundering bull" underwriter Merrill Lynch, Boston

Chicken sold an 11 percent stake consisting of 1.9 million shares and raised $38 million. With revenues exceeding $36 million for the four quarters preceding the offering, and negative earnings, Boston Chicken was valued at 9 times revenues and at an "N.A." (not applicable) times earnings. And as they used to say on the classic TV show *Laugh In*, that is not another chicken joke.

As we mentioned, obtaining the highest valuation for your business should not be the determining factor when seeking to place a value on your business, nor should it determine which route you take to unlock the value of your business. Value is intertwined with your overall corporate objectives. And, often, you may have to consider the investment banker's objective and point of view. If your underwriter insists on a lower valuation of your company than you envisioned for your dream IPO, you might want to listen carefully. Starting at a lower valuation allows the stock to grow and to deliver a return on investment, which encourages investors to make future investments in your company and in future IPOs of your underwriter. This can make you happy and your underwriter happy at the same time.

VISHAY GOES CONVERTIBLE

In his book *Never the Last Journey*, Felix Zandman, the founder of Vishay Intertechnology, Inc.—the now $1.2 billion multinational electronic concern, which he founded in the early 1960s—speaks of the importance of his long-standing investment banker in making his success possible. (After we spoke with Zandman, he referred us to his recently published book, which describes in detail the accounts of growing Vishay.) Vishay had gone public in 1972 with the firm of Bear, Stearns. A friend of Zandman had been a stockbroker at the Philadelphia office of Bear, Stearns and had introduced Zandman to the investment bankers. Personal contacts can be one of the better ways to go if you should decide on the public market route.

In 1980, Vishay wanted to tap the market with a convertible bond, and Zandman decided to split the mandate between Bear, Stearns and the firm at which Zandman's friend and broker now worked. At the moment of truth, the new firm on the offering seemed unhappy with the pricing and the way the deal was shaping up. The investment bank intimated that it wanted to "pull the deal"; such a move could have limited the future access of Vishay to the market.

It was at this point that one of the most charismatic figures on Wall Street stepped into the picture: Ace Greenberg of Bear, Stearns. When Ace Greenberg saw what was happening he said, "What the hell is this? I'll take the whole issue myself." With but a few more words, Zandman and Greenberg made a deal. As Zandman puts it, "Since then Ace Greenberg has handled all our public offerings. Our relationship quickly developed to the point where we could and did take care of everything over the phone; I had found him a person of utter trustworthiness as well as great professional acumen."

Although Zandman's experience took place when his company was already beyond the emerging growth stage, it is still worth noting, since it demonstrates the importance of factors other than price when you make the decision to tap either the private or public markets. As we can all learn from the story, you should not choose a banker on price alone; rather, the quality of the person should weigh heavily in your decision. Indeed, for those of you who decide to take the public offering route, we hope that in looking back over the experience you will be able to sing the same praises as Zandman.

Before concluding the discussion on valuation, we would like to share with you some observations that we have gleaned on valuation and that can further assist in demystifying the valuation process. First, many financial advisers put significant emphasis on "positioning" your company—or, stated another way, on how to present your company in a positive light to prospective investors. Whether you are a tech, biotech, or neither-of-the-above tech firm, you must "position" yourself in the broader social, cultural, and economic mix taking place in the marketplace. Yes, that sounds like a high-minded and abstract statement. Nonetheless, the burden is on you to present to the prospective investor the larger context in which your firm can offer an attractive rate of return to that investor.

It's the big-picture game that many investors are playing, and you will significantly enhance the value of your firm by articulating the context in which your firm can yield returns for prospective investors. Fore Systems can be viewed as a company that has positioned itself well, since these are times when there is a proliferation of LANs (local area networks) and WANs (wide area networks).

VISIONS AND PARADIGM SHIFTS

Now, for some more important concepts that can help in your self-presentation to those prospective investors. Talk about the "vision thing." Investors are not buying what they see in front of them. They are buying the future—the future with all its hopes and illusions of unlimited growth and, of course, untold capital gains. By convincing a prospective investor that you have a "realistic" vision, you enhance value. We have heard from many analysts that they were attracted to Starbucks, for example, because the founder, Howard Schultz, is a "visionary." Similar statements have been made about the individuals who operate Boston Market, the former Boston Chicken, including Scott Beck.

Another good concept to dazzle the prospective investor with is: "paradigm shift." As in, "My company is part of a global paradigm shift." (We caution you to limit the paradigm shift to global trends, rather than getting into what some may consider to be "extraterrestrial" trends; otherwise you may not be taken seriously.) Being part of a "paradigm shift" is slightly different from the "vision thing."

The "vision thing" grounds your company's value in existing trends and then extrapolates them to the future. The "paradigm shift" focuses more on the potential changes that can and will take place. We think that's what people like Michael Moe, principal at Montgomery Securities, believe when he tells us that "Netscape is like a castle in the sky." Part of the cachet of Netscape or other cyberspace companies is that they have convinced people that the Internet will fundamentally change the way people do business and, indeed, even change the way people live their daily lives.

Finally, another important qualitative factor has recently gotten wide attention. An article in the April 29, 1996, issue of *Fortune* discussed one of the most important concepts for emerging growth companies: the law of increasing returns. Classical economics has a primary tenet: the law of diminishing returns. In other words, the more you make or sell, the harder it gets.

By contrast, the law of "increasing returns" states that the more someone makes or sells something, the easier it becomes. W. Brian Arthur, a Stanford economist, put it this way: "The more people use your product, the more advantage you have—or put another way, the bigger your installed base, the better off you are." This can be summed up as the tendency for something that has gotten ahead to get still further ahead. Indeed, the principle explains the success of such firms as Microsoft and ADP. In his book *The Road Ahead*, Bill Gates refers to the law of "increasing returns" as "positive feedback." When presenting the rationale for the future growth prospects of your business, you can harness this concept to demonstrate that your growth rate can be sustainable many years into the future and that you are thus entitled to a higher valuation.

Valuation is an art rather than a science and that art becomes a very fine art, indeed, when you are valuing emerging growth companies. Michael Moe, an emerging company analyst with Montgomery Securities and formerly with Lehman Brothers, has adopted a philosophy for assessing the value of emerging growth companies: the "4 P's"—people, product, potential, and price. When speaking of price, he states that he looks for "reasonable price, which doesn't mean cheap." The investor should look 3, 5, even 10 years into the future and so should you when valuing your business.

Moe also cautions emerging growth managers to avoid being shortsighted by taking "everything off the table." It's better for managers to create reasonable expectations that can be met and to build goodwill when valuing their businesses. The goodwill created by a fair valuation of your business also enables the emerging growth company manager to tap financing sources again. As we said before, focus on obtaining fair value for your firm, rather than on the highest possible price.

Moe's advice is astute, especially since it does come from someone who has been to the inner sanctum of the Temple of Finance. However, when valuing your business, you should take into account many different perspectives, including those of merchant bankers or other entrepreneurs. Thomas Itin, founder and cofounder of many firms and current CEO of Williams Controls, has a longer list than the 4 P's of Michael Moe when it comes to valuing businesses; some of the criteria do overlap.

The number-one criterion for Itin in valuing a business is "positive cashflow" on a monthly basis. The manager must have adequate financing at the beginning and adequate financing to do what he or she wants to do in the future. Itin focuses on the E (earnings) in the P/E multiple. Other attributes that he looks for are self-assurance of the manager and the key people who are going to carry the business forward; the market and product knowledge of the managers; the focus of the company; and hands-on management balanced by the ability to delegate.

Finally, as long as we have made the circuit of people we have talked to about valuation, we would also like to include an important perspective from Chip Ottness, a small-cap portfolio manager at J. P. Morgan Investment. "There is a band around fair valuation," says Ottness. In fact, there is no ground zero when it comes to valuation.

The point that Ottness was making was that the market risk adjusts around this "band of fair valuation." For example, assume that a projected earnings stream, X, should yield a valuation of Y on a business. However, if there are certain obvious risks associated with achieving that X stream of revenues, it makes people nervous, and "I'll give them a 'haircut' because the company will never make it to Y—and the market adjusts for it," says Ottness.

For example, Ottness points out that one of the key factors in this risk adjustment process is the management team. The emphasis in this instance is on the "team." The value of a business is directly related to the entrepreneur's ability to delegate and share power with other members as the company grows in size. If the market perceives that all the power is concentrated in the hands of the founder and CEO, it will make people nervous and the market will adjust accordingly by giving the stock a "haircut" for that risk. The company may be inhibited from achieving its full potential.

You might conclude from these discussions with Messrs. Moe and Ottness that the "numbers" are not important; "numbers" certainly are important to these individuals. Be assured that they will do their homework in "spreading" your financials on the most sophisticated valuation software—either developed by their own firm or bought from third-party vendors. Moe, however, appropriately puts the valuation of an emerging growth company in context. As a company moves up the market capitalization curve—from micro, to small, to mid, to large, the fundamentals do make more of a difference. After all, there's more data upon which to base a fundamental analysis of a large-cap company. But for the emerging growth stock company, it's more qualitative and more fun. And, to keep things in perspective, the valuation process should be fun for you as well.

As important as it is for you to have fun with the valuation process, you should remember that valuation is only part of the overall dynamics of the business. As Henry Taub of ADP mentioned to us, after his company went public he did not check the price of the stock every day. Instead, the founders of ADP went on with the business of their business; they continued to build and to diversify ADP.

THIRTEEN BIG RULES

It is time to sum up the lessons we learned from the analysis and examples in this chapter. These are the rules which we believe you must follow to obtain the best *fair* valuation for your company, and to create a goodwill with your investors and strategic partners. This formula of fair valuation and goodwill not only will attract them to support you in this round, but will bear fruit into the future and propel your company into healthy and hopefully fast growth.

1. If you shoot for the stars in valuation, you might get shot down.

2. Be very high on your company's potential. If you don't believe in yourself, who will? But explain your vision and prove its uniqueness and feasibility.

3. Enhance your team with people who have what's considered by investors to be desirable management qualities. Share and delegate responsibilities to show team play. And don't forget to share the riches.

4. Estimate the full scope of your needs 5 years ahead. Always stay overcapitalized. In each financing stage take more than you need—no matter what the exact valuation is.

5. Do not split raising capital into too many stages just because of valuation considerations. Dilution and control are important, but never as important as healthy growth.

6. Study other, similar cases and be prepared to present them as support for your valuation estimate. People feel comfortable with precedents.

7. Make the rounds, but stay focused. Evaluate all reasonable modalities, but don't make the quest for higher valuation consume too much of the time you should devote instead to growing your business. If the company grows, you'll be rich anyway; if it fails, current valuation won't help you.

8. Use emissaries (board members, intermediaries) to feel the pulse and to create trust.

9. Get quality sources, even if they offer less current valuation. Investment source identity is worth more than current valuation in the emerging growth years.

10. Get expert advice. Experts know better what's accepted and reasonable.

11. Accounting practices that affect valuation should be carefully considered. People who pay too high because of creative accounting that manipulates the company's distribution of sales, profits, or expenses might sue later, or kill your future capability to access investment sources.

12. Look to the future, not the present. Create goodwill with investors by establishing current value that has ample space to grow and delivers profits to them. Choose your strategy on the basis, not of current valuation, but of potential future growth—which means future valuation.

13. As always, your perceived value *is* your value. Asking unreasonably high valuation, or selling out for too little, are both a turnoff.

When a company is perceived by many to be overvalued, in these times, we could call it Netscapism. But, then, the higher-than-traditional valuations accorded many companies might just be a sign of the times when companies such as Fore, Boston Chicken, and America Online can grow tenfold in a couple of years. And, similarly, companies like Microsoft, ADP, and Compaq seem to defy the basic laws of classical economics of diminishing returns and continue going and going and going, but are never gone.

THE ATTRACTIVE BUSINESS MODEL FOR THE EMERGING COMPANY AND ITS STAGES OF EVOLUTION

INTERNAL GROWTH, GROWTH BY ACQUISITION, GROWTH BY UNIT MULTIPLICATION, AND SOMEWHERE IN BETWEEN

How would you characterize the explosive growth of America Online (AOL) in the first half of the 1990s? You might say that's easy—AOL grew by internal growth. Its product line expanded, its number of subscribers grew, and the usage per subscriber also grew. Case in point: AOL's client base grew from 200,000 in 1992 to over 5 million in early 1996. Basic membership revenues are proportionate to the number of members—who pay approximately $120 each annually in membership fees. Therefore, basic membership revenues increased 25-fold in that period. AOL revenues have also increased in another way. The average revenue per subscriber has risen steadily, primarily because subscribers use more paid hours (those that aren't included in the basic membership).

But was AOL's growth really an *internal* growth per se? AOL's brochure states that providing consumers with breadth and depth of content has always been a key component in AOL's formula for success. And it has been indeed adding content that provides differentiation, ranging from special-interest to branded content that offers mass-market appeal. How did AOL accomplish that? Well, a major part of the formula included strategic investments in, and acquisitions of other companies, those we call content providers. It looks like internal growth was highly leveraged by acquisitions and the contributions of other companies. Seems like a different business model, doesn't it?

The attractive business model for the emerging growth company of the 1990s and into the twenty-first century is not like the Model T of the Henry Ford era. You can have it in any color you like, so long as it's "black." In sifting through the formative stages of emerging growth companies, we realized that many shades of "gray" characterize the genesis and growth of these companies. In fact, after viewing the many shades of gray of the current era, we were unable to distinguish between the black and white of simpler times.

Still, we find that these gray areas are not made up of a purely homogeneous distribution—that, so to speak, anything works—but rather are built around distinct clusters of strategies and tactics with overlapping boundaries.

THE BUSINESS OF BEING

Business models are associated with two distinct areas: being and growing. Being relates to the basic premise that the company was founded upon. Growing is the process through which company development is achieved. Growing has two components: the how and the when—how the growth is achieved, and in what stages.

THE HERD PHENOMENON

From the macroinvestment perspective, at times it appears that trends or "herd" phenomena dictate business models. In the 1980s, we were flooded with emerging PC and software companies—all of which were seemingly built and functioned in similar ways. At the start of this decade, the biotech sector had its moment in the sun. The fountain of youth and panacea for all that ailed us was supposed to be found in the test tube at the neighborhood "biotech store." But lo and behold, again, all these companies looked like genetic clones.

Now, as we move forward toward the end of the century, new principles are appearing: for example, satisfying consumer needs with designer coffee beans or catering to drivers in the fast lane on cyberspace's highways, on which only information can travel.

This kind of clustering by popular sectors definitely proves the important role that "trends" play in boosting and propelling a *basket* of emerging growth companies. In the early 1980s they used to say that *any* company that had some reasonable product and fair management would be funded or even taken public—if the company's product was related to computers or medical electronics. Later, in the second part of the 1980s, apparently, more stringent criteria were developed to measure which company had what it takes. These criteria didn't change much in essence—they only shifted the burden of proof. Adding executives, preferably from companies with three initials (IBM, ITT, AT&T), or Nobel laureates to a team of otherwise talented hungry entrepreneurs seemed to be one way to curb the adventuresomeness of the early 1980s.

Today we are more sophisticated and we recognize that the factors which measure a company's potential to grow fall more into gray areas. There are no prescriptions—only guidelines. But the recent Internet craze proves that the herd effect in business will be around probably as long as businesspeople are around.

Trend following, or the herd system, actually fits well with the paradigm, attributed to the venture capitalists, that you might have heard whispered in the halls of finance. The claim is that as a rule of thumb, out of 10 companies you invest in, 5 will go bust, on 3 you break even, and on 2 you make a killing—and hopefully recoup your other losses, and even manage to turn a profit. The fact that many such venture capital firms didn't manage to start new funds after the first or second were fully invested may be a not so subtle indication that, perhaps, following trends is not sufficient.

The public markets are more forgiving toward the underwriters, and therefore on Wall Street the trend system works even better. Not that there are no failures; to the contrary, there are plenty. But the early investors in an IPO—who are the core infrastructure crucial to the underwriters—usually manage to make money even if later the stock takes a dive.

But the real issue becomes poignant. Here you immediately encounter an obvious paradox or more accurately, a big dilemma.

The trend or much-maligned herd phenomenon raises a key concern, or more appropriately a perplexing dilemma, when you switch from the statistical views of investors to the individual impact on each emerging company. As an emerging growth company founder and manager, if you ride the bandwagon of a trend and go with the flow, you will share in the updraft bestowed on all similar companies. You will be the subject of less scrutiny, since at least some of the due diligence has already been performed on other ventures. On the other hand, a prospective financier or attractive business partner might look the other way and proclaim your firm as just a "me too" company.

TWO SCENARIOS

In our nature, we seek to be unique, and it is these fascinating, innovative companies that can attract some of the most talented people and most lucrative financial backers. But the agony of being a "one of a kind" company in the business world is that you have to learn everything through your own mistakes. You are the trailblazer and that trail is blazed by mistakes that can cost you your corporate existence. Whether in Eastern philosophy or business philosophy, you have to position yourself to avoid being the high-risk, unproved "new kid on the block," while still coming early enough to the table that your company avoids being called just a "me too." As such, there are two scenarios.

In the first scenario, if you are one of the early entrants, you have the chance to become the victim of the natural weeding-out process. (A chance you may prefer not to take.) While you have the advantage of being there first with a particular product or service, you also have the disadvantage of being first with making all the mistakes. Where do you market your product? How do you fine-tune the manufacturing process? Who will be interested in investing in you?

By contrast, in the second scenario—if you are a latecomer—the interest of the market might already be shifting to another sector. Stated another way, the growth potential of that market might have already been absorbed by the first entrants. By being a "me too" company under such circumstances, you'll encounter not only a lack of enthusiasm but also the sediments of possible disappointments with other companies in the trend sector and the most common of all objections: Why do we need another whatever-you-call-it widget company?

To spend another moment dwelling on the dilemma. Let's say, you are the new kid on the block—a pioneering first (or second) in your market. Ask people and they'll tell you that it's tough and getting even tougher. The reason is simple: Businesspeople, whether they be the truly adventurous capitalists or potential customers, are risk-averse. Everybody talks about taking calculated risks, but the new kid on the block is not included in any definition of calculated risk.

Microsoft, which in the late 1970s and early 1980s was the quintessential new kid on the block, had practically no infusion of outside capital until it went public. Granted, Bill Gates built the business on alliances with larger and smaller corporations, but these were de facto client/vendor relationships. By the time that major investors were knocking on the doors, Gates didn't need them.

Java, Sun Microsystems' language for interactive computing, is one of the current Internet megaproducts. It's a programming language that's designed to run on the Internet and other computer networks. With Java, users can download bits of programs from the Internet, as needed, instead of buying today's operating systems and application of software, such as word processors. Java was first developed over 10 years ago, but its developer didn't get the recognition and resources until Sun Microsystems turned it into one of the most revolutionary products in current vogue. This brings us to another observation and that is that new kids on the block might have to wait many years until they are accepted as "one of the guys."

So, how should you position your emerging growth company to be attractive? Let's be practical. You can't take a new kid on the block and reposition it as a "me too" company or vice versa. Both extremes are dangerous, and therefore your goal is to move away from the extremes. Repositioning must allow you to turn a me-too company into a *somewhat* unique company, and a new kid on the block into a *somewhat* familiar company.

The emerging growth company strategies of Lehman Brothers, as reflected in a document called *Philosophy, Strategy & Product* (for growth companies), clearly emphasize product differentiation as a criterion for choosing high-growth contenders. Michael Moe, formerly first VP and emerging company analyst with Lehman and now principal at Montgomery Securities, looks at better mousetraps as "recipes for disaster." Again, a better-mousetrap strategy can serve a small, steady family business very well. But high growth requires product differentiation.

You might justifiably argue that the boundaries of product differentiation must be very vague. After all, you can't claim that successful companies like Wal-Mart and Boston Chicken invented the "wheel" in their market sector. So, perhaps, we should look to some well-known examples to get a clearer understanding of the boundaries of product differentiation.

Take, for example, the emerging years of Sam Walton's Wal-Mart. Wal-Mart, which developed out of Walton's five-and-dime stores, could have been perceived for all practical purposes as a me-too company. Walton didn't invent the concept of variety stores; in fact, he started his retail career by buying a Ben Franklin franchise. Then, in some locations, for example, he was competing head on with two other, "similar" stores in the center of the same town. (Doesn't appear like too much of a product differentiation, does it?) Even as he moved to larger-format stores, which evolved into Wal-Marts, Walton basically followed the general concepts of preexisting retailers. Discount retailing wasn't his brainchild either.

Nevertheless, Wal-Mart was growing, and through its emerging growth years Wal-Mart was always perceived as unique, and Walton was considered to be a major innovator—so much so that he practically shed the me-too stigma. Walton achieved this by a very innovative business model, which as we suggested previously repositioned a me-too concept (with a twist) into *somewhat* unique—a new stigma which later, as Wal-Mart developed, reinforced itself.

Wal Mart's business model included first and foremost the concept of *deep* discount. Walton admits in his book *Made In America* that in the early days of Wal-Mart they didn't have anywhere near the emphasis on quality that they had later. What they were obsessed with, according to Walton, was keeping the prices below everybody else's. The "dedication" to that idea was *total*. Then, came the famous Small-Town America strategy, whereby Walton discovered that *small towns* in America's heartland can support *large stores*—if the price is right. A less-publicized but crucial component of Walton's business model was the concept of saturating geographical markets with Wal-Mart stores before expanding to new territories. This is a strategy that many of the retailers now follow routinely. Today, for example, in certain areas in New York City, you have three large Staples office supply stores in an area that includes less than ten city blocks and two avenues. Finally, one might say that Walton's "people" strategy of associates and partners completed the loop of differentiation, which later reinforced itself.

In the opera *Barber of Seville,* one of the lead characters describes how creating a rumor works. It starts with a very light breeze entering one person's ears, which when expressed by the mouth enters other people's ears as a light wind, which then multiplies and amplifies into a strong wind which finally ends up becoming a tornado.

Creating a successful product differentiation early on is like starting a long journey with the first step. As we already mentioned in this book, small differences at the initial stages can result in major differentiation as things unfold in the life of a company and the market it represents. Microsoft's Windows operating system is an excellent example of a small early differentiation that turned into a major difference in the final count. In fact, Apple claimed that Windows was practically copied from Apple's operating system.

Starbucks, which created the concept and first chain of coffee bars in the United States, could have been considered at that time a new kid on the block. After all, the health authorities were for many years proclaiming the hazardous effects of coffee. And those people who didn't pay attention to the health fanatics could get their coffee in countless coffee shops or even regular bars. When Starbucks started establishing "coffee bars"—dedicated to coffee and its derivatives—it had what we call a differentiated product, perhaps even too differentiated.

To prove that the coffee bar is a viable business model in the United States, it wasn't enough to compare it to the success of its cousins in Milan, Italy—where Schultz (Starbucks' founder) picked up the concept. It was also not enough to point out the me-too ingredients of coffee bars—by comparing the enterprise with, say, a fast-food chain. The Starbucks business model wasn't even as close to the ubiquitous fast-food chain concept as, for example, Boston Market (once Boston Chicken) was.

How did Starbucks prove its viability? It first had to established and prove the success of its first three stores. But that's not so bad, because if you know anything about retail chains, you would know that almost all of them had to prove first the viability of their business models on a small scale—namely, a few units. The advantage of being a new kid on the block in such a business is that you can develop into becoming the number-one "name brand," a position that usually presents your followers with a tough barrier for market penetration.

THE BUSINESS OF GROWING

Up to this point the discussion has focused on the "being" aspect of the emerging growth company's business model. We have demonstrated how companies should adapt to the gray areas, between the extreme stigmas of me too and new kid on the block. The next step is to consider the "growth" aspect of an emerging company. There are three fairly distinct business models for growth:

- Internal or "organic" growth
- Growth by acquisition
- Growth by multiplication or franchising

INTERNAL GROWTH

The internal or organic growth of the emerging growth company is characterized by the development of new products or services and markets—thus fueling its growth. Improving on the products or services, increasing their scope of applications, and growing the customer base are all part of the internal-growth business model.

We wish to point out that there is another form of internal growth, and it is not a contradiction in terms. It is growth by a multitude of small tuck-in acquisitions. The main difference between this category and our second business model for growth is that the purpose of small tuck-in acquisition is to enhance the same product the company has or to increase, say geographically, the same market segment. Good examples are the acquisition of small content providers in the early emerging growth years of America Online, or the acquisition of small service bureaus by ADP when, after its IPO, it wanted to expand nationally.

GROWTH BY ACQUISITION

Growth by acquisition, the second business model, refers to purchasing other synergistic or quasi-synergistic emerging growth businesses that fit with the company's general strategy. These acquisitions usually add complete product lines and may open totally new market segments. Furthermore, the purpose in these acquisitions is to bring a large chunk of income to the company, because you can simply add the revenues of the acquired company to your balance sheet.

Thomas Itin, CEO of the emerging growth Williams Controls, put an interesting twist on growth by acquisition. He told us in an interview: "Growth by acquisition gives you insights into how people are doing things. Are they doing it better? It brings in 'new blood.'"

GROWTH BY MULTIPLICATION

Growth by multiplication, the third business model for growth, refers mostly to the retail or service chain stores (fast-food, clothing, office supply, tax preparation). In this model a company uses an initially successful formula and gradually increases the number of units by expanding first locally, then nationally, and eventually internationally. This expansion can manifest itself through company-owned or franchised operation.

There are some interesting advantages to growth by unit expansion, which makes this business model one of the favorites among investors. First, the development costs associated with growth are relatively low. Once the company has developed its flagship unit, and rolled out two or three units which were proven successful, it can grow a hundredfold with very modest improvements. At the same time, a company relying on internal growth has to continue developing new products and spend heavily on research and development.

Then, of course, there's a reduced risk involved in the growth. It is safe to assume that if the business is successful in three existing locations, it will be successful in another 100 carefully chosen locations. The increased buying power of an organization that's growing by unit expansion makes the cost of goods decline and consequently the profits grow as the number of units grows. The corporate overhead doesn't increase proportionally with the number of units. As a result, the corporate overhead per operating unit declines with the number of units—a very favorable outcome. Training and assembling new teams become easier as the company grows. Increased efficiency and the usage of the same training personnel and facilities for a larger output allow the company to turn out new well-operating units faster and at a lower cost. Finally, the presence of more units provides the company with increased exposure and popularity—the equivalent of added advertising without spending additional advertising dollars.

There is a growth model for the emerging growth company which we don't list separately, because it works together with the other three—that is, increasing growth by corporate partnering and strategic alliances. All three models of growth can be leveraged by strategic alliances to enhance growth, often significantly. You'll find an elaboration on this area in the various examples to come in this chapter, and in a dedicated chapter on corporate partnering.

Which business model is the best? There's no such thing—each product, market, and management team must be designed to fit the business model to its particular environment. Which business model is preferred by investors? Well, different strokes for different folks.

Chip Ottness, manager of a large small-cap fund (over $1 billion in assets), at J. P. Morgan Investment in New York, told us in an interview that from his experience companies that grow internally are more successful than companies that grow by acquisitions (in the context of the second business model, as defined in this book). In acquisitions, companies often pay a high price to acquire a company which eventually will not produce as much profit as projected. Ottness also feels that many companies that make acquisitions are sometimes compelled to become, what he calls "poor corporate citizens"—that is, they fire a lot of people and might demoralize the remaining employees who are supposed to lay the golden eggs for them. Furthermore, acquisitions often involve payment by stock, which increases dilution and creates what Ottness calls "funny money." Although Chip Ottness doesn't believe in "wide-angle" synergistic acquisitions (like ITT acquiring all kinds of businesses), he does believe in tuck-in acquisitions (like the consolidation in the waste management industry led by Browning-Ferris).

At the same time, Stanley Trilling—a senior VP of investments at Paine Webber in Los Angeles, and *Money* magazine's repeating top-ranked stockbroker—told us that he considers Williams Controls to be one of his favorite emerging growth companies and stocks. Williams Controls is a company whose highest growth was achieved through acquisitions. It's interesting, though, that Trilling believes that Williams Controls is now in a position to grow *internally* in a big way, with what he calls "huge gangbuster products."

THREE COMPANIES FOR THREE ATTRACTIVE BUSINESS MODELS

To underscore the point of the different business models, we have selected three distinctly different businesses that were designed to fit their particular industry and selected different business models. Each company falls into one of three domains—the "high tech," the "no tech," and the "somewhere in between tech."

In most situations the business model is hybrid, with one dominant business model laced with one or both of the other two. Fore Systems was basically an internal-growth play in its emerging growth years, yet it has made a few acquisitions. And now that it has crossed beyond the emerging growth stage, its acquisitions are getting bigger (e.g., Alantec). Starbucks is a growth-by-multiplication play, yet during its emerging growth years it constantly developed internally in terms of products. Williams Controls is primarily a growth-by-acquisition player, with some internal growth. In the future, however, internal growth will play an important role at Williams, according to Stanley Trilling and to CEO Thomas Itin.

To begin at the high tech: Fore Systems proudly calls itself in the "forefront" of what it does. What Fore does is as important as the how of what it did. And most of what it did was through organic growth, although Fore did try its hand at acquisitions as well.

The company produces a product with the familiar-sounding initials ATM. This particular ATM is not to be confused with those comfortable machines that we all turn to when we're in a panic for a quick fix of cash. Fore produces asynchronous transfer mode (ATM) switches, the products that integrate other "initials" that have come into the workplace: the LAN (local area network) and WAN (wide area network). Too much information crossing all those wires that connect corporate networks creates problems which need a sophisticated solution. Enter the new "money machine," the ATM created by Fore Systems.

When reading the credentials of the founders of Fore Systems, you may walk away and just say, "Well, another group of Silicon Valley geniuses." Yes, they may be geniuses, but they're not from Silicon Valley, and from the beginning they started very modestly with their own funds and not a lot of splash from overeager valley capitalists.

Four researchers from Carnegie Mellon University in Pittsburgh started with $100,000 and, just as important, with a federal grant. In an interview with *Network World*, Eric Cooper, Fore's CEO, stated that they are pretty conservative and risk-averse. To reinforce the point, Cooper added that the federal grant money they received initially covered only engineers, but when they started hiring sales and support staff, they agreed not to do it unless each new position could pay for itself. In fact, as John Baker, then with Patricof & Co. Ventures who eagerly backed the new company, said to us, some of the first orders for Fore Systems' ATM products came through selling on the Internet by e-mail.

Although Fore turned a profit quickly, it realized that to sustain its growth momentum, it had to tap the public markets. In the spring of 1994, Fore found that the IPO market was awaiting its arrival. Originally, it planned to sell 3 million shares, with insiders selling 1 million, at $12 to $14 a share. But, when it was finally priced, the company sold it shares at $16. Even so, the stock opened at $21.25. Fore, of course, had the help of Goldman Sachs.

The true forte of Fore is that it is very cognizant of designing its products and its business to fit its customers and potential partners. Fore has introduced the ForeThought Partners program. The program, which had 35 "partners" at the close of its fiscal year, ensures network interoperability throughout the industry. *Webster's* defines *interoperability* as "the ability of one system to use the parts or equipment of another." Whatever interoperability really does, it certainly ensures revenues. In FY1993 Fore had $5.4 million in revenues; by the close of FY1996, Fore had $235 million in revenues.

Fore has complemented this ForeThought Partners strategy with strategic alliances and modest acquisitions. In 1995, Northern Telecom teamed up with the company to offer the "first seamless desktop-to-desktop" ATM architecture. Fore has also signed alliances with the ever-present Microsoft and TCI.

Recognizing the limitations of internal growth and the opportunities that "partnerships" can present, in 1995 Fore implemented an acquisitions strategy. In mid-1995, the company completed two stock acquisitions to fill in its product line— Applied Network Technology (ANT), a developer of Ethernet switches, and RainbowBridge Communications, a developer of routing software. Finally, to complete the year, Fore acquired Alantec, a leader in multilayer LAN switching. All the acquisitions were consummated for stock, and for accounting purposes were done on a "pooling basis" to avoid dilution of earnings. So Fore represents a company that grew in its emerging growth years primarily by internal growth, and very little by acquisitions. Now that it has graduated, its appetite to grow by acquisition grows.

FROM HIGH TECH TO NO TECH

Howard Schultz, chairman and CEO, does not have a Ph.D. like the founders of Fore Systems, but he did have an epiphany when he was on a business trip to Italy.

Convinced that the hurry-up 1980s were due to shift into an emphasis on quality of life, he was "starstruck" by the promise of a café society in the United States similar to the culture that had been spawned by the Italian espresso bars. With a talent to convince a local coffee roaster to brew a special mix, in 1985 Schultz opened his own café. Eventually, he was able to acquire the roaster, and thus today's Starbucks was born.

Starbucks' goal is "to be an integral part of consumers' lives," sums up Michael Moe, emerging company analyst and principal at Montgomery Securities and formerly with Lehman Brother. "Starbucks' management wants Starbucks to be part of a customer's day from daybreak to midnight. Consumers can start their day with a cup of Starbucks coffee at home, visit

Starbucks stores or one of the many other outlet locations (such as at Barnes & Noble, Crate & Barrel, and Delta Airlines) during the day—and meet up with friends at the neighborhood Starbucks in the evening. The average customer visits Starbucks stores 15 to 20 times per month."

Starbucks has stayed focused by operating its own stores; in fact, it followed a clustering or saturation strategy similar to that of Sam Walton's Wal-Mart. Howard Schultz chose to grow his business "organically"; indeed, you might expect nothing less of a company that brews designer coffee beans. Nonetheless, recently Starbucks has modifies its go-it-alone approach and become the partner of favor among the consumer-brand companies in the United States and elsewhere. "Rogers & Hammerstein. Abbott & Costello. Tracy & Hepburn. Michael Jordan & Nike. Peanut Butter & Jelly." heralds the letter to the shareholders of Starbucks' 1995 annual report. What does "Peanut Butter & Jelly" have to do with espresso? Starbucks is "exploring new ways to share the Starbucks' experience."

Howard Schultz states that he has, thus, "chosen the road less traveled" by entering into partnerships with Pepsi and Red Hook Brewery, and on and on. Despite his humility, the road he is traveling is exactly the one that the emerging growth company of the 1990s must follow.

Starbucks embodies the notion of growing a business through unit multiplication by internal means—to produce a company that fits the aspirations of other consumer products or service companies. In this case, Schultz designed a company with a powerful brand name and a loyal constituency. The franchise has enabled Starbucks to enter into major strategic alliances. In the air you can sip a Starbucks brew either on United or Horizon Airlines. You can sip beverages designed by Starbucks with Pepsi or Red Hook Brewery, while listening to music that Starbucks has orchestrated with Capitol Records. Just to make sure that he is keeping Ben & Jerry's on its toes, Howard Schultz is developing a premium brand of ice cream with Breyer's.

And when Schultz decided to venture abroad, he found a local partner to suit the taste of his Starbucks customers. Starbucks' first offshore venture wasn't to Schultz's country of inspiration, Italy, but to Japan. We may think of Japan as a land of tea drinkers, but Schultz knows that Japan is the third-largest coffee-drinking nation.

When Starbucks ventures abroad it picks a partner that is in keeping with its image. SAZABY, Starbucks' partner in Japan, is not a coffee brewer or even a coffee shop. Instead, SAZABY is billed as one of Japan's "most creative high-energy and dynamic retailers." Yes, that's a bit of hype, but SAZABY has collaborated with other brand-conscious businesses seeking to enter the supposedly impenetrable Japanese market, such as the very trendy Agnes b. clothing company. SAZABY helped Agnes b. establish one of the most sought-after apparel products that only young Japanese women can wear along with the waiflike models of the Parisian runway.

FROM NO TECH TO SOMEWHERE IN BETWEEN

We all know that where there's a will, there's a way, and the "will" in this chapter is Williams Controls. One of the most colorful entrepreneurs we interviewed in writing this book is the chairman, president, CEO, and individual extraordinaire of Williams, Thomas Itin. Itin's approach to building a business embodies what is and will increasingly become an even more important method for the Emerging Growth company: Buy it and grow it. Although Itin does not forsake internal growth, he knows the importance of playing the "deal" game. Why build it from scratch if you can buy it?

Williams Controls is in the "somewhere in between tech" business of "sensors, controls, and communications systems." That sounds much more interesting than the basic "brake" business that was purchased from Dana Corporation in 1988. Sensing the need to transform the company from the mundane to something more, Itin took Williams public in 1989, thus giving the company a "currency" with which to make acquisitions.

Itin is a financially savvy businessman who has been at the helm of other firms. At one time he was "master of the road"— that is to say, he was the cofounder of Road Master, a bicycle manufacturer. Unlike Starbucks' management, Itin believes in and has mastered the art of the deal. From 1993 onward, he has acquired at least one company a year.

The core business acquired from Dana is a leading manufacturer of electronic pedals for heavy-duty vehicles. In other words, it makes things for trucks. Making anything for the trucking industry is something that most people would hardly consider an emerging growth business. Thomas Itin, however, has redesigned his business to add to the core strengths and to complement the business through acquisitions. The acquisition footnote to the financial statements of Williams' 1995 annual report is longer than the balance sheet.

In January 1994, the company acquired Michiana Performance Group to extend its product line to the more popular light truck and sport utility vehicle market. That same month it acquired National Energy Service Company, moving Williams into the natural gas metering business—in other words, into the sensors business, which has more value-added cachet.

The year 1995 started out with a similar aggressive mergers and acquisitions posture. In February, Williams acquired Hardee Manufacturing and Waccamaw Wheel. Hardee is a manufacturer of equipment used in highway and park maintenance, landscaping, and farming, while Waccamaw manufactures rubber wheels from recycled tires. Back again to adding to the core business.

The list goes on and the acquisitions get even more interesting, but the important observation is that Itin has grown his business through a two-pronged strategy: complement the core business he acquired from Dana and add to the core businesses outside the transportation business, such as telecommunications and agriculture, with an emphasis on "electronic sensors and control systems." In the philosophy he expressed to us, his acquisitions focused on those industries that would give the company better technological products. Itin is designing his company to fit the expectations of a market that places higher valuations on "higher value-added" products such as "sensor, controls, and communications systems." That certainly sounds better than just making something for trucks.

Reflecting on these three companies, we are left with what

we see as three trends for business models of emerging growth companies in the latter half of the 1990s:

- The niche-focused company that initially grows internally— as quickly as the market presents it with opportunities and then opens up to acquisitions.
- The company that fiercely guards its franchise and positions itself to multiply fast while at the same time improving and expanding its product and service base, and drawing the brightest strategic lights into its orbit.
- The astute and experienced entrepreneurial "deal maker" that takes advantage of the opportunities that grow in corporate America and repackages them into a new business, which he can then also grow internally.

QUANTUM LEAPS

Now that we have taken care of the "how" of growing we want to close this chapter with the "when" of business models for growth. This component, more precisely, relates to an emerging growth company's growth timewise.

If each minute you put a penny in your piggybank, you'll have $5256 at the end of the year. If you deposit the same total amount in a bank, in 12 consecutive monthly deposits, you accrue interest and your balance will be a few percent higher. If you put the same amount in a CD you stand to make an additional few percent. This kind of growth model based on gradual progress doesn't necessarily build attractive emerging growth companies.

For the attractive emerging growth company, developing products and markets is a quantum process—you must grow by jumping steps. Archimedes said, "Give me where to stand, and I will move the earth." Once you get a foothold with a product in the market, you have a place to stand, so to speak. Now, if you want to "move the earth," you must achieve growth by quantum leaps.

Advancing in quantum leaps is almost natural in the growth-by-acquisitions business model. Every time you buy a new company you add a meaningful chunk of revenues to the pie and you increase the total number of employees in one step. How many new stores you have to open per month to qualify for being branded with the superlative of a *quantum leaper* is perhaps more difficult to define, and hence in the multiplication model it is more appropriate to consider quantum growth in relation to other standards of the industry.

But even the internal-growth business model allows for growth in quantum leaps. Compaq, for example, leapfrogged in less than 2 years from nil to $100 million in sales, and became a major player in the computer business. In another example, by introducing major new products and constantly expanding into new markets, Fore Systems grew in its emerging growth years in quantum leaps.

In the very early emerging growth years of the now huge Microsoft, Bill Gates hired Steve Ballmer—his old Economics 2010 pal from Harvard—to run the business. Microsoft had 30 employees at the time. Within 3 weeks of Ballmer's arrival at the company, he came to Gates and requested to hire an additional 50 employees, a number that would almost triple Microsoft's head count—a would-be quantum leap on all accounts. After Gates' initial resistance, he conceded to Ballmer's request and told him to keep hiring smart people as fast as he could. He, Gates, would tell him when he was getting ahead of what they could afford. Gates admits that he never had to tell Ballmer to stop hiring, because Microsoft's income grew as fast as he could find great people.

Being *poised for growth* means, also, that you are setting the stage to grow in quantum leaps.

POOLING OF RESOURCES: DEMYSTIFYING BUSINESS INCUBATORS

WILL YOU BECOME A MORE ATTRACTIVE COMPANY IF YOU BEGIN YOUR LIFE IN ONE OF THE FIVE TYPES OF BUSINESS INCUBATORS?

In our interview with Henry Taub, cofounder of the now $3 billion ADP—one of the best and most profitable companies of this half of the century—he told us that in the first decade of ADP "we were 'incubating' ourselves." Taub, now director, honorary chairman, and chairman of the executive committee of ADP, was 21, his brother Joe was 19, and the now famous senator from New Jersey Frank Lautenberg was 26 when they got ADP on the road. ADP, which is now a diversified data processing and communications conglomerate, has always billed itself as a service company. It started as a provider of "manual" (nonautomated and noncomputerized) accounting services—mainly payroll—to small businesses.

When we asked Taub what he meant by "incubating," he explained: "We were learning how to manage a small business, and manage people." He believed in division of labor, and in fact when ADP had 20 people there weren't more than 5 who knew how to put together a payroll. Someone would analyze time cards, someone would do taxes, and so on. "We created a paperwork factory. But first we had to develop as managers rather than technologists," concludes Taub.

In an article titled "Innovation and Diffusion in Small Firms: Theory and Evidence," in *Small Business Economics* (Kluwer Academic Publishers, Volume 6, November 5, 1994), researcher Bart Nooteboom of Groningen University in The Netherlands indicates that small firms are known to be good innovators and will spend relatively large sums on R&D, but they are far behind their larger competitors in the ability to translate their innovations into salable products, and they are especially behind in marketing know-how and muscle. They also lack the "internal knowledge network" of larger companies such as IBM, Hewlett-Packard, and 3M—which are restructuring and becoming internally more entrepreneurial and which manage to translate innovation to products and markets more readily and effectively.

The Economist (February 18, 1995) feels that clustering together in "protective" groups can ease these problems. High-tech zones, such as Silicon Valley between San Jose and San Francisco, Route 128 in the Boston area, and even the newly forming Silicon Alley in New York, can help small firms achieve the critical mass they need in terms of professional and management expertise as well as administrative support services. You could call these zones "incubator belts."

So while the founders of ADP or the architects of Silicon Valley had one or another "incubation" concept in mind, the incubators that we want to concentrate on are the actual incubator organizations. The purpose of these organizations is to deal with the early problems posed by Taub and the economists in a structured and concrete format. These incubator organizations, or as they are called *business incubators,* are far from being homogeneous—they come in a multitude of "shapes" and "forms," as you'll learn later in this chapter. They incorporate the incubation concepts we mentioned above. But, in terms of these modern business incubators, the early-day ADP, Route 128, or Silicon Valley concepts amount only to virtual incubators.

THE STRUCTURE OF THE INCUBATOR INDUSTRY

Today's business incubators are structured organizations which provide a way for companies to pool and share resources. These resources can be financial, intellectual, or administrative in nature. In a very simplistic view, incubators are there to cut operating costs—such as rent, computers, copiers, fax machines, and secretarial services—for each tenant company. But in the modern world of incubators, there's much more to it than simple cost cutting. Furthermore, even the cost cutting goes beyond rent, furniture, and equipment.

Although each company in a business incubator is relatively independent, the existence of an umbrella supervisory "management" provides the tenants with an additional benefit of drawing on sources of valuable advice in business building. Also, the relatively "protective" environment somewhat muffles the typical hectic neurosis that the highly competitive and volatile business world imposes on young companies. This gives the companies some breathing space and comfort, as they go through the learning curve of growing a business. Finally, since young companies have to meet certain standards (which vary from place to place) before they get accepted into an incubator, there's an element of added credibility once they are accepted, which helps open doors.

In synergistic incubators—where all the companies are functioning in a similar market, such as information technology, food businesses, or medical devices—professional talent may also be shared among companies. In addition to being economically lucrative, these scenarios can also create cross-nurturing creative and strategic partnerships.

Next, if you look at the incubators that are located in major institutions, such as the 50 or more university-based incubators in the United States, you will find that here the tenants can draw on an even wider support system, either from the faculty for business or from facilities and experienced professionals in the technical faculties.

Before we get into the fascinating issues of the structure of the incubator industry and its possible effects on emerging growth companies, let's put the issue of incubators in perspective. To use an analogy, let us suggest that you poll promising, progressive people in their twenties about their backgrounds. Various studies will try to give you a statistical measure of their success potential versus the availability they had of the tools needed for the individual to develop. Social and economical backgrounds are definitely a factor in development, but success comes in a great variety of forms.

You can't grow a plant or a tree without the proper soil, water, and sunshine—and that's true too when you look at the analogous resources needed for emerging growth companies. Yet plants and trees do grow in a great variety of environments—from rain forests to deserts—and so do companies. Some compare the role of the business incubator, and hence the name, to the role of the incubator in the life of a prematurely born baby, or even to the parents' protective nourishing care in the early years of a child's existence. We think that this analogy has many limitations and it needs a great deal of explanation.

For one thing, we've never heard of a baby who didn't grow up in some sort of a protective unit of "parenting" or other equivalent environment. Yet most companies in the United States even in the past 10 or 20 years—including the fast-growth ones—didn't start in business incubators. Now, you may justifiably argue that the concept of business incubators—at least as an omnipresent phenomena—is relatively new. In fact, over half the business incubators in the United States are less than 7 years in operation. In industrializing (not industrialized) countries, the average incubator is less than 4 years in existence. There is also a learning curve in operating incubators, promoting them to attract high-caliber tenants, and establishing the parameters for successful operation and growth within this environment.

There is no doubt that a business incubator environment can be quite beneficial at the startup stage. After all, the statistics are unequivocally conclusive. Some 80 percent of companies that start their life in an incubator survive, while the reverse statistic is true for companies that start on their own—nearly 80 percent fail. This survival rate for incubated companies applies in industrializing countries as well. Still, the focus of this book is not on survival, but rather on growth and on achieving a high degree of company attractiveness in the emerging growth stages.

In this respect, the 20 percent of companies that survive from among the nonincubated population are the ones that *currently* constitute most of the high-growth attractive companies. One might claim that this is due to a Darwinistic "survival of the fittest" phenomenon. In other words, a company that survived on its own had to learn how to "hunt" in the "wild" and has a better chance to grow and dominate its market.

At the same time, you can argue that the incubation industry is too young, and that the success of incubated companies—from the emerging growth perspective—might be just now on a cusp of significant outburst. Or, as Richard Frank, director of the University of Maryland TAP Incubator, told us, "By the nature of the process, it takes a long time to see the results." Some examples in this chapter will show that indeed the incubator system in the United States has been, slowly but surely, producing some interesting results in recent years.

There is a crucial underlying reason for the surge in business incubators and incubated companies. The winds of change are blowing. It is becoming more and more difficult to fund startups, even to the degree of taking care of basic needs. The average venture capital fund is abandoning the startup sector in favor of emerging growth companies. The glut of venture capital funding for startups in the 1970s and 1980s is over. Business models that were right for the 1980s are not necessarily good enough any more. Companies whose major growth might take place in the first years of the next millennium could significantly benefit from exploring the incubator option.

A study reported in the *NBIA Review* (January–February 1996)—a publication of the National Business Incubation Association (NBIA)—found that there are many similarities between incubator and tenant company sizes and company survival rates in the United States and in a sample of seven industria*lizing* countries. It is reasonable to argue that, proportionally speaking, incubators will play a more *decisive* role in the industrializing countries, because of the very different financial and investment environment—especially in their private sectors. But, in light of the shift of financing in the United States toward the later-stage emerging growth sector, and considering the more agile, entrepreneurial internal systems that large companies gravitate to, business incubators may become very important for building the next generation of emerging growth companies in the United States.

ROCKING THE CRADLE OF GROWTH

So, while the numbers even in the United States might be changing as we speak, we wish to give this matter an analysis from the perspective of a current snapshot of the cradle of fast-growth companies—which is the United States. Accordingly, for the rest of this chapter we'll focus on the business incubator systems in the United States and its implication on the growth factors of companies. The following statistical data, which originate with the National Business Incubation Association (NBIA), refer to North America as a whole—that is, the United States, Canada, and Mexico.

A BRIEF HISTORY

While the concept of sharing space, services, and even management has been around for a long time, U.S. business incubators as we know them today emerged in the 1970s (although the oldest began in Batavia, New York, in 1959). There were three major forces that propelled the establishment of incubator organizations. The first started as an experiment by the National Science Foundation to foster innovation and entrepreneurship at major universities. The second was the attempt to use old, abandoned buildings in distressed areas by partitioning them for the use of small firms. And the third emanated from initiatives by investor groups and successful entrepreneurs to utilize their company building experience and expertise, and provide them to new companies in environments which can be conducive for successful innovation and commercialization.

Business incubators got their first big momentum from the office of Private Sector Initiatives of the U.S. Small Business Administration—which promoted their development from 1984 to 1987. The SBA held a series of regional conferences, and published a newsletter and several handbooks to promote the concept. In 1985 the National Business Incubator Association (NBIA) was formed by industry leaders, and by 1987 it became the primary source for incubator information.

There are currently over 500 small business incubators in North America. They host a total of more than 8000 entrepreneurial firms, and have more than 4500 graduates. In North America, new business incubators have opened at an average rate of one per week since 1986. As we mentioned previously, research shows that more than 80 percent of the firms that have ever been incubated are still in operation—a very high percentage compared with the survivability rate of an average startup, which is either 20 percent or 30 percent, depending on the sector. Typically, 30 percent of incubator companies "graduate" each year. Clients normally graduate in 1 to 5 years, with 2.3 years as the average time a firm spends in a business incubator.

NEW INDUSTRY TARGETS

According to the NBIA, the earliest incubation programs were focused on technology in general, or on a combination of light industrial, technology, and service firms. In recent years, however, new incubators that target industries such as space and ceramic technologies, food processing, medical technologies, and even woodworking have been established. Incubators have been even targeted for arts and crafts people, for retail firms, or specifically for software development. For example, in the Denver Enterprise Center, a 7000-square-foot kitchen incubator was opened, to serve the needs of new food companies.

Incubator companies may be statistically classified to belong to the following sectors:

- Service—36 percent
- Technology products and R&D—27 percent

- Light manufacturing—20 percent
- Other—17 percent

As you may note, slightly more than a quarter of incubator companies are technology-based. Most of them traditionally resided in the 50 to 55 university-based incubators—especially those which deal with cutting-edge technologies. The reason is simple. The community-based incubators, which represent 75 to 80 percent of the small business incubator network, usually can't provide the extensive specialized support systems needed to develop major innovative, technology-rich products. This trend is, however, changing. You'll find a few dozen high-tech companies in what we call incubator corporations—which incubate companies and then spin them off. There are also other developments taking place in community incubators, such as those in what's called Silicon Alley (in New York City), which attract certain families of high-tech companies—in this case, mostly related to media applications.

Business incubators accelerate the successful development and growth of entrepreneurial companies. They provide hands-on assistance—a variety of business and technical support services for fragile firms during their most vulnerable years. They charge reduced fees, and receive a small percentage of equity for each year the company resides in the incubator. As we noted earlier, there's also a class of corporations which incubate companies and then spin them off. As you will learn later on, the incubation process in incubator corporations is much more intimate, and these organizations own a much higher percentage of their incubated companies.

TYPES OF SUPPORT

In a nutshell, business incubators provide a supportive environment for a number of businesses under one roof. This support includes:

- Flexible space and leases
- Office services and equipment on a pay-as-you-go basis

- An on-site incubator manager as a resource for business advice
- Organized exposure to a network of business and technical consultants
- Assistance with financing
- Opportunities to network and do business with other firms in the facility

Incubators impose business and technical selection criteria upon prospective companies. When a company is accepted, they reduce the business risks involved by providing facilities, equipment, and business advice that might otherwise be unavailable or unaffordable. While the phenomenon of attractive emerging growth companies that began life in an incubator might not yet be statistically substantial, there is a nonnegligible number of attractive emerging growth companies that have benefited from a wide array of business incubator environments.

For a better grasp of the role that early-stage incubation plays in the emerging growth sector, we should note that there are five distinct types of business incubator systems. We feel that this classification, which is a somewhat modified version of the five categories adopted by the NBIA, provides a better understanding of the role of incubation when examined from the perspective of the emerging growth sector. Here they are:

- The incubator corporation
- Incubators for economic development (government, community, not-for-profit)
- University incubators
- Incubators originated as a business of the host, and potential hybridization with government and not-for-profit organizations
- Financial organization driven incubators (FODIs)

The five systems have very distinct characteristics. According to the National Business Incubation Association (NBIA), the second and fourth categories host the numerical majority (75 to 80 percent) of incubated companies in North America, but there is very little statistical data concerning the nature of company growth in these types of incubators. A few years ago the NBIA did initiate a joint program with Dun & Bradstreet titled "NBIA Partnership with Dun & Bradstreet to Track Success of Graduates/Clients," but we were informed at the writing of these lines that not much is currently available in tangible measures. We will therefore treat these sectors of the incubator system more in terms of foresight than hindsight.

It will probably take a few more years until companies from the second and fourth categories of incubators become effective case studies for high growth in the context of this book. These incubator environments currently provide mostly space and other shared amenities. The strategic support in terms of close hands-on business and financial assistance has yet to be developed further. We believe, however, that as these types of incubators develop, they will be able to provide a strategic environment that draws on the experience of the other highly effective incubator systems. Therefore, we feel that studying some well-documented results from the other three incubator categories could be very valuable for companies considering an incubator environment as a cradle for producing their future emerging growth business.

INCUBATOR CORPORATIONS

The first and fifth sectors, and to a growing extent the third, have produced some powerful success stories. The incubator corporation is a company whose charter is to identify and develop new products or technologies—in the incubation stage—and then spin off a company that produces and markets the product. Notable incubator corporations include the much publicized ThermoElectron, Teknekron, and Safeguard Scientifics. Let's look at two of those. ThermoElectron and Safeguard Scientifics take completely different approaches to the incubation process. ThermoElectron epitomizes a "nonsynergistic" business incubator, whereas Safeguard Scientifics heralds itself as an incubator concentrating on information technology.

FOCUS AND DIVERSIFICATION AT SAFEGUARD

Safeguard, a $1.5 billion New York Stock Exchange–traded company, has 22 "partnership" companies; its equity investments in those companies range up to 100 percent. Most of the "partnership" companies are engaged in information technology, primarily the distribution of microcomputer hardware, software, and telecommunications technology. One of its best-known partnership companies is the well-known Novell. However, Safeguard has diversified beyond information technology, and other companies in Safeguard's portfolio provide specialty metal finishing, interactive marketing consulting, relationship marketing, and commercial real estate.

If that level of focus and diversification is not enough to impress its shareholders, Safeguard also participates in managing three venture capital funds. Those venture capital funds, in turn, are coinvestors in 9 of Safeguard's "partnership" companies and are invested in over 30 additional development-stage businesses. In contrast to Safeguard, the focus of the venture funds is in biotechnology, health-care and service-related companies.

An example of the nurturing process in which Safeguard engages is demonstrated through its relationship with Cambridge Technology Partners (CTP), a company that provides systems integration, consulting, and custom system development services for a fixed price, in a fixed time. Safeguard assisted in both the financial and managerial development of CTP. On the financial front, Safeguard made a loan to the company's founder, guaranteed a bank line of credit, converted a working-capital loan to equity, negotiated the rights offering, and in 1994 helped the company complete a secondary offering. Yes, all in a day's work at Safeguard.

Money isn't everything, so Safeguard assisted in the restructuring of the management and operation of the firm. Safeguard helped find and secure clients, advised on strategic initiatives, and arranged for a new headquarters building. In building a management team, Safeguard identified and helped recruit a new chief executive officer, chief administrative officer, chief technology officer, and several directors.

Among the "partnership" companies in its portfolio are several other publicly traded firms that are worth mentioning. Coherent Communications, a NASDAQ-traded company, develops, manufactures, licenses, and markets voice enhancement products for wire, wireless (including digital cellular), and satellite-based telecommunications systems throughout the world.

As mentioned, Safeguard has diversified itself beyond the technical, and National Media is a company which embodies that diversification. National Media, a NYSE-traded company in which Safeguard now owns only convertible preferred stock with warrants, is a worldwide leader in the home shopping infomercial industry, now doing business in over 40 countries in addition to the United States and Canada. National Media is off the beaten track from the major focus of Safeguard, but its investment in the company highlights the flexibility of Safeguard to capitalize on a trend. Who of us has not turned to a cable TV channel and sat back in our favorite "couch potato" couch to see a once-famous actor begin to tell us about some miracle that has just taken place in his or her life? It usually turns out to be an infomercial, and sometimes the "miracle" that has taken place in the actor's life turns out to be a check from the advertiser.

Finally we turn back to one of the more traditional companies with which Safeguard is involved: CompuCom Systems. CompuCom Systems, a company with which Safeguard has been involved since 1984, is a leading personal computer services integrator that provides corporate customers services ranging from product delivery to network integration and support. When you consider that computer integration has been the hot thing for the last several years, you realize that Safeguard was prescient in getting involved in that business over a decade ago.

THERMOELECTRON'S PERPETUAL IDEA MACHINE

In its annual report Safeguard presents itself as a business incubator. By contrast, the chairman and president of

ThermoElectron, George Hatsopoulos, agrees with a securities analyst who characterizes ThermoElectron as a "perpetual idea machine." An October 9, 1995, *Forbes* article notes that in the past dozen years ThermoElectron, a "technology greenhouse," made public offerings of 12 businesses. As the article put it, investors thrust money on the company. And why not when, on average, the return to investors has been over 30 percent a year?

ThermoElectron is viewed as a "family of companies" in a diverse range of businesses. The company is a world leader in environmental monitoring and analysis instruments and a major producer of paper-recycling equipment, biomedical products (including heart assist devices and mammography systems), alternative energy systems, and other products and services related to environmental quality, health, and safety. Well, we told you it was a nonsynergistic company, and that list certainly proves it.

Harvard Business Review (January–February 1996) featured ThermoElectron as a model of how a big company keeps the entrepreneurial spirit alive. Quoting Hotsopoulos, the article states that ThermoElectron may have to change a goal if it decides it is not realistic, but the company does not fire people for taking a calculated risk and failing.

. The Thermo Instrument Systems segment of ThermoElectron's "family of businesses" demonstrates the parent company's unique approach to doing business. In 1994 Thermo Instrument, which had been spun off from ThermoElectron in August 1986, spun off its first "offspring," ThermoSpectra. In general, Thermo Instrument is in the analytical, environmental-monitoring, and process control instrumentation business. ThermoSpectra focuses on high-speed imaging, inspection, and measurement systems. The following year, 1995, after Thermo Instrument spun off its first "offspring," it completed one of the largest acquisitions in the history of ThermoElectron. ThermoElectron acquired the Scientific Instruments Division of Fisons plc, one of the largest manufacturers of high-performance analytical instruments, for approximately 202 million British pounds, or over $300 million.

We thought that ThermoElectron's array of businesses was particularly interesting and wanted to share more of the substance with you to stimulate ideas about how you might invent businesses within your own company. In addition to the instrumentation business, alternative energy systems is another major segment. ThermoEcotek, one of the firms within the alternative energy segment, builds and operates power plants that make use of environmentally responsible fuels, such as wood and agricultural waste. In addition, the Thermo Power subsidiary produces refrigeration systems that are free of chlorofluorocarbons (CFCs); those refrigeration systems use ammonia.

The next major business segment for ThermoElectron is the biomedical products group. One of the companies, Thermo Cardiosystems, made medical history when the U.S. Food and Drug Administration approved its left ventricular assist system. It is the first and only implantable heart pump to achieve this status.

In the environmental services segment, Thermo Remediation, which was spun off by ThermoElectron in 1993, is already spinning out a second-generation company, Thermo Process Systems. Thermo Process Systems, performs soil remediation and recycles waste fluids.

The last noteworthy area which we would like to discuss is the advanced technologies segment, from which future spinoffs will likely arise. Thermedics, which from its name does sound like a biotechnology company, actually manufactures equipment that detects compounds in refillable bottles. For example, a company such as Perrier, which has in fact purchased equipment from Thermedics, would use the equipment to detect soaps and detergents in recycled bottles that are being refilled with, hopefully, pristine mineral water.

ThermoTrex bills itself as a next-generation technology for breast digital-imaging, sonic-computed tomography. Finally, a highly marketable product is being developed by ThermoLase. ThermoLase, which was spun off in 1994, is a laser-based process to provide painless, long-term removal of unwanted hair.

All these companies and more than we could write about add up to a "ThermoDynamic" company called ThermoElectron. It's a business incubator which is a perpetual idea machine.

FODIs

The financial organization driven incubator (FODI) can be a physical or virtual system. The system is originated or devised by the group that intends to fund the companies. Since funding is usually the number-one problem of early-stage companies, it consumes a very large percentage of the time and effort of a young company's management. A relatively high financial security in this early stage will allow managers to focus their energy on product and market development and hence achieve faster growth. In addition, managers in venture funds, for example, have ample experience in growing businesses. The fact that they "parent" the incubator means that the young company will receive advice and direction from people who have hands-on experience and are aware of the many pitfalls such a company faces.

In the case of the Nucleus Group—a FODI which was created in 1990 by the Minneapolis-based Medical Innovation Partners (MIP)—a number of companies in synergistic areas share physical facilities, intellectual resources, and the initial funding and guidance of MIP. The Nucleus Group believes that it represents a new breed of incubator which emphasizes sharing intellectual resources, rather than just physical facilities.

Venture Capital Journal (May 1994) characterized just how the Nucleus Group operated with three synergistic companies: InoMet, Diametric, and CorTrak. InoMet was created by MIP to commercialize a patent that MIP had obtained for a noninvasive blood glucose analysis system. About the same time that InoMet was being launched, the founders of Diametric and CorTrak sought financing from MIP.

CorTrak is a developer of site-specific drug delivery systems, and Diametrics is a maker of point-of-care blood gas analysis systems. MIP identified synergies among the three medical device companies and proposed that they share physical facilities and, more important, intellectual resources. In fact, MIP identified a common base of technical and research needs among the trio. MIP encouraged the companies to assist one another on an as-needed basis. All the principals of the Nucleus

Group were encouraged to help one another, since each would benefit financially by being granted stock options in the companies that it assisted. In addition, engineers and scientists at each of the incubator companies are awarded stock options when they assist another company. As one of the founders of CorTrak said, there was a sense that if one succeeded they would all succeed. It does sound like the Three Musketeers— all for one and one for all.

In the final addition to the Nucleus Group incubator, two more companies were admitted: Cardia Catheter and TranCell. Admittance of these two companies to the Nucleus Group was contingent upon approval of all the other Nucleus Group companies. In 1992, when these two companies were added, the group decided that it had "maxed out." Five was probably the maximum number of startups that could be effectively managed in the "one for all and all for one" environment of the Nucleus Group.

A virtual FODI is created by partners (and consultants) affiliated with a financial organization such as a venture fund that decide to fund and provide their own management expertise to develop ("incubate") a company which has a product and technology they believe in. Once the company stands on its feet, the temporary management usually returns to its funds and a management team is brought in to take over the further development of the company. Kleiner Perkins Caufield & Byers (KPC&B) in Menlo Park, California, scored such a home run with the famous Tandem Computers, Inc., and with other investments.

As computers were completely taking over in storing data for banks, insurance companies, accounting firms, and more, the question "What happens if something goes wrong with the hardware or the software?" started bothering more and more users. After all, if all the information on transactions of a bank for a particular day is wiped out, it will constitute a disaster. KPC&B, henceforth, recognized a great market opportunity for fail-safe or fault-tolerant computers.

Tandem Computers was incubated internally. Two of the partners left the daily work of KPC&B to become president and vice president of finance, and a third became the chairman. This formula worked well—not the least because all three partners had extensive managerial experience in the computer industry.

This opportunity justified the investment of capital and partners' time at "incubation," and resulted in one of the most successful venture capital investments ever. Tandem, 3 years after its foundation, became a public company and continued growing at a fast pace. It became a "100 bagger" for KPC&B (in other words, a return on investment 100 times over).

Investment companies like KPC&B, which use the "significant involvement approach," are actually more than virtual FODIs—they are actual FODIs—in that they provide close guidance and support at the early critical stages of companies. Viewing things from this perspective, one might argue that Tandem Computers, which became a high-growth company very fast, originated in a business incubator.

Indeed, today, venture funds such as KPC&B, the Mayfield Fund, and Onset Enterprise Associates, as well as Medical Innovation Partners whose Nucleus Group we described previously, operate business incubators, each in select areas of investment in which the partners of the funds have significant experience.

A hybrid incubator corporation and FODI was created by the venture capital arm of Xerox—Xerox Technology Ventures. It created a corporate incubator operated by Xerox to nurture promising technology that springs up within Xerox but does not fit into the company's main strategic thrust. Sorry, Fred Wilson from Euclid Partners. You probably won't be able to fish at Xerox for projects which are developed in the bosom of corporate America but which the parent company no longer wants to fund—as you so successfully did at ADP and Ingram Industries.

UNIVERSITY INCUBATORS

The third category of business incubators—the university-based incubator system—is perhaps the most accessible to candidates from among the widely used incubator formats, and for which there are documented results for success in creating emerging growth companies. A recent national survey of more than 30 5-year and older university-sponsored technology incubators (USTIs) concluded that the USTIs appear to provide an environment conducive to the development of new technology-based firms.

There are over 50 university-based incubators in the United States, with a total of 1000 companies (including recent graduates). This university-based business incubator format has many advantages—some of which we'll talk about later in this chapter. But, after spending some time talking to incubator directors and companies in a number of university incubators, and after working with two companies closely, we have determined that clearly "money talks"—in this case, very loudly. And the message is very clear: Incubator corporations and FODIs have produced, up to this point, companies with higher success rates than those in university incubators.

And the reasons are quite obvious. While incubator corporations and FODIs naturally take care of the early financial needs of their "children," the companies in university-based incubators are "on their own" when it comes to funding resources. That's not all. You see, university incubators have ample access to a lot of *academic* talent. Incubator corporations and FODIs, on the other hand, have access to hands-on *experienced company builders*. Also, university incubators usually host a wide variety of companies—with no inherent product and market synergy among them—in nonrelated market segments such as computer software, environmental, biotechnology, food technology, and more.

But things are changing as we speak. There is enough evidence now to show that university incubators can produce successful emerging growth companies. We'll discuss three examples in this chapter. One of the companies was incubated in the TAP Business Incubator at the University of Maryland, and the other two at the Long Island High Technology Incubator (LIHTI) at Stony Brook.

THE UNIVERSITY OF MARYLAND TAP

The University of Maryland, the seventh-largest public research and teaching institution in the United States, bills itself as an organization that maintains close ties with business and industry. "In its role as a leader for economic progress," says the brochure, "the University creates opportunities for the business community to interact with University faculty and students, and to use its extensive physical resources."

The TAP (technology advancement program) Business Incubator is putting the resources of the university to work for technically oriented early-stage companies. TAP has been helping such companies grow since 1984, and today it is one of the most respected business incubators in the United States. At the end of 1995, TAP had 10 diversified companies—in areas such as computers, medical technology, aeronautics and more—and it boasted over a dozen successful graduates.

From a strategic perspective, the TAP incubator provides four essential elements, which you'll find characteristics of most university-based business incubators.

First, it is a resource. It provides space that may allow for flexible expansion. It also opens the institute's vast facilities and creative talents to support the incubated company's technical and business needs. *Second*, TAP is support. It provides the companies with essential business and technical services at very low cost, and consequently it allows a company to concentrate its limited resources on the critical functions of product and business development. *Third*, the business incubator is a unique environment. It is an ensemble of motivated entrepreneurs working to achieve success within a stimulating intellectual environment. It is a fertile atmosphere for ideas to be born into and for business to grow from. *Fourth*, TAP offers affiliate programs which provide access to the full range of support services for companies that do not wish to physically be located on campus.

Moving from the strategic classification to the more tactical aspects, let's look at what a typical university-based business incubator provides to its incubated companies. This support can be divided into two categories: facilities and logistic support, and university resources. In the first category you'll find cost-effective office and R&D/ limited production space; reception and some secretarial services; central copying and fax machines; conference rooms and audiovisual equipment; and PCs and network access. In the second category you'll find resources (some of which involve additional fees) such as faculty expertise; short-term technical assistance; campus libraries; fabricating shops; specialized instrumentation; computer resources; business and management assistance; related seminars and lectures; and—what can be very useful—a student labor pool (smart people at low cost).

An example of a successful emerging growth company which graduated from the University of Maryland TAP incubator is Martek. Martek Biosciences Corporation—a public company traded on the NASDAQ—bills itself as a company engaged in the research, development, and manufacturing of nutritional supplements, drug design tools, diagnostics, and pharmaceuticals derived from microalgae.

It might sound a little abstract, but it's not. Martek has created a baby-formula ingredient which has been proved, by independent researchers, to enhance mental development in infants (IQ boosters). The product, Formulaid, was licensed to a number of infant-formula makers, which represent close to half the $5 billion worldwide formula market. These firms, some of which are already selling Formulaid in Europe, are taking Formulaid through clinical trials. The company is also working on bringing other consumer nutritional products to market.

Although most of the company's $2.5 million revenues for the quarter ending January 31, 1996 are from licensing and related fees, the figure represents a fivefold growth compared with its revenues for the same period a year before. Looking at the company's performance for the 9 months ended July 31, 1996, the growth is less "meteoric"—only $3.5 million in revenues compared to $1.5 million for the comparable period in 1995. The company's market capitalization is over $250 million.

But look at this. The company boasts strategic partners and licensees like Sandoz Nutrition S.A. (a division of the Swiss giant), Nutricia, American Home Products, and Mead Johnson

& Co. (a subsidiary of Bristol-Myers Squibb—another giant pharmaceuticals conglomerate).

If that's not enough, 3 years after the company went public and raised $9 million, it raised another $40 million in a secondary offering in late 1995—with underwriters that bear the names Hambrecht & Quist LLC, Bear, Stearns & Co., Inc., and Salomon Brothers, Inc.

LIHTI

The Long Island High Technology Incubator (LIHTI), founded in 1986, is located on the State University of New York (SUNY) campus at Stony Brook, New York. It lists on its roster over a dozen companies. LIHTI provides early-stage companies and *new ventures of existing industries* (an interesting twist) with a nurturing environment. Campus facilities allow access to high-caliber professionals as well as business development services. This environment, combined with support in the areas of financing, business planning, and management assistance, naturally enhances the probabilities for company survival in critical growth periods.

Practically all the strategic and tactical support services provided by LIHTI are identical to the ones provided by the TAP Business Incubator we described above—so we will not elaborate on those. We do want, however, to present two sample successful high-growth graduate companies.

Curative Health Services, through its national franchise of over 85 outpatient clinics, is a leader in the treatment of chronic wounds. Curative's care centers are complemented by a novel therapeutic technology. The company, a graduate of the Long Island High Technology Incubator, went public in 1991, at that time functioning as a biotechnology company. After 3 years of underperformance, Curative changed its focus and became a service-oriented company, aided further by a new CEO, John Vakoutis, who was formerly COO of Critical Care America. The company's $52 million in revenues for the year ending December 31, 1995 (close to a 30 percent increase from the year before), its $31.3 million in revenues for the 6 months ended June 30, 1996 (another 26 percent increase compared to the same period of 1995), and over $200 million market capitalization leave no doubt that Curative made a healthy transition to the emerging growth sector. We can further enhance Curative's accolades by pointing to a successful $21 million offering in August 1996 through Smith Barney, Hambrecht & Quist, and Vector, and a new "buy" rating in September 1996 by Hambrecht & Quist.

Another LIHTI graduate is Moltech Corporation—which, in contrast to the previous examples, is, as we're writing these lines, still a private company. Moltech was incubated from 1989 to 1994, and in mid-1995 it moved to Tucson, Arizona, in order to scale up the process to high-volume manufacturing of its high-energy, high-density, rechargeable battery cells for portable electronic devices—which is the core business of Moltech.

The company has yet to generate revenues, but in light of the huge potential market for its products—which eventually get integrated into many consumer electronic devices such as portable communication equipment and notebook computers—it is attracting people, capital, and corporate partners.

In mid-1996 Moltech staff was approaching 100. Many that the company attracted are in high-skilled areas such as R&D, product development, and manufacturing engineering, which require many years of experience. Moltech has obtained more than $5 million in government grants to develop its basic technology. Up to the present, the company has raised approximately $22 million from its strategic partners and private and venture capital sources. Of this the Long Island Venture Fund, which works closely with the business incubator, provided $2 million. And the kind of strategic partners Moltech has? World-class names like Electrolux and Ericsson of Sweden, the latter of which infused $3 million. And Moltech's cash position is pretty good; in early 1996 it had $13 million on hand. No doubt that the 5 years in which Moltech was incubated paid off.

An important observation is that despite the technological bent of Martek, Curative, and Moltech, all three of these companies are developing products for "consumer" markets.

IN SUMMARY

Since this book is about growth, it focuses on those specific cases where growth has been demonstrated and documented. With the aim of demystifying incubators, we tried to present an objective picture of the current situation. But the fact is that nothing is stationary, and everything is evolving.

We can't decide in which family we will be born, and similarly a company can't decide to be created from within an incubator corporation such as ThermoElectron. Still, incubator corporations like ThermoElectron, Safeguard, and Teknekron—which are business incubators that consistently produce high-growth companies—will probably be willing to discuss the "importing" of your early-stage technologies and products to be considered for their "greenhouses."

Since like most companies you probably need funding, you may first want to approach the venture funds that operate business incubators, such as Kleiner Perkins Caufield & Byers (KPC&B), Mayfield Fund, Onset Enterprise Associates, and Medical Innovation Partners (MIP).

University-based business incubators offer a wider choice of possibilities, but they are suited mostly for technology-based companies. If you fit within the selection criteria of the more than 50 such incubators in the United States, or if you are in other countries, and fit into the appropriate systems there, it would be quite worthwhile to investigate the potential of this environment. University incubators have been producing some well-documented positive results in terms of company growth. The strategic and tactical benefits you may be able to receive could be important in allowing you to move to the next step— as Martek, Curative, Moltech, and others did.

Finally, the community and government incubators which were founded to facilitate economic development or to take advantage of underutilized buildings, or for hybrid situations, offer the most available sites and openings. There are about 450 such incubators in North America, most of them in the United States. The Denver Enterprise Center is a good example. If nothing else, you can benefit from this kind of business incubator environment because of your ability to reduce your costs by sharing services and by virtue of operating in an entrepreneurial environment. Many of these incubators are extending their strategic and tactical support services to include help in areas of business development and access to local capital sources. Contact your state, county, or city authorities to find out more about the options available in your area.

Before you start your incubator hunt in the United States, we recommend that you contact the National Business Incubation Association in Athens, Ohio. Happy hunting.

TEN

GUIDELINES FOR CRAFTING A STRATEGIC BUSINESS PLAN THAT WORKS

BECAUSE YOU DON'T GET A SECOND CHANCE TO MAKE A FIRST IMPRESSION

Can you imagine the two Steves—Jobs and Wozniak, who later became two of the most famous and rich entrepreneurs of the 1980s—toiling over a business plan in Jobs' garage, then going out to the investment community and having hardly anyone be interested? Well, that's exactly the picture you get if you read *Odyssey—Pepsi to Apple,* by John Sculley, who in the 1980s became Apple Computers' CEO.

According to Sculley, the real propellant for Apple's takeoff was Mike Markulla, an Apple director and vice chairman who always stayed in the shadow and turned the limelight on the Steves. In those early days Markulla went to Jobs' garage, rewrote the business plan, and lined up the capital sources to transform the two kids' dream into a business that later became the shining star of the early PC industry.

Could it be that Apple wouldn't have taken off without Markulla? Well, that's really not the question. The relevant question is whether Apple would have had an early entry into the PC business, before powerful competition had sprouted all over. You see, a business plan that doesn't sell for a long time often becomes stale, and with it the business itself. According to Sculley, Markulla did much more for Apple in its early days than rewrite the business plan and take it to the venture capital industry which he knew. He put in his own personal money, recruited all of Apple's outside board members, and lured away from the big names like Intel and HP many of Apple's early professional managers.

But, in our experience, the fact that Markulla knew the investment community, rewrote the business plan, and shopped it around constituted his most critical early-day contribution. Why didn't Apple sell to the investment community with the business plan of the Steves? What was wrong with it? Well, we haven't seen that plan, but we have seen many others which are produced under similar conditions.

THE SALABLE BUSINESS PLAN

Before elaborating on the principle of the "salable business plan," let's get two issues out of the way. First, Markulla not only rewrote Apple's early business plan, but also shopped it around in the venture capital industry which he knew to a certain extent. This alone was an important factor, on which we elaborate in a number of places in this book, but which is not our thrust here. Second, Apple was a startup when Markulla reworked its business plan, whereas this book deals with emerging growth companies—more mature entities that should have more experience in putting together the right business plan. However, our experience shows that a significant portion of the business plans written by the emerging growth constituency are somewhat or significantly deficient.

By now you say: Why are these guys making such a big deal about writing a business plan? For one thing, today you can buy a software template for business plans for less than $100. Then, you have probably written a few business plans already, and it wasn't that difficult. Well, that sounds like Mark Twain's famous quote: "To cease smoking is the easiest thing I ever did. I ought to know because I've done it a thousand times."

What putting together a good, *salable* business plan really boils down to is *understanding the third party's point of view*— whether it's an investor, a large corporate partner, or even a highly desirable top manager or board member. And most company founders and managers are not fully acquainted with the details of such a perspective. That's the key reason that Markulla, who knew the venture capital industry and had experience developing and budgeting new projects, was able to transform a business plan that would sell to hardly anyone into a hardworking successful business plan which brought in the required capital.

In contrast to the business plans which fully *capture the third party's point of view,* many plans that investors receive fall into two other extremes categories. One we call the "storyteller" business plan, and the other the "junk mail" business plan.

The *storyteller* business plan is actually a very pleasant document. It tells you about the product—every technical detail. The writers describe how interesting and ingenious it was to develop the product, how much they think customers will like it, how 1 in every 5 people in the world will be interested in it and 1 in 25 will actually purchase it in the first year. You'll also find 5-page résumés of every soul who has any connection with the company, and finally, even though you are by now sinking in detail, you might find some abstract general financial projections—giving the impression that making money is really not important when a project is so interesting. This storytelling business plan is thick, reads like a dissertation, and is actually very pleasant, except that after browsing through it, the busy investment executive will say: "Well, let me get back to some real business."

The *junk mail* business plan is concise on information and analysis and very big on promotion. With such a plan, even a great business can give an expert the impression that there is very little substance here and a lot of hype and hot air. In such a business plan you'll find a lot of newspaper and magazine clippings, and abstract opinions from many important and not-so-important people. Often this business plan comes with a video that resembles an infomercial, rather than an audiovisual presentation of those aspects of the business for which the "audio-visual" can enhance the print presentation significantly.

This style of document has financial projections galore—tables after tables filled with zillions of details. You'll even be told that in the fourth month of the third year after funding, expenses for repairing the company's PCs will be such and such. If you think that much thought and analysis are behind the numbers, you are grossly mistaken—and investment executives can tell. Their response to this kind of business plan will be: "The business could be interesting if we believed in all this hype." Then they will do to the plan what they usually do with other junk mail—a slam-dunk in the basket.

Now to the good news. You can avoid becoming one of those who submits a storyteller or junk mail business plan by understanding what serious third parties are looking for. Tune in for the rest of this chapter.

Every big and worthy project involves a multistage decision process. That's why only a small percentage of the companies seeking funds get it. In this multistage decision process Murphy's Law applies—everything that can go wrong will. You need to leverage what you've got to offer with help, know-how, and contacts of other people. The team that gets to the finals in the NFL or NBA has to prove its leadership and worthiness step after step.

But in order to be considered for this multistage process, your company's calling card—its business plan—has to be taken seriously, and has to elicit enough interest to get you to first base. That's why the cliché "You don't get a second chance to make a first impression" is so appropriate. Yes, contacts are very important—they will get you in the door. But contacts are effective only in conjunction with an impressive, hardworking business plan. Such a document must predict and answer all the key questions a typical investor or corporate partner is interested in, and it must do so in a way which the third party can identify with. This brings us back to the necessity to understand *in detail* the typical *third party's point of view.*

The emerging growth company sector has unique characteristics when it comes to the rules for crafting the strategic

business plan and presenting it to investors or strategic partners. The key words are *track record*. While a startup is fat on
projections and very lean on performance and market indicators, an emerging growth company has some of both—and with
time the performance and market indicators grow in quantity
and reliability.

On the road to becoming an emerging growth business, the
emerging growth company, after all, had to deal with presenting
a business plan and soliciting investment or corporate clients. It
usually even accumulated some well-positioned supporters and
interested parties, and can draw on these resources. So what is
there still to know? Everything.

The business plan is only a dry document. What's behind it
is the vision, feasibility analysis, product paradigms, strategic
plans, management skills, market projections, and financial
savvy of the company.

THE COMPOSITE INVESTOR

Who will be reading your business plan—a document which
you may very well consider to be a labor of love? (At least, the
business you are describing in your business plan is your labor
of love.) From our experience in advising emerging growth companies and operating in the investment community, we based
our analysis and guidelines on a composite figure of the person
who will be turning the crisp pages on your freshly bound business plan.

This person will sit in judgment, evaluate, dissect, and
decide, with the help of a staff, whether your business—as
reflected in the business plan—is worthy of the firm's time and
attention and the risk of funding. This is what we call the "third
party's" point of view.

There is no reason to be intimidated by this abstract, composite figure. In reality, the person is exactly like you: a busi-
nessperson. Take it from us—we have met the composite
investor many times—sometimes in the mirror. That person is
attempting to make a rational decision on the basis of informa-

tion available at that point in time. Dispensing money is the person's business, just as producing and selling a product or service may be your business.

Books and software programs are a good starting point for writing a business plan. But only people who have to face those whose money was invested, whether those are institutional entities, qualified investors, or corporate sources, and be held responsible for gains and losses, can really tell you about the important elements of a business plan and the key stages of deal processing.

So, back to the composite investor—possibly one of the major players investing in high-growth companies—and that person's road map for a strategic business plan whose impact not only will get you through the door but will get you to the bank.

The system we present is especially applicable for companies in their emerging growth stage—the focus of this book. For start-ups—or at the other end of the spectrum, for mature large companies—there might be situations in which changing emphasis and/or the order of presentation would be appropriate.

Finally, before we roll up our sleeves to present you with the full scope of what serious third parties will look for in your strategic business plan—on the basis of which they'll determine whether they want to meet you or do business with you—it's important that you fully understand the unique angle of this presentation.

Besides basing the forthcoming rules on the composite investor—whose point of view we know and identify with, and who will judge our business plan in his or her daily investment activities—we also base it on another kind of experience: the due diligence process. We had the privilege of doing ample due diligence ourselves, and we especially appreciate what we gleaned by sitting in on due diligence meetings of what we consider top-of-the-line investment groups. One of them, for example, is an affiliate of the Soros Funds, which invests in emerging growth companies.

When an emerging growth company is being evaluated by this Ivy investment group, a series of meetings are held over a period of a few months in which a close, extensive, and very astute investigation is made of the merits of the business. Much of the forthcoming material is synchronous with such a systematic due diligence process.

First and foremost, for a business plan to attract the attention of major players—private, institutional, or public investors, large potential corporate partners, and key people or board members—it has to answer the *fundamental* question: *Can this be a big company, and can the people make it happen?*

THE *EXECUTIVE* SUMMARY

Successful entrepreneurs will tell you that a business plan should begin with an executive summary. But if you had the privilege of reading a large number of business plans, such as we in the business do, you'll notice that in many cases the preparers of the plan remember only the "summary" and forget the "executive." In other words, they forget who the typical executive is who will eventually open the book at the executive summary, and whom they want to impress, excite, or even dazzle.

Often the executive summary reads like a short story—a condensation of the ideas and concepts on which the business is based. That's not what an investment or large corporate executive—whom you usually want to interest in your business—is looking for. The main purpose of the executive summary is to answer the *question* a busy executive will unavoidably ask: "Why should I read the rest of this book?" In other words, why should the executive spend time learning all the details about your company?

To answer this fundamental question, seasoned investors expect you to cover *five crucial points*—and convince them that there's enough substance there to make them interested to learn about your company in more detail. Before you decide to skip over these points with a smirk on your face and a statement like "Well, everybody knows this stuff," we urge you to reflect on the matter and make sure that you are not among the *majority* of people whose business plans prove that they are unaware of this important piece of how-to advice.

Yes, you need to tell the reader what this "book" he's holding in his hands is all about. But at this stage, approach the matter in terms of a very general statement—almost as if it was a subtitle to the "book." For example: "We are a software company that produces innovative enterprisewide total financial management and planning software for the Fortune 1000 corporate market." Or, "We are a physicians practice management company specializing in providing complete management for small group practices in the northeastern USA."

But once you've made the introductory statement, for most major investors, the *number-one point* is to demonstrate that the company has an *outstanding, experienced, repeater management.* We wish to point out that not all investors require the *repeater* quality. Repeater management means that at least one member of the management team has grown a similar business to a point of profitable exit—that is, the manager is a "repeater." But for some investors like the Sprout Group, it's a prerequisite. As you recall, we reviewed the advantages and disadvantages of different management backgrounds in our chapter on attracting people.

How to qualify the terms *outstanding* and *experienced* is as much subjective as objective. First of all, we are dealing not with pure startups, but rather with emerging growth companies which already have something meaningful going in a business sense. Many third parties will agree to consider the experience of management in building up *this* company to the current level—in terms of staff and market entry—as the *previous experience* which will give them confidence that the management can take the company to the next level. Others will strongly prefer that management learn to shave on someone else.

Either way, investors and corporate partners want to see, in the words of Michael Moe, an emerging company analyst and principal with Montgomery Securities: "sharp on-the-ball guys with a plan, visionary leaders who can articulate a vision and who have the type of experience and presence that other people believe in, and people who are fully committed and not just checking in and checking out every day."

In the *second point* of the attractive executive summary, you want to present clearly the issues of *market size and growth* potential, and whether there are *any dominant competitors.* Again, as you see, the executive is probing to see whether the medium in which your company is and will be operating will allow it to grow—under reasonable competitive conditions—and provide investors with the level of total returns they are looking for and at the rate they are looking for.

The *third point* in the ideal executive summary is embodied in the issues related to the *product or service.* The investment or corporate partnering executive wants to know about the proprietary aspects of your product or service, whether it constitutes a *superior customer value,* and whether it has *sustainable advantages.* It is not coincidental that the section with the information on the product or service is in the middle of the list and not on top of it. This is in contrast with the practice of most preparers of business plans, who open the executive summary with the issues related to the product or service.

You might have heard the cliché that investors prefer a B product with an A management over an A product with a B management. Well, we might argue that investors prefer a C product, with a B market, and an A management, over an A/B product with a C/A market and a B/C management.

The *fourth point* you want to cover in the executive summary is the financials. You need to provide 3 *years of history and 3 years of projections.* In this respect you want to focus on *revenues, gross margins,* and *EBITs.* Although startups do not have financial data going back 3 years, emerging growth companies usually do.

Omission of a substantial snapshot view of the financials is quite a common "disease" associated with executive summaries. Most business plan preparers either skip this part altogether or provide some very limited information. They, of course, expect the reader to turn to the back of the book or somewhere else, and dig out the most crucial portions from among the sea of spreadsheets and charts. Well, if you remember the purpose of the executive summary—to answer the question of the executive: "Why should I read the rest of this book?"—you know that the above approach is wrong. It simply becomes a Catch-22: In order to whet the appetite of investors or corporate executives and entice them to read the book, you need to provide a snapshot of the financials, which unfortunately, in those popular tomes, they can find only after reading the book! (Assuming they don't appreciate fishing around for the relevant pages.)

In the *fifth point* (and not first and foremost), you want to talk about *capitalization: how much money you need, when* (and in what stages) *you need it,* and *what percentage of the company you intend to give* in exchange for the investment. Here too, many business plan preparers have the habit of placing this information at the top of the list. As in any commerce, first you must interest the party in what you have to offer and then discuss the price. Placing the capital requirements at the top of the list is equivalent to saying: "Look what a deal I have for you—it will cost you only $5 million. It's ridiculous, isn't it?"

Now, you might say, investors would want to see whether the investment size falls into their category before studying the detail. That might be an adequate argument for a startup or when a company is blanketing the investment community— both of which are not in line with the spirit and focus of this book.

An attractive emerging growth company should have the ability to target investors that fit the range. And even if there is a slight difference in numbers between what the company needs and what a particular investor might invest in such a deal, investors do work in syndicates. This financing system will take care of any possible discrepancy between what the company thinks a group can invest and its actual needs. If the business plan and executive summary are targeted at a potential strategic corporate partner, the argument for not putting the capitalization requirements at the top is even stronger. After all, a large partner can usually afford any investment size within a reasonable range. Furthermore, corporate partnering doesn't always start with monetary investment; it often starts with shared development and marketing synergy.

In the case of strategic partnering, the fifth point of the executive summary must deal with issues related to the proposed exchange of information, services, and processes, as well as a possible cash investment. Here you must include the general concept of what you propose as the rights and obligations of each side. You should discuss ownership issues of proprietary developments and market rights, and how much equity you will give in exchange for cash or other tools of investment.

When a business plan is furnished to attract a potential key employee or board member, it is obvious that the company's capitalization requirement can wait to the end of the executive summary, without diminishing its importance.

Most executive summaries we've seen do not follow the five rules presented above. Instead of providing a complete *condensed version of the crucial aspects* of the business plan, many executive summaries provide essentially *background information*. The two are very different. The first does answer the executive's question: "Why should I read the rest of this book?" while the second doesn't. Guess which one will work and which one will not?

MANAGEMENT BACKGROUNDS

Now to the business plan itself. Keeping with our priorities the first chapter should present the *management backgrounds*. This section has to answer the simple question "How good are they?" Off the record: In cases where the company has really exceptional and unique products and markets, you can get away with placing the management backgrounds chapter as the second chapter—provided that you gave a clear snapshot of your management team in the executive summary.

In order to answer the question "How good are they?" satisfactorily, you must elaborate on the following. *Prior positions*—we want to learn about managers' previous positions so that we can have a frame of reference with regard to their experience, responsibilities, and the type of environment in which they are used to functioning. Then we want to hear about their *real accomplishments*—their major impact on the company. This can be related to building teams, channeling the effort to highly successful products, or opening new markets.

Again, as we mentioned previously, many but not all investors will accept the accomplishments of management in bringing *this* company to the current emerging growth stage, as a track record which will make them feel confident about the future—the next level.

Next you want to discuss the managers' achievements in terms of *sales and profit building*. After all, at the end of the day, a company's performance will be measured by its sales and profits. The ability to build teams and come up with new products without growing sales and profits in a meaningful way might have worked once in a government-sponsored environment, or might still work for a startup or for a very early-stage company. But the inability to generate growth could never be sustained in an emerging growth for-profit business operation—especially the kind that requires significant risk taking on behalf of investors, corporate partners, key people who came to grow with the company, or public investors on Wall Street.

Next, you want to mention the *closest analogs*. Since there is no way to predict the future by looking into the future, the only way to estimate the future success probabilities of someone's endeavor is by looking at his or her past performance in a similar or closely analogous environment. The reasonable assumption behind this approach is that someone who successfully grew a company—say, in the retail chain sector—has a higher chance of repeating the success in building another, similar, successful retail operation than an executive who comes straight from the environment of a Fortune 500 organization, or someone who grew a successful company in a nonrelated sector such as biotech.

As we emphasize throughout this book, success comes in various shapes and forms and so does successful management. Certain parties you want to attract will stress one or another component—which they will consider a make-or-break quality for a member of management. Others might want to get a fair mix of each. It is as subjective as it is objective, and it's as much art as it is science. All you can do is put your best foot forward and present things according to the rules outlined in this book.

Finally, *disclose problems early.* If you feel that there are issues which could be perceived in the eyes of third parties as factors that might critically hinder the ability of a key member of the management team to perform—such as legal proceedings or serious medical problems—it is better to bring those issues out. If you don't and something goes wrong, it can lead to a lawsuit for losses incurred as a result of holding back critical information. Of course, this is easier said than done, but in some cases such straightforwardness can build additional trust.

An executive in a major investment company told us some time ago that the company intended to invest in a particular business because it would be run by an executive who successfully grew a previous business on which this investment firm made a huge profit. A few weeks later we were told that the "star" who was to run the company suffered a heart attack just a few days prior to signing the papers with the investment group.

The would-be success-repeater claimed that the whole medical incident was a minor problem and that he could carry out the original plans without any limitation or interference. Nevertheless, the investment group halted the investment process and referred him to two cardiologists retained by the group. Evidently, from the point of view of the investors, they felt lucky that they found out about a potential problem before the money was committed. This story happens to have a happy ending, because evidently the medical opinion was favorable and the investment was made.

PRODUCT OR SERVICE DESCRIPTIONS

The second chapter of the business plan should deal with the *product or service* in an all-inclusive manner. This chapter should answer the question: "Why is it a winner?"

You might note that in the executive summary we advocated telling the "market size and growth" story before the issues related to the product or service. There is a good reason for that. If you remember, the purpose of the executive summary is to whet the appetite of our "composite investor" to continue reading the rest of your business plan. Well, a typical composite investor is more market-oriented than product-oriented. Then, also, some larger investors would be interested only if the market and growth rate are beyond a certain minimum—something other, smaller groups might view in a more flexible manner. Once you've convinced the "composite investor" to continue reading the plan, you want to explain every important facet of your product or service, before you put it in the context and perspective of the market and its growth potential.

First, you owe the reader a *description* of the product or service. You might elaborate on prior art, methods of operation, methods of production (if applicable), potential future by-products, or derivative products and services.

Then you want to describe and explain how and why your product or service has a *superior performance*. After all, it's very rare that a company invents a totally new field. More often than not, what the company is offering is a *superior* product or service.

Product or service economics is of course important when it comes to production and operating costs as well as when it comes to the cost to the customer. In both respects, you want to elaborate on *substantial cost savings* associated with your product or service. The cost savings can be passed on directly to the customer, as in the Wal-Mart or Compaq growth model, and hence can generate significant increases in sales volume. Or, by reducing operating costs and increasing efficiency, you can reduce expenses and increase profit margins. Consolidations, such as the one Browning-Ferris orchestrated in the waste management industry, can effectively achieve cost advantages by reducing operating expenses.

MARKET SIZE AND GROWTH

Since becoming a winner product depends as much on the market for the product or service as on the details of the product or service itself, in the third chapter you must deal with the prime issues of *market size and growth*. A product without a clearly defined market is like a submarine without water—both are useless. A thorough market research, analysis, and segmentation is a prerequisite to embarking on a journey for growth. Calling potential customers or assembling focus groups can teach you more than reading a bunch of reports. But gathering information from research reports, on-line services, trade publications, and trade associations is probably the basis on which you build the customer interviews. We advised some of our clients to run trial ads in the relevant trade magazines (when applicable). You'll be amazed what a treasure such an approach comes up with.

Market size, of course, tells you whether you are currently operating in a medium that can support a big company. Projections as to *market growth* tell you how far you can go. Sometimes you are one of those lucky companies that's creating the market, as in the early days of Apple or Microsoft. There are markets, however, in which the growth potential is enormous, but because the *existing* market size is small, and the transition from the initial state to the final one requires significant time and cost, a small or midsize emerging growth company might not have the capability to sustain itself and survive the transition, whereas a larger company would. In other cases, an emerging growth company with a visionary and innovative management team is able to devise a strategy for "crossing the chasm."

Take, for example, America Online (AOL)—the quintessential emerging growth company of the first half of this decade. AOL, with FY1995 revenues of almost $400 million and with FY1996 revenues in excess of $1 billion, is beyond the range of our upper limit for emerging growth companies. But the transition beyond the emerging growth company limit of this book happened only in the 1995 fiscal year. In fact, AOL's market grew *tenfold* in just 2 years, between 1993 and 1995—from 400,000 to 4 million subscribers (and in early 1996 estimated at 5 million subscribers)—a quantum leap. In this transition, AOL surpassed the previously dominant on-line service provider CompuServe—which was owned by the deep pocket H&R Block (and raised a few hundred million dollars in an IPO). Thus AOL became number one in the market.

In the process of AOL's growth, Steve Case, its CEO, has studied the evolution of TV and radio. The on-line service market, as in TV and radio, depends on content to attract users, and the ability to create content depends on the number of users—a closed feedback loop. It's obvious that the potential size of the on-line services market is huge—almost everyone who has a PC is a latent user—although some consider the Internet to be the eventual executioner of on-line services as we know them today. In 1993 it was also obvious that AOL's customer base, at 400,000 users, was small. Having the ability to show that an emerging growth company, without the resources of a large corporation, could increase market share tenfold in 2 years can be a great challenge for the preparer of a business plan.

An often cited example from recent history involves the VCR manufacturers' battle to win the VHS versus Beta wars. There was no question that the potential for market growth was huge. After all, it is a consumer product. But it was only after years, when the VHS started winning out, and the number of titles stocked by video stores increased in a positive feedback loop, that the market really opened up and boomed.

Even before VCRs, there was television. In fact, without TV we would not have VCRs. In 1946 only 10,000 television sets were sold in the United States, and in 1947 sales increased by 60 percent to 16,000. Then, in 1948 the number increased by 1200 percent to a couple of hundred thousands. As more sets were sold, more programs were created, and by 1955 more than 30 million sets were sold per year. Again the potential for market growth was huge, the initial market was low, and in the transition only large companies could participate. There are other examples such as audio CDs, but we don't want to go on like a broken record.

In the early 1980s one of us was involved with a small emerging public company that developed a completely pioneering turnkey product. At the time the company finished the development, there was only one additional source for this kind of system—but unfortunately this source was a division of American Hospital Supply (AHS), a large corporation. Guess what happened? The smaller company, which managed to strike a major distribution contract with a large distributor, still got stuck in the mud. The FDA limited the number of units a company could sell, before full multistage testing and approval, to 20 per year.

Selling only 20 units per year for what was estimated as an approval period of 3 to 4 years would not allow the small emerging company to survive in the market (which was now being entered by new players). But the division of AHS could survive the waiting period and capitalize on its early entry. Here is a clear example where the current market size was small, the future market size was large, but the inherent market growth was too slow to allow an emerging growth company to survive in it.

You'll find a very similar phenomenon with regard to pharmaceuticals. Many new drugs have a huge potential market, but their current market is minuscule and limited by the regulatory authorities to research applications. Only large corporations or extremely well-funded emerging growth companies (often themselves backed by large corporations) can sustain themselves for the 7 to 10 years it takes to bring a new drug to market. No wonder that most of the popular drugs on the market were developed by large corporations.

An example of an emerging growth company which managed to sustain itself on the promise of future market growth, in spite of a minimal current market size, is QLT PhotoTherapeutics, a company we feature in other chapters. It has been 9 years since the company embarked on the development and testing of its applications based on Johnson & Johnson's original Photofrin drug, and it's just now that the regulatory approvals are coming in and the markets are opening up. But QLT couldn't have achieved any of the above without the crucial strategic partnering with, and investment by, American Cyanamid. This alliance gave the company cash, access to development and regulatory know-how, and the prestige which allowed it to raise large sums of money in the stock market.

For an emerging growth company, and the investors in such a company, not trying out a futile road is a blessing that can be ensured by careful analysis of market size and market growth.

It's not enough to look at the current and future potential conditions; this section of the business plan must also analyze the possible roadblocks in getting from A to Z. Only with such detailed analysis will the investor or the corporate partner be able to judge whether the risk is contained enough, so that the current and future potential markets will allow this company to survive and then grow to become a big company—the question that was asked by the reader of the business plan in the first place.

PRODUCT PROTECTION

In this chapter, you also want to elaborate on whether and how the product or service is *protected from competition*. The most effective, but not always applicable, way to protect a product from competition is by filing a patent and expanding the filings as new developments are added. You must state clearly whether you have filed a patent or patents on your product and in what stage of approval these filings are.

If the company's products are not patentable, they can still be protected from competition by the nature of using proprietary processes and methods, which are kept as trade secrets. Keeping trade secrets is difficult in a growing organization, but it is not impossible. You must elaborate in your business plan whether this is the way you envision protecting yourself from competition.

Another way a product becomes effectively protected from competition is if the company penetrates the market very fast, and gets so far ahead of the competition that it becomes the brand that everyone remembers. "Having the lead is self-reinforcing, and a dominant leader gets the first call," said John Baker, head of Baker Capital and formerly with Patricof & Co., in an interview with us.

Case in point: Starbucks Corporation has successfully graduated from its emerging growth years in 1993 as the dominant brand name when it comes to coffee bars—and its meteoric growth proves it (although some like George Naddaff, former chairman of Boston Market, think that it can't last!). Starbucks, at the time these lines were written, had only *one* patent—for its coffee-on-tap system—which can't be considered in the core of its success, plus several patents in application. It had 37 U.S. trademarks, and over 55 foreign registrations—all of which protect its brand name—the most important asset at this point, but not its products per se. It also has proprietary roasting methods which are kept as trade secrets.

If you're preparing the business plan to raise capital—for example, for a fast-growing retail operation, such as the route that Office Depot took in its emerging growth years (and which received money, among others, from Patricof & Co.), or which Staples took in its emerging growth years (and which received money, among others, from the Sprout Group)—you must clarify in your business plan that the large sums you're seeking will allow you to become the dominant leader *fast,* a position that will effectively protect you (to a certain degree) from competition.

Finally, a hard-to-copy product with, say, trademark and/or copyright protection, which is introduced to the market in an expedient manner can be effectively protected from competition to a fairly acceptable extent. A good example of this kind of protection is the mainstream software industry. Although in some limited cases you'll find programs which are protected by patents, most of the large commercial success products on the market enjoy the above-mentioned kind of protection.

In conclusion, there are many ways in which your product or service can be protected from competition, and this chapter of the business plan must clearly demonstrate "what color your parachute is." Not clarifying the modality in which you plan to protect your product from head-on competition is almost like signing a death warrant to your business plan. This point alone can make your plan unattractive and rejected. A well-proven strategy for protecting a product or service from competition can go a long way in attracting investors and corporate partners to your business plan.

Let's see what you have accomplished up to this point. With the executive summary you convinced the reader to go on and read the rest of the plan. In the first chapter you proved that the management team is good, solid, and experienced, with past accomplishments. Then, in the second chapter, you showed that the company has a winner product or service—one that gives major benefits to its potential customers. In the third chapter you demonstrated that your product has a large potential market which the company could capture, and one that is fairly protected from competition, to the extent that market penetration and growth could not be seriously eroded by competition. This approach doesn't assume no competition; it just wants to establish that the company's efforts would not be in vain—that there is a reasonable potential to grow without being shot down before taking off.

SALES AND DISTRIBUTION FACTORS

You may look at the above as establishing the axioms for the business—management, market, product. Now it's time to plot the map for execution—to go from the what to the how—and to call attention to possible roadblocks in executing the growth plan for the company.

So the fourth chapter will deal with the issue of *sales and distribution*—providing the answer to the question "Can the company get to market effectively?" You should note that investors' experience, for example, shows that *distribution challenges are often more difficult than product development challenges.* This means that you should expect significant scrutiny in this regard, and your business plan has to provide satisfactory answers in the following respects.

How are you going to get the product to consumers—via *direct sales, telemarketing, distributors,* or a combination thereof? Direct sales, for example, require that you spend money on establishing a sales force, usually before you have the revenues to cover the expense. It's usually done by raising capital through equity or debt. Telemarketing is less expensive, but the "hit" rate is much lower. With distributors, you give up a significant portion of the revenue and you don't control the supplier-customer relationship, the latter of which might hurt you in the long run. And, in the age of the information superhighway, and its predecessor the Internet, cyberspace becomes a marketplace and distribution channel too, especially in technical markets where you may assume more subscribers.

If you are lucky enough, the potential investor or corporate partner might even guide you. Don't count on it when you are preparing a plan to attract an investor, but if it happens, all the better. For example, as a partner in the large Patricof & Co., John Baker invested $4 million in Fore Systems. He told us that one of the three requirements he posed to the founders before investing was that Fore hire its own sales force, and that the company sell internationally. In fact, in its first couple of years, Fore managed to generate a meaningful part of its sales through the Internet, but of course this modality was not adequate for the huge growth that Fore experienced in recent years.

All in all, the executive who reads your business plan must be convinced that your plan is practical and is the best route to market. Then, you must specify your *sales pipeline*—at what stages you stand with previous customers, and customers that were solicited lately. An adequately full sales pipeline, with a reasonable spread of prospects and orders in process, shows that your system of getting to market works. If there are current problems, you must point them out and describe how you plan to solve them.

The *sales and distribution economics* is as important as the system on which it is based. Theoretically, you could go out tomorrow and hire 100 additional salespeople, by which you'll triple your sales force. This significant increase in sales power will most probably increase company sales, but can you afford it? And, even if you get funded, will the money be utilized best by massive investment in direct sales? Or in the long run might you be better off spending only half the sum on the sales force and the other half on product development?

When considering the sales and distribution economics, you might find that a hybrid formula will generate the best results. For example, a common strategy is to differentiate between large-volume customers, and low-volume buyers. The first type—which includes companies with multiple sites or multiple users, original equipment manufacturers (OEMs), and value-added resellers (VARs)—you'd service with your direct sales force. At the same time, you'd utilize distributors to handle the second type. Add to this formula a few telemarketers and you might have structured the most cost-effective sales and distribution system for your company. And the readers of your plan will surely take notice.

The last point you want to touch on in this chapter is the possibility of drawing on the experience of the *distribution of similar products*. Nobody is required to reinvent the wheel. In fact, most third parties who would be interested in your company prefer that you don't. If you can show that your distribution system is based on a proven approach to distributing similar products, you will drastically increase your plan's reliability.

For example, if you are an emerging growth software company, you might want to follow the general distribution strategy of a successful emerging growth software company that services similar markets. (Choose a public company for which you can obtain information in public reports.) Alternatively, you can look back at the emerging growth years of a large player in the market, and try to model its sales and distribution tactics, which evidently worked quite well. Both ways, you're giving the third party you want to attract to your business an added feeling of comfort and security by relying on what we may call a proven *prior* art.

UNIT ECONOMICS

The fifth chapter should deal with *unit economics*. Its purpose is to answer the question "Can the company grow profitably through unit expansion?" What we mean by unit expansion is a multiplication of the basic unit on which the business is based. The expansion can be based on company-owned units, franchising, or a combination of both.

Since this growth modality doesn't apply to every business— not, for example, to the manufacturer of a new series of software applications—the chapter should be dealt with accordingly.

There are quite a few types of businesses which grow mainly by unit expansion. One thing is for sure: Investors like this relatively easy business model for growth. In Chapter 8, which covers business models, we deal with this issue in more detail. It is sufficient to note that the economics of growth by unit expansion are characterized by low development costs, a "repeater" success model, and reduced cost of goods and operating costs—all a result of expanded buying power and the sharing of central management. Here we'll list three of the most notable categories of businesses whose growth is based on unit expansion.

First there are what we may call *care centers*. The most popular of those are health-care units, which provide a variety and a mix of health-related services. They may include medical centers with an assortment of medical specialties, or nursing homes. Choosing the right locations through demographic studies and maintaining good cost control are key factors in determining the viability of growing profits by an expansion of the number of units locally, nationally, and perhaps internationally. Even an education-related chain such as Nobel Education—characterized by providing care with professional services—would fit into this category.

Retail chains are another category of businesses that grow by unit expansion. Wal-Mart, the Gap, Starbucks, and Lenscrafters are all variations on the theme. Location, pricing, and competition are important factors in determining whether the business can be profitable and grow both on the unit and the corporate levels.

The third category of businesses that grow by unit expansion is *warehouse distributors*. These businesses do not occupy prime real estate, because the square footage is very large. Yet they must be located in easily accessible, usually suburban crossroads of fairly populated counties. IKEA furniture and Home Depot are good examples of fully grown distributor companies. Since warehouse distributors cut out one middle layer, they can be highly competitive pricewise—one of the chief reasons that customers will make the trip. Another factor that attracts customers to warehouse distributors is that usually everything is in stock and the customer can pick it up on a first visit. So the company must allot major resources to inventory, and at the same time try to practice some kind of just-in-time system—a fairly complex balance.

THE COMPETITION

Next stop, *competitors.* This sixth chapter must answer the question "Will others tolerate your success?" Competition is a great motivator, but it is also the source of a lot of headaches. You may have a great product, but if five other companies are selling similar contraptions or providing similar services, you enter a cutthroat competition—and who knows whether your throat will emerge intact. Even if currently you are alone in the market, competition can pop up faster than you think—especially if you don't have foolproof patent protection.

And what if you have a better mousetrap? You might be surprised, but a large competitor with huge marketing, distribution, advertising, and customer support muscle may win customers over with a product of lesser performance than yours. Would your three-store quality hamburger joint be able to compete with a few McDonalds, Burger Kings, and Kentucky Fried Chickens in the neighborhood? Or would your two stationery stores, with added personalized service, be able to compete with the prices and product availability of a few Staples and Office Depots in the neighborhood?

We don't say you couldn't compete, but the facts must be analyzed and the conclusions presented clearly. In fact, Sam Walton's Wal-Mart, the emerging growth discount chain with 19 stores and $9 million in revenues in the late 1960s, was competing with the giant S. S. Kresge's 250 Kmart discount stores, which at that time had $800 million in revenues, and with at least two other major discounters—F. W. Woolworth's Woolco chain, and Dayton Hudson's Target Stores. Still, not only did Wal-Mart not fold up, but it grew ferociously and took over the lead in the number of stores, total sales, and profitability.

Another case in point. Up until 1993, America Online was the smallest on-line service, with 400,000 subscribers, significantly behind CompuServe, which led with more than five times the number of subscribers, and Prodigy, which was somewhere in the middle. Moreover, AOL was an independent emerging growth company, while CompuServe (which since went public and raised close to $450 million in an IPO) had the deep pocket H&R Block as a daddy. And until recently, when it sold to management and an investment group, Prodigy was jointly owned by two giants, IBM and Sears.

Still another, Boston Market (formerly Boston Chicken), which in FY1992 had total revenues of $8.28 million, finished with FY1995 revenues of $159.5 million—a multiple of close to 20 in 3 years—in spite of the fact that it was surrounded by giants such as McDonald's, Burger King, Roy Rogers, and Kentucky Fried Chicken. Granted Boston Market's meals are of higher quality, but how many moderately priced quality restaurants manage to break into the mass market of fast-food chains?

ADP, in its emerging growth years, was competing with data processing services that were provided by the likes of IBM and Remington Rand. Still, in this market segment ADP became the largest service provider. On the other hand, coffee bars like Timothy's and others manage to survive side by side with the now huge Starbucks. Still, they don't manage to grow significantly because of a crowded and highly competitive market.

So, the first thing you have to do in analyzing the competition is to provide a *description of the companies and their profitability*. If you have been in a business segment for a couple of years or more, you probably know the names of your major competitors. It might still be worthwhile to check some databases, and perhaps contact the trade association for the business segment you are in. Get up-to-date data. Old information is not good enough in rapidly changing market scenarios.

It is also important that you discuss the profitability of your competitors. If some of your competitors are not profitable, they might not be around for too long. Furthermore, you might arrive at the conclusion that the market you are entering will not allow profitability on the basis of current costs and product pricing. Then, if you prove that you can be profitable—because you have a way of producing the product at a lower cost, or because its premium value can fetch a higher price—the existence of competitors might not matter that much.

Next, you want to discuss *technical advances in the pipeline,* if applicable. Imagine that your company today has a unique product with very little competition. Will your competitive position be retained? In order to make a fair judgment, you must know the technical developments in the pipeline of the industry in general, and at your competitors in particular.

Will a new, advanced technology make your product obsolete, or invade on your current proprietary position? Keeping tabs on the latest developments—through networking, reading the literature, participating in conferences that report on the state of the art, or even hiring away experts from other companies (a habit that is nowadays considered to be part of the business reality)—is crucial to understanding whether you'll be able to maintain a competitive position, and what kind of action you'll have to take if you sense imminent danger.

You also want to touch on the *distribution position of your competitors.* If they have a way of getting their products to the market more efficiently than you, you'll have a problem competing with them, even if your product is of higher value, lower cost, or both. If a major competitor has a huge sales force which gives it a clear advantage in getting to market, and if your resources don't allow you to match that sales force, you must find other ways to get to the market. You might want to associate with a major distributor, or strike a strategic alliance with a larger company which has sales and marketing muscle.

Finally, in the competition chapter, you want to qualify the *nature of the competition.* Is it a head-on competition—with fairly similar products? McDonald's and Burger King can clobber each other in commercials and still survive. But could an emerging company survive with the same burger concept? Is it a competition for the lowest price? Is it a competition for the best and highest-quality product? Is it a competition between a high-performance/quality high-cost product and a low-performance/quality low-cost product? Finally, is it a competition among fairly equals, or does one or another competitor stand out as much larger and richer?

Armed with all the above information about the competition, the party examining your business plan can judge not only how good you, your product, and your market potential are, but also what the chances are that your company can survive, and then grow, among the predators in the jungle called your market.

THE CUSTOMER

In the seventh chapter you want to discuss the issue of *customers*. Here you must answer the question "Who is already using your product or service?" Let's preface our discussion here by saying that at a growth stage, as early as it may be, you have one or another kind of customer. In the best scenario, which many investors would highly prefer, you have a growing constituency of outright buyers of your product or service. In the second-best scenario you have people who are testing and evaluating one or two units of your product, whether they have purchased it or only have purchase in mind. Then you might have strategic and joint venture partners that have started using your product on a joint evaluation basis.

What things boil down to is very simple. The people who examine your plan want to hear from third-party users how good your product is, how it compares with other things they've tried, and whether they feel that it's worth the price. Sampling existing users of your product or service is equivalent to having a mini market research and focus group combined. The assumption, which is usually statistically correct, is that if x people think that your product is desirable and worth the price, probably another y will want it—and vice versa.

Many entrepreneurs and managers omit from their strategic business plan information about customers. Well, we have news for you. Investors, corporate partners, and even good people who would want to join your management usually insist on being informed about that part of the story. We have seen major investors ask companies, again and again, for more and more names and telephone numbers of what we call in the general sense *customers*. (How early-stage customers pay for the product, and how much, is much less important than the firsthand, expert input they provide as users of the product or service.)

In this chapter you want to present the *names* of your customers, their *purchasing patterns,* and their *buying cycle.* The names of your customers are sometimes important to establish credibility. In this respect, you'll find that blue-chip and Fortune 500 customers usually carry a lot of weight. The names are also important to establish demographics and size of operation, and to determine whether the typical user is financially solid, will possibly be a multiple user, or will be the kind who tends to upgrade to next-generation products and hence will become a long-term customer. For example, large successful corporations with multiple terminals and networked operations will buy large quantities of PCs and software packages, and will tend to upgrade them to keep up with the state of the art. In smaller firms you might find fewer terminals and more outdated hardware and software.

The purchasing patterns and buying cycles are important in a number of ways. First, you want to establish whether your future revenues might be seasonal. You also want to discuss whether the typical customer is an OEM (original equipment manufacturer) or a VAR (value-added reseller) that incorporates your product into a "larger" product. Selling to OEM users and VARs is great, because with one sales call you sell many units, and usually business-to-business dealings of this sort require less free customer service.

The drawback is best understood if we recall a strike at GM's brake manufacturing plant which halted many car production lines. Thousands of small OEM suppliers suffered a major loss of business. If you sell to OEMs, you also depend on the success of a product that's not under your control. Finally, if you lose one large OEM customer, you can lose a large percentage of your business. Many of these problems also apply when a large percentage of your business is conducted with a few multiple-user large companies.

These considerations are as central to evaluating your business as any other. That's why you'll find that the readers of your plan will insist on having the maximum amount of data about your customer base, and might avoid taking a chance with you if they are not intrigued with what you present in your strategic business plan.

FINANCIALS

The next, and eighth, chapter covers the *financials*. We can't describe vividly enough what a turnoff it is when an expert finds high-flying, unrealistic projections that do not have a solid factual basis in the preceding chapters of the business plan. Presenting pro forma revenue growth, profit margins, and cashflows that are way out of line will work against you.

At the same time, we have met people who claim that their advisers advocate being highly conservative, which leads them to prepare financial projections that systematically assume worst-case scenarios. If your plan lacks excitement and optimism with regard to the company's financial growth potential, you are back to square one. As you recall, the fundamental question a business plan has to answer is "Can this be a big company, and can the people make it happen?"

Third parties examining your plan assume that you are putting your best foot forward in the financial projections. They tend to discount some of your projected results. Using worst-case scenarios will throw you completely out of the game. If, on the other hand, you are exaggerating too far up, you lose credibility and you won't be taken seriously. The best advice is to be *carefully optimistic*. After all, investors are used to some phenomenal growth in companies—even as much as tenfold in a matter of 2 years (AOL, Fore, Boston Market). So take your vision, mix in some careful market analysis, add some comparative case studies (analogous companies), stir and present.

The technical part of presenting the financials is pretty straightforward. First, present *detailed projections and assumptions*—3 to 5 years into the future. This includes *income statement, balance sheet, and cashflow*. Next, present your *very recent financial performance*—a couple of years back. *Show sales momentum if it exists*. If your business consists of a chain of units, you must present *actual results by unit over time*.

The existence of sales momentum implies that in all likelihood, next year, the company will continue growing. In presenting past financial performance, keep in mind that the reader of your plan is really not interested to know that when you started the company 5 years ago, you generated $10,000 in revenues the first year. It is really the most recent couple of years that constitute the more reliable, updated information as to where your company stands, and how you might evolve in the future—if you receive, for example, the funding you're looking for.

Finally, a point that's neglected *very frequently*: Sooner or later, you must turn a profit to stay a viable, desirable, growing business. Investors and corporate partners would like to know for how long you'll be dependent, and how much more funding you'll need before you become self-reliant. They also want to know if you expect them to take responsibility for funding beyond the current round, and if not who will provide the funding you need—after all, their return on investment will depend on it. In sum, you must estimate the *total time and funding required for cash breakeven,* and the sources you expect to provide you with the required funding.

It is true that many investors manage to cash in their investment in certain companies before those companies break even. It happens when a company is bought by a larger concern, or has a lucrative IPO. Still, in foresight, people who examine your plan want to know the odds, and make their own decision.

THE DEAL

You'll conclude your strategic business plan with a chapter that covers the proposed *deal*—the reason you did all this work in the first place.

In this, the ninth, chapter you must present the *pricing* of the deal *and the logic* behind it—namely, how many shares or warrants, or how much interest, royalties, patent rights, market rights, or exchange technology a lender, investor, or corporate partner will receive, and why. In order to substantiate your deal proposal, you want to present *comparable private pricing,* if available, or *public comparables* (comps) if the company is already public or in a very late private stage. Information on comparable private deals is harder to obtain than public company information. Still, you may have friends, associates, or a previous experience that might help. Chapter 7 of this book, which covers valuation, should serve as a guideline for preparing these data.

You must also incorporate company capitalization, including information on previous investors and the prices they paid. Everybody wants to know who else thought your company was worthy of investment. The herd effect is known to be a contributing factor in drawing capital, corporate partners, and good people. If a famous industry player thought you were worthy of his or her time and money, others will feel more comfortable, too. JAFCO America Ventures, for example, will categorically not consider investment in U.S. companies unless the investment is referred to JAFCO by a well-recognized entity that has already invested, or unless a clear reference to such an entity is made in the business plan. Most firms will not have such a strict policy, but the emerging company is definitely subject to the rules of positive spiral and chain reaction when it comes to people, capital, and corporate partners. An important finance or industry personality who put money in your company, and say, is also on the board, can carry more weight than you could imagine.

In addition to knowing the identity of past investors, people who are considering investment or other involvement with the company want to know how much those previous investors paid. Nobody wants to randomly overpay for anything. If the price is increased significantly, there must be a good explanation for it, or there must be such a demand for the company's shares that it becomes the explanation.

Investors and potential corporate partners will also insist on having full information about previous investors and the prices they paid because of issues related to dilution and control. Some companies obtain financing in such a haphazard, shortsighted manner that in a few short years they have diluted the company significantly, and spread control (in board seats or some other form) among too many parties. A new investment group or corporate partner will often pass on such opportunities because it does not want to get involved in what's already a messy situation in terms of control problems and future valuation.

Finally, investors will want to know if the deal is *negotiable.* In other words, *should they bother if they find it too expensive?*

At the bottom line, your strategic business plan can be only as good as your business. But if your conclusion from the above is that only *function* is important not *form,* you are wrong. A deficiency in form will probably not take away from an otherwise superb and flawless opportunity. It is also safe to assume that form, as good as it can be, will not turn a complete "dog" into anything else. But, then, most situations are gray, and not black or white.

Your business plan represents your business and the people behind it. But it represents more than the dry factual information. It represents style, knowledge, understanding of priorities, accuracy, attention, and character—qualities that the readers of the plan who might tie their fortunes to that of your company want to see. You can cook the same food and present it in many ways. One restaurant might get $10 for the dish; another will be able to charge $25 or $50. One restaurant will have lines waiting; another will have more tables empty than full. It's the form that makes the substance count.

If you want people to line up to get a piece of the action in your business, form and function—image and substance—must work in synergy. Your strategic business plan must satisfy the intellect, increase confidence, reduce fear, excite the imagination, and stimulate the greed glands of its readers.

THE GOOD, THE BAD, AND THE UGLY

Turning Everything into Good to the Power of 3—at the "Speed of Light"

"The good, the bad, and the ugly"—the title of Clint Eastwood's early spaghetti western blockbuster—is the expression that came to mind when we were defining the parameters for a book about emerging growth business. What we wanted to come up with was a framework which would give a growing company the tools to turn its experience into the good, the good, and the good. We decided to achieve that with our EAIR method of examples, analysis, insight, and rules. But let's review first why it seemed so appropriate to think of a famous movie title to describe the conditions of emerging growth businesses.

The good is obvious. It's exciting and often very rewarding to build up a business. There's the intellectual stimulation, the creativity, the sense of achievement, the sense of power and control, recognition, and the creation of your own new social family. The financial rewards can be huge. Sam Walton, Bill Gates, Steve Jobs, Howard Schultz, Eric Cooper, Jim Clark, Steve Case—these are all people whose fortunes are larger than those of most movie stars, sports personalities, TV anchors, surgeons, high-visibility lawyers, and CEOs of large corporations. Even many less well-known company builders made out extremely well—sometimes beyond their wildest imagination.

Granted, as Bill Gates commented when he was named the richest man in America, much of those people's wealth is in the form of their company's stock, and not in the bank. But, still, if the company does well or is eventually sold, the stock paper turns into money.

Is there anything else we can term "good" for the emerging growth company? Yes. The economic system and government policies in a capitalist nation encourage entrepreneurship and the creation of wealth through industrious methods. Take, for example, one simple fact—that much of the U.S. economy is built around public companies, those traded on one or more stock exchanges.

The stock market functions because of one axiom: appreciation and return on investment beyond what one can get in the bank, via Treasury bonds, or similar "safe" investments. That's why people and institutions take the risk. Now, when a company reaches a point where its earning prospects are clearly analyzable, the only way its stock value can increase is by increasing earnings. But when a company is in its emerging growth stage, stock value is usually based on a combination of growth expectations and current performance. For some biotech stocks or cyberstocks, expectations are so high that stock value is driven primarily by potential growth and very little by earnings.

On the basis of the above analysis, it is obvious that the stock market is much more forgiving and lenient toward the emerging growth company than toward large corporations. Take, for example, a large $10 billion company. In order for its stock to appreciate it has to constantly increase earnings. But by virtue of being a large company, it has already reached a relative plateau—or quasi-equilibrium, so to speak. While many in the company would be happy to keep their performance steady or with little growth, they can't; the stock market doesn't let them. And if they disappoint the market, people dump their stock and the whole kit and caboodle goes haywire. Look what happened to IBM and DEC just a few years ago.

So the large corporation often has to resort to massive layoffs, to a reduction in developing the products of the future, and sometimes to a compromise in quality—all in order to cut costs, and improve the bottom line. The company's growth in such cases is paper growth, but not actual growth. Paper growth without actual growth can backfire.

Now with all fairness to large corporations, we must say that some large companies manage to grow continually in a positive way. Good examples are Intel, ADP, and Microsoft. In fact, they are defying the law of diminishing returns and keep growing and growing. But for every Intel, Microsoft, and ADP there is an Apple or an AT&T—companies which are retrenching to regain a bottom line that will allow them to survive, especially in the public stock market, where survival means first and foremost paper growth.

For the emerging growth company, growth is natural—and once a company is public the market capitalization follows. After all, the company starts with close to 0 percent of the market, and when it graduates from the emerging growth stage, there is usually still a huge market growth potential ahead—whether the company grows internally, by acquisitions, by unit multiplication, or by a combination thereof. Stock market growth is highly leveraged by *potential* growth, which gives the growing company a nice cushion for a few years. The market often looks at growing companies as young college graduates who come to work for a large company—where they are given a few years to grow into their roles—rather than as full-grown adults who are held accountable for every action and hence must expect an equal reaction.

Finally, the government—on the federal and local levels—encourages small emerging growth businesses with a variety of programs that provide them with financial and other support. Emerging growth companies are engines of economic, innovation-related, and employment growth—and local and federal authorities want them to grow and prosper, for the sake of the whole community.

So with all that "good," what's bad? First and foremost, it's the Catch-22 phenomenon: In order to attract _____, you have to prove that you don't need _____. Of course, what you want to do is turn some of the Catch-22s into well-defined problems that need solutions. But before we point to the solution, let's look at the problem in more detail.

"People will take their shirts off their back for you—if you already have a shirt." Sounds sarcastic but familiar? It is well known that during the early emerging growth years of Microsoft Corporation, many investors approached Bill Gates and wanted to put money in the company. But Microsoft didn't need the money for its growth—which was financed by its revenues, at least until its IPO. Nevertheless, they say that one investor was really "lucky," because Microsoft agreed to take $1 million from him. Of course, that investor made a "killing," and many feel that Bill Gates did him a favor by accepting his money.

In a more recent example, Fore Systems, the superfast growth company which we often feature in this book, was courted in 1992 for 11 months by John Baker, then senior VP at Patricof & Co. Ventures—one of the biggest venture funds—to finally get a 33 percent stake in the company for an investment of $4 million. And, for its IPO in 1994, Fore was again courted by a variety of midsize to large Wall Street firms. The lucky winner for the lead was Goldman Sachs—another Ivy League investment banking firm. Of course, Fore has an excellent product line and market potential, and for FY1996 its revenues grew to $235 million from minimal revenues in FY1992 and zero in FY1991. But Baker pointed out to us in an interview that the four founders of Fore came from Carnegie Mellon University's computer science and related departments. So what's the big deal? Well, in the past 10 to 20 years, most of the Department of Defense (DOD) computer research budget has gone to three universities: MIT, Stanford, and (guess who?) Carnegie Mellon—each sharing approximately one-third of this huge bounty.

We do have Microsofts and Fores, but most companies, even some that later become very successful, face a harsher environment—one which is characterized by a series of Catch-22 situations.

For example, the same quality people that a company would need to help in its growth would prefer to wait until the company's growth is secured before joining. Corporate partners look for a company with proven products and markets, when the company actually needs them to help in the process of developing the products and markets. Because of the increased risk of businesses competing in saturated markets, investors look for sales, profits, and liquidity before investing—when at the same time we know that a company's sales and liquidity depend on investments. Bankers who provide business loans represent the extreme of this tendency. They might court businesses that don't really need the money, or that could finance things in alternate ways, and impose enormous difficulties in the way of other viable companies.

And Wall Street—that's a classic. The public markets want to invest in companies whose stock is on the rise, yet we all know that what makes the stock rise are those buy orders. Emerging growth company managers are therefore faced with a tremendous challenge: how to counter and overcome the impediments of these Catch-22 trends that are at the core of their businesses. We say *c'est la vie*—that's life—and the purpose of this book is to turn these apparently negative conditions into manageable and solvable problems.

But let's see what else is "bad." While a large corporation can afford to follow a number of alternative paths simultaneously and devote the proper humanpower and resources to each, the emerging business is often forced to gamble on one, or a very limited number of routes. In a fast-paced *Darwinistic* global and local economy, things are changing so fast that competition pops up like mushrooms after the rain. Designs become obsolete by the time you gear up to full production. Market penetration, especially for products that need mass advertising, is costly and often prohibitive for a small emerging company. (As Augustine's Law Number IV puts it: "If you can afford to advertise, you don't need to.") Meeting product regulations often requires resources beyond the means of an emerging business. Small, emerging businesses are constantly scrutinized by creditors, customers, and competitors, and they have very little to fight back with.

In an article titled "The Puzzling Infirmity of America's Small Firms," *The Economist* (February 18, 1995) goes one step further and claims that in some ways small firms are being driven out by large firms which are continually adopting behavior patterns of...small firms. That is, they emphasize entrepreneurship, agility, and the passing of decision making to lower levels of management.

If that's not enough, here is another catch. Small emerging companies usually can't keep up with the salaries needed to attract an excellent staff. Perhaps ironically, however, the massive wave of layoffs in the Fortune 500 companies, with all its negative connotations, not only forced many people to establish their own businesses, but also provided a large pool of highly experienced professionals, which emerging growth companies can tap as management candidates or as members of the board of directors. Investors, in fact, like businesses with this kind of experienced personnel at the helm.

We have talked about the "good," we have talked about the "bad." Now to the "ugly." The "ugly" is what often you've got to endure and go through to get your emerging growth company to the next step, and then to the next step, and so on. Another way to put it is that it takes blood, sweat, and tears to get your emerging business "up the hill"—and none of those three "excretions" is beautiful.

Let's just name a few of those "ugly" things:

- Cashflow emergencies, in which you don't know where your next payroll will come from, but the banks won't increase the line of credit any further

- Unexpected product development problems, which may require a large amount of capital and will result in major delays in producing revenues

- A sudden soft economy, beyond your control, which turns the market for your products soft and leaves you with excess inventory or significantly reduced revenues

- A new competitor that bites into your market share, especially when it's a large company with huge marketing and distribution muscle

- Companies that infringe on your patents, but you don't have the resources to litigate them

- Good people leaving for greener pastures

- Wall Street speculators shorting your stock, sending it into a nose dive, and your phones are ringing off the hook with hundreds of calls from disappointed investors

Yes, all these are quite "ugly." This book, with its EAIR system of experience, analysis, insight, and rules, provides you with the means to turn the "bad" and the "ugly" into "good"—or at least "fairly good."

Let's take as an example one of the major components of the "bad"—the series of Catch-22s that an emerging business is subjected to. Instead of looking at those apparent Catch-22s as a trap with no way out, the positive thinker will arrive fast at the conclusion that the Catch-22 phenomenon we described is nothing more than a risk-reward game. It therefore follows that the risk that good people, providers of capital, and corporate partnerss will be ready to take depends on how positively they perceive the reward and how detrimental they perceive the risk.

It is the entrepreneur-manager's job to demonstrate that the reward is high enough and that the risk is contained enough. The better you can maximize the perceived reward, and contain the perceived risk, the further away you get from the terribly frustrating Catch-22s, and the closer you get to solvable problems. The rules of this book, which among others demonstrate how to attract PCCP—people, capital, and corporate partners—clearly provide solutions and can turn the "bad" into "fairly good."

Another "bad" we discussed was the disadvantage of the smaller versus the larger company—especially with respect to chaos and change. Here again, an emerging growth company which attracts good people and capital can employ the best talent and stay overcapitalized, and thus diminish or totally eliminate the damaging aspects of fast change, and perhaps even capitalize on them. Furthermore, an emerging company that attracts large corporate partners can utilize those companies' marketing and distribution networks and have the best of both worlds.

Finally, eliminating the "ugly" or perhaps even turning it into "good" is again tied to PCCP. M. Scott Peck, in his megahit

The Road Less Traveled, makes a point that life is a problem-solving sequence, a fact that shouldn't be taken as a detriment. Business is even more so. Therefore, by encountering some of the problems in the "ugly" category and solving them, the company becomes more agile and stronger. Except that sometimes those problems can pull the company down the helix of a negative spiral—the famous chain reaction.

Here again, following the examples and rules of the book, and attracting PCCP, will reduce the hardship and turn the problem-solving experience into a positive factor that will enhance the growth process and produce a stronger and healthier company. The "ugly" can actually be turned into the "beautiful" or at least the "good."

Now that we have turned the good, the bad, and the ugly into the "good"— to the power of 3—all that is left to talk about is the pace at which an emerging growth company should grow. It is a well-known fact that the once-patient capital market is not so patient any more—it's looking for a fast return on investment. Also, good people are not so patient any more, and are looking for the best place to gain the maximum rewards, and sooner rather than later.

In today's highly competitive and fast-paced environment, you can't stay floating in a state of "quasisurvival" for too long. Either you take off fast or you sink. It's like treading water in quicksand. *If the transition from survival to success is not fast enough, the survival itself is jeopardized.* Again, in order to accomplish a fast transition, you need—you know what: you need to *attract good people, quality capital, and the right corporate partners.* And this book is your guide.

A big bank blew its horn in a popular commercial: "Because Americans want to succeed, not only survive." For today's emerging companies, survival depends on *expedited* success, which requires them to become *emerging growth* companies in the fullest sense. Homogeneous, gradual progress is "out"; quantum leaps are "in." Today's emerging business can't afford to follow a path of trial and error, because if it doesn't make it "soon" it might never make it; chaos will propel it to disorientation and disintegration.

To attract PCCP—good people, quality capital, and the right corporate partners—you must be, or at least must be *perceived* as, a company which can make the transition from "guerrilla warfare" to "statehood" very smartly, and at the "speed of light." Conversely by having PCCP, you can speed up the transition. The good ol' chain reaction of attractiveness, or the positive spiral, guarantees that. In fact, if you have the P (people), you'll probably be able to get the C (capital) and the CP (corporate partners).

Finally, Dan Lufkin said that in 1963 he developed the seven corporate objectives for the investment banking firm that he cofounded, Donaldson, Lufkin & Jenrette (DLJ). The seventh corporate objective was to have fun doing what you're doing. DLJ has since been acquired by the Equitable Insurance Company, and Equitable restated the corporate objectives and produced a modified list. Guess what is one of those objectives? Have fun doing what you're doing, because it's not only about "return on investment," it is also about "return on life."

We believe that the emerging growth business sector is exciting, and has a lot to offer to individuals as well as to a community and to a country. So much so that we took the liberty of modifying one of our country's most famous creeds:

> *"The business of America is business."*   —CALVIN COOLIDGE

> *"The business of America is emerging growth business."*
> —THE AUTHORS

ABOUT THE AUTHORS

GABOR BAUMANN is founder and president of Noveltek Inc., a venture and investment banking firm that specializes in working with emerging growth companies. He is also corporate finance advisor to the Ray Dirks Division of National Securities, a major investment banking firm. He is a member of a Washington, DC-based Small Business White House Task Force and was on the Economic Steering Group of Business Executives for National Security.

JACOB WEINSTEIN was with The Bridgeford Group, the mergers and acquisitions arm of The Industrial Bank of Japan (IBJ). He was also an attorney with Willkie Farr & Gallagher.

INDEX